A History of Building Control in England and Wales 1840–1990

A History of Building Control in England and Wales 1840–1990

A.J. Ley, MBE, BA, M.Phil., FRICS, FBEng.

RICS BOOKS

Published by RICS Business Services Limited, a wholly owned subsidiary of
The Royal Institution of Chartered Surveyors,
under the RICS Books imprint
Surveyor Court
Westwood Business Park
Coventry CV4 8JE
UK

No responsibility for loss occasioned to any person acting or refraining from action as a result of the material included in this publication can be accepted by the author or publisher.

ISBN 0 85406 672 1

© RICS Books 2000

The right of A.J. Ley to be identified as the author of this work has been asserted in accordance with the Copyright Designs and Patent Act 1988 Sections 77 and 78.

No part or parts of this publication may be reproduced by any means electronic, mechanical, photocopying, recording or otherwise, now known or to be devised, save by prior consent of the publisher.

Typeset by Wyvern 21 Ltd., Bristol
Printed in Great Britain by Page Bros, Norwich

Contents

xi	List of illustrations
xi	List of abbreviations
xii	Acknowledgements
xiii	**Foreword**
xiv	**Introduction**
xvii	**Chronology**
Page 1	**Chapter 1: The Building Regulation Bill (1841–1842): Antecedents and Failure**
Page 1	The origins of building control
	London Building Acts 1667–1774
	The Bristol Building Acts 1788–1840
	The Liverpool Building Acts 1802–1825
Page 6	The role of local authorities
	Spread of disease
Page 8	The Health of Towns Select Committee and Building Regulation Bills 1841–1842
	Evidence presented to the Committee
	Findings of the Committee
	Recommendations of the report
	Adoption of the Building Act
	The Marquis of Normanby and the 1841 Building Regulation Bill
	Reintroduction of the Bill
	Objections to surveyors' efficiency
	Extent of the Act
Page 17	Failure of the Bill
Page 20	**Chapter 2: Local Improvement Acts and the Health of Towns**
Page 20	Edwin Chadwick
	Solutions for improving conditions

Page 22	**Proposals for Improvement**
	JC Loudon
	Captain Vetch
Page 23	**Chadwick and the issue of building control**
	Avoidance of Building Acts
Page 26	**Chadwick and the issue of central control**
Page 27	**Local Improvement Acts**
	Differences between local Acts
	Influence of the London Building Act 1844
Page 30	**The Health of Towns Commission**
	The Commission reports
Page 32	**The Health of Towns Bill 1847–1848**
	Controls over building
Page 35	**Chapter 3: The Local Government Act 1858 and Building Bye-laws**
Page 35	**Reappearance of cholera**
	Formation of the Board of Health
	Opposition to the Act
	Opposition to Chadwick
	Chadwick's proposals for a General Building Bill
Page 40	**Local Government Bill 1858**
	Creation of the Local Government Act Department
Page 41	**Weaknesses of the Local Government Act 1858**
	Building requirements
	Development of the Local Government Act Department
Page 45	**Chapter 4: The Growth of the Building Bye-law System**
Page 45	**Model bye-laws**
	Local practices
	Speculative building
	The effects of bye-laws on technology
Page 49	**Variations to bye-law requirements**
	The St Helens Improvement Act 1869
	Failure to improve uniformity of requirements
Page 53	**Need for a central body**

Page 56	Development of philanthropic housing Establishment of Garden Cities
Page 57	Housing Demand
Page 58	Public Health Act 1866
Page 59	The Royal Sanitary Commission (RSC) Rural districts

Page 64	A period of consolidation 1871–1875
	    Local Government Board Act 1871
	    Public Health Act 1872
	    Public Health Bill 1873

Page 65	Sanitary Laws Amendment Bill 1874
Page 66	The Public Health Act 1875
Page 69	**Chapter 5: Bye-laws and the Anti-bye-Law Lobby**
Page 69	The introduction of a model set of building bye-laws

Page 71	New technology
	    Cements
	    The use of concrete at upper floor levels
	    Role of the surveyor
	    The Local Government Board

Page 75	The Public Health (Amendment) Act 1890
	    Adoption of bye-laws in rural areas
	    Lucas' alternative proposals

Page 80	Application of bye-laws in rural areas Isolated buildings
Page 84	Public Health (Amendment) Act 1907
Page 85	The continuance of objections to bye-laws
Page 86	Housing of the Working Classes Bill Resubmission of the Bill
Page 90	**Chapter 6: Committees, Commissions and Circulars**

Page 90	The Departmental Committee on Building Bye-laws
	    National Federation of Building Trades Employers
	    The Royal Institute of British Architects
	    The presentation of other evidence

	Methods of updating
	Enforcement of bye-laws by surveyors
	Reaction to the report
Page 98	The Housing (Building Construction) Committee
	Construction after the war
	Differences between the two committees
	The Housing Acts of 1923 and 1925
	Public buildings
Page 107	Ministry of Health circulars
	Circular of 1st September 1922
	Circular 56 of June 1926
Page 110	Effects of the circulars
Page 112	Chapter 7: The Professional Approach
Page 112	Establishment of the Building Research Board
	The use of steel
	The Building Research Department
Page 117	The appointment of surveyors
	Publications
Page 120	Consolidation of the law
	The appointment of officers
Page 122	Second interim report of the Local Government and Public Health Consolidation Committee
	Revision of bye-laws
	Complaints
	The London system and the new model code
Page 128	Chapter 8: Towards a Building Act
Page 128	Rebuilding after World War II
	National versus local bye-laws
	Prefabricated buildings
Page 130	The Public Health Act 1961
	The Building Regulations Advisory Committee
Page 131	Means of escape in case of fire
	The Building Regulations Advisory Committee

Page 135	**The effect of building failures on building control** Notable failures Compensation claims
Page 137	**Reviews** Fees One single Act
Page 142	**Chapter 9: A New Beginning**
Page 142	**The 1984 Building Act** Approved documents London Approved Inspectors The National House Building Council Competition between the NHBC and local authorities
Page 147	**Conclusion**

Appendices

Page 151	*Appendix 1:* The City of Bristol Building Act 1788
Page 154	*Appendix 2*: The Bristol Building Act 1840
Page 157	*Appendix 3*: The Liverpool Improvement/Building Act 1825
Page 159	*Appendix 4*: Bill for Regulating Buildings in Large Towns 1841
Page 163	*Appendix 5*: Building Regulation Bill No. 2–Bill No. 371 1842
Page 165	*Appendix 6*: The Liverpool Building Act 1842
Page 168	*Appendix 7:* Structure of Building Bye-laws Made Under Section 34 of the Local Government Act 1858
Page 170	*Appendix 8:* Sections 124 to 142 Relating to Building Control Matters St Helens Improvement Act 1869
Page 172	*Appendix 9*: Model Building Bye-laws 1st series (Local Government Board 7th Annual Report 1877/78)
Page 174	*Appendix 10*: Model Building Bye-laws 1899
Page 176	*Appendix 11*: Model Building Bye-laws – Rural series
Page 177	*Appendix 12*: Model Building Bye-laws Series 4 Urban – 1912
Page 180	Appendix 13: Model Bye-laws – Means of Escape from Fire in Certain Factories and Workshops 1935

Page 181	*Appendix 14*: The Public Health Act 1936 – Sections of the Act which enabled local authorities to refuse or conditionally approve deposited plans
Page 183	*Appendix 15*: Model Building Bye-laws, Ministry of Health 1937
Page 186	*Appendix 16*: Model Building Bye-laws 1952 and 1953
Page 188	*Appendix 17*: The Building Regulations 1965, 1972, 1976
Page 190	*Appendix 18*: The Building Regulations 1985 and the Building (Approved Inspector etc.)Regulations 1985
Page 192	*Appendix 19:* Legislative Growth of Building Bye-law Powers
Page 194	Notes to the text
Page 211	Bibliography
Page 218	*Index*

List of illustrations

Figure 1:	Front page of the Bristol Building Act 1788
Figure 2:	Appointment and Oath of Surveyors, Bristol Building Act 1788
Table 2.1	Average age of death (in years)
Figure 3:	The differing standards of rear open space required to houses
Figure 4:	City of Bath Building Bye-laws 1866
Figure 5:	Amendments to the City of Bath Building Bye-laws 1868
Figure 6:	Terrace of the future on refuse of the past
Figures 7a & b:	Improvements to cottage construction

Plates

Plate 1:	Terrace of early 19th century town houses, Southernhay, Exeter.
Plate 2:	Jettied housing, St Mary's, Exeter
Plates 3a & b:	Back-to-back housing, Thorville Row, Thorville Place, and Thorville Street, Leeds
Plates 4a & b:	Back-to-back housing, Norman Row and Norman View, Leeds
Plate 5:	Pre-1912 housing, Jubilee Road, Exeter
Plate 6:	Post-1912 housing, First Avenue, Exeter
Plate 7:	Rural estate housing, Duke of Bedford's Estate, Ridgmont, Bedfordshire
Plate 8:	Early bye-law housing, Normanby Road, Exeter
Plates 9a & b:	Pre-fabricated buildings
Plate 10:	Modern lightweight industrial/commercial building
Plate 11:	The challenge for modern building regulations

List of abbreviations

ABE	Association of Building Engineers
BB	Building Bye-laws
BRAC	Building Regulations Advisory Committee
BRB	Building Research Board
BRD	Building Research Department
BRE	Building Research Establishment
BRS	Building Research Stations
BSI	Building Standards Institute (now British Standards Institute)
DSIR	Department of Scientific and Industrial Research
FRE	Fire Research Establishment
HC	House of Commons
HL	House of Lords
IAAS	Incorporated Association of Architects and Surveyors
IBC	Institute of Building Control
I.Mun.E.	The Institution of Municipal Engineers
LGB	Local Government Board
LGO	Local Government Office
MH	Ministry of Health
MOH	Medical Officer of Health
NALGO	National and Local Government Officers' Association
NFBTE	National Federation of Building Trades Employers
NHBC	National House Building Council
NHBRC	National House Builders Registration Council
PP	Parliamentary Paper
RC	Reinforced concrete
RIBA	The Royal Institute of British Architects
RICS	The Royal Institution of Chartered Surveyors
RDC	Rural District Council
RDCA	Rural District Council Association
RSC	Royal Sanitary Commission
UDC	Urban District Council
UDCA	Urban District Council Association

Acknowledgements

I should like to thank the following people for their help with this book:

Kenneth Hunt, FLA, former Area Librarian, Devon County Council, for his valuable assistance in obtaining relevant literature.

The staff of the libraries of the Department of the Environment, House of Lords, The Royal Institution of Chartered Surveyors, and The Incorporated Association of Architects and Surveyors.

Arthur Curtis, FIBCO, formerly Chief Building Control Officer, City of Exeter Council, and Dennis Mosely, FIAS, FIBCO, formerly Assistant Director of Planning (Building Control), City of Bath Council, for their valuable assistance in locating and obtaining public Acts, local Acts, building bye-laws and records in respect of building development within the cities of Exeter and Bath.

George Baxter, MIAS, former Senior Building Control Officer, City of Leeds Council, for his valuable assistance on information relating to back-to-back housing in Leeds.

Copyright acknowledgements

Figures 1, 2, 4, and *5*: reproduced by kind permission of Her Majesty's Stationery Office.
Figure 6: based on a drawing from T. Pridgin-Teale's *Danger to Health* (1878), published by J & J Churchill. Redrawn by F. Gaynor.
Figures 9a and b: reproduced by kind permission of the Royal Agricultural Society of England (*RASE Journal*, 1892, pp 634–635).

Dedication

To my wife Valerie, for her encouragement and support

Foreword

Building regulations provide the central core to all construction, and are foremost in the minds of the development team. The provision of a safe and healthy environment is paramount. However, history has shown that man has developed and often abused the built form, and in many cases created an environment which has been detrimental to health, safety and welfare. Building development often ignores the social needs of the majority of the population whilst meeting the financial demands of the few. This text shows how this was reflected in land ownership and property development in and around factory sites and watercourses, with the development of industrial complexes and conurbations.

History has also shown that the impact of this on the social well being of people frequently has been one of devastation resulting in plague, pestilence and often major disasters, such as the Great Fire of London.

Over time legislation has sought to develop building regulations which are simple in format, easily applied and enforced, with regulation often resulting from a knee-jerk reaction to a disaster taking place. Problems relating to the consistency of application throughout the country became apparent, and where there was inconsistency the resultant building was often detrimental to the users. This book provides the opporunity to view both social and technological development and see how requirements were built into the legislation.

The reader is helped to explore the development of legislation in response to the physical and social needs of the population with the emphasis on housing and improved standards. This process enables the reader to feel the demands of society, and to understand and grasp the development of legislation from the earliest times through to 1990.

This book allows the reader to grasp the dimensions relating to public health, safety and welfare which are achievable through building regulations, and encourages a reasoned and logical approach to the legislation of the future. A comprehensive text which makes a positive contribution to the study of building control and building regulations in a historical context, it will be of significant benefit to both professionals and students alike.

David Gibson
Chief Executive
Association of Building Engineers

Introduction

The evolution, development, problems and achievements of the control of building construction, with regard to the interests of public health and safety, have not been widely researched. This book is an attempt to explore this area of public administration, its development and the socio-technological implications of this form of control. Little has been written on the subject as it applies to England and Wales, although Knowles and Pitt [1] have produced a good survey of the London system of building control which mainly centres around the work of the district surveyor.

The system in the rest of England and Wales developed later than the London system, and in this book I aim to establish the origins, influences, the roles of national and local government, and the demands of society in the development of building control law. I chose the year 1840 as a starting point as during that year the first parliamentary moves were made to obtain a Building Act for England and Wales, although the origins of control outside London with the introduction of a Building Act for Bristol in 1788 and Liverpool in 1825 will also be examined. The year 1990 was chosen to end the period of study as by that date a national Building Act with functional building regulations, advocated for so long, had eventually become a reality. The new Act brought about a change in the system of control. No longer were local authorities the sole body responsible for administering building regulations. Independent professionally-qualified and experienced individuals and corporate bodies were recognized and granted authoritative status, and by 1990 this new system was beginning to evolve.

A detailed study cannot begin until it has been established what occurred during this period. Very few studies on the subject of building control exist and the main sources for this book were primary material such as Parliamentary Papers. These, along with journals and standards, were consulted at Exeter University Library, whilst secondary material was obtained through the Devon County Council library service. As the study developed, I found additional material in the libraries of the Department of the Environment, the House of Lords, The Royal Institution of Chartered Surveyors, and the library of The Incorporated Association of Architects and Surveyors. I visited Leeds, Bath, Exeter and Barnstaple to find out more about local issues. Other material was taken from *The Builder* and *The Times*. A full list of reference material can be found in the Bibliography at the end of this book (see p.211).

Parliamentary Papers provided the structure on which this book is based and in relation to which the local issues are discussed. Arguments about some of the points raised are supported by extracts from the books referred to. Some of the reference material is more related to the development and social aspects of local government, housing and public health, and therefore limited in its contribution to building control. However, it has been included as it is important that the evolution of the control system should be seen in the wider social, political and economic environment of the time. Local material is often poorly referenced or sometimes not available, making research into local issues difficult.

Building control is one of the oldest forms of local government responsibility, from which has developed the provision of public housing, construction of streets, public drainage and town and country planning. All of these topics provide many avenues to explore. However, this book will not include bye-laws relating to streets as these were not specifically related to buildings, although they did provide spaces between them which had the effect of restricting the spread of fire and offering light and air to buildings. Public health laws relating to drainage, means of escape in case of fire, and to dangerous buildings have been included, as these are matters of public safety encompassed within the normal building control responsibilities of a local authority.

This book will show that broadly applied, building regulations and bye-laws did provide the control necessary to raise the standard of construction in the interests of health and safety, especially in the building of houses. The specific terms in which bye-laws were framed resulted in minimum building sizes and specification of particular materials. However, this frequently restricted innovation within the industry, and invariably resulted in increased construction costs. A more flexible type of bye-law was required, one in which a more varied specification could be acceptable without affecting the bye-law's overall aim. The industry had to wait until November 11th 1985 [2] before this came into place.

The rate of progress in achieving the aims of building control varied considerably. The administration of the law, and particularly of bye-laws, was very weak. The flexibility sought by builders required a functional form of bye-laws and a more professional approach by local authorities. However, this was likely to increase the cost of administration, and was therefore not welcomed by many local authorities. (This area of conflict did not apply to London, which had a separate system financed partly through the fee system, and partly by the surveyors having private practices.)

The discretion given to local authorities produced unevenness of control and achievement, with some acting responsibly and others not. This resulted in the government increasing the bureaucracy of control and conflict between national and local issues. In retrospect, it can be seen that the manner in which central government became involved in local issues was a mistake. The approach should have been the removal of local authority discretion, the imposition of a statutory duty and the provision of comprehensive sound enforcement law.

One thread running through this is the balance of interests needed to produce housing for the working classes which not only provided acceptable accommodation in terms of health and safety, but was within the economies of profitable construction and renting. It is in the provision of low cost housing that the greatest conflict on these issues took place. Chapter 1 sets out to trace the origins and examine the factors that influenced the development of a building control system in England and Wales. Chapters 2 and 3 examine the role of the public health movement and the way it affected the growth and pattern of building control, leading to the introduction of building bye-laws as a means of controlling building. How this system developed, and the opposition which grew with it, will be examined in Chapters 4 and 5. Chapters 6 and 7 will explore the interaction between central and local government, the difficulties of achieving uniformity without legislation, the growth of professional involvement and consideration both of the law and the system.

During the period of my research, Roger A. Harper was undertaking research into the evolution of English building regulations between 1840 and 1914.[3] His work was primarily concerned with the actual technical regulations, the way in which they grew and changed, what prompted them, how their standards were set and how they worked in practice. Harper's thesis is unpublished but he has published a book on Victorian building regulations based on his work,[4] in which he briefly describes their evolution and proceeds to detail and illustrate their requirements and changing pattern. S. Martin Gaskell has also taken this as the basis of a book on building control which deals with national legislation and the introduction of local bye-laws in Victorian England.[5] In this he examines the evolution and establishment of building bye-laws as a means of controlling building and urban development during the period 1840–1880. My book touches on this subject, but expands into the problem area of control and examines the solutions developed in response to social and technological change. The period covered is from 1840–1990, and includes the investigation of the Departmental Committee on Building Byelaws and the introduction of its recommendations. This resulted in greater central control (every local authority having building bye-laws) and a more professional approach to the making and enforcement of standards beneficial to public health and safety.

A.J. Ley
Braunton, Devon

Chronology

CHAPTER	YEAR	EVENT	PRIME MINISTER	GOVERNMENT
1	pre-1840	London Building Act 1667 London Building Act 1772 London Building Act 1774 Bristol Building Act 1778 Liverpool Building Act 1825		
	1840	Bristol Building Act Report of Select Committee on Health of Towns Building Regulation Bill Building Regulation Bills	Viscount Melbourne	Whigs
2	1842	Report on Labouring Population of Great Britain (Chadwick's Report) Liverpool Building Act		
	1845	Health of Towns Commission Report	Peel	Tory
	1846	Metropolitan Building Act Liverpool Building Act		
	1847	Town Improvement Clauses Act Bristol Building Act		
	1848	Public Health Act	Russell	Whigs
3	1854	Public Health Act	1852 Earl of Derby	Tory
			Earl of Aberdeen (Peelite)	Peelite–Whig Coalition
	1855	Metropolitan Management Act	Viscount Palmerson	Liberal
	1856	Public Health Act Local Government Act		
	1859	Public Health Act	Earl of Derby	Conservative
4	1866	Public Health Act	Earl of Derby	Conservative
			Disraeli	
	1869	Stockton Improvement Act	1868 Gladstone	Liberal
	1871	St Helens Improvement Act Report of the Royal Sanitary Commission Local Government Board Act		
	1872	Public Health Act		
	1874	Sanitary Laws (Amendment) Act		
	1875	Public Health Act	Disraeli	Conservative
5	1885	Report of the Royal Commission on Housing	Marquis of Salisbury	Conservative
	1888	Local Government Act		
	1890	Public Health (Amendment) Act		
			Gladstone	

A HISTORY OF BUILDING CONTROL IN ENGLAND AND WALES 1840–1990

CHAPTER	YEAR	EVENT	PRIME MINISTER	GOVERNMENT
5 cont	1894	Local Government Act	Earl of Rosebury	
	1901	Factories and Workshops Act		
	1905	Public Health (Amendment) Bill		
	1906	Public Health (Building Bye-Laws) Bill	Campbell-Bannerman	Liberal
	1907	Public Health (Amendment) Act		
	1909	Housing & Town Planning etc. Act		
	1911	Housing of Working Classes Bill		
	1912	Housing of Working Classes Bill	Asquith	Liberal
	1913	Housing of Working Classes Bill		
	1914	Housing of Working Classes Bill		
6	1918	Report of the Departmental Committee on Building Bye-Laws		
	1918	Report of the Housing (Bldg Const) Committee (Tudor Walters Report)	Lloyd George	Coalition
	1919	Housing and Town Planning Act		
	1923	Housing Act	Bonar-Law	Conservative
		Report of the Commission on Fire Brigades and Fire Prevention	Baldwin	
	1925	Housing Act		
		Public Health Act	D Baldwin	Conservative
	1930	Building (Escape from Fire) Bill		
7	1933	First Report of Local Government & Public Health Consolidation Committee	Ramsay MacDonald	
		Local Government Act		National
	1936	Second Report of Local Government & Public Health Consolidation Committee	Baldwin	
		Public Health Act		
8	1956	Clean Air Act		
	1957	Thermal Insulation (Industrial Buildings) Act	Eden	Conservative
	1961	Public Health Act	Macmillan	Conservative
	1971	Fire Precautions Act	Heath	Conservative
	1972	Local Government Act		
	1974	Health & Safety at Work etc. Act	Wilson	Labour
	1982	Local Government (Miscellaneous Provisions) Act	Thatcher	Conservative
	1984	Building Act		

CHAPTER 1

The Building Regulation Bill (1841–1842): Antecedents and Failure

In 1840 a move was made to introduce building regulations to control the construction of buildings in the interests of public health and safety. This was the first attempt to encourage a building control system in the United Kingdom, and this chapter traces the origins of, and examines the influences on, legislation as a means of regulating the construction of buildings.

The Origins of Building Control

London Building Acts 1667–1774

Control over the construction of buildings in the interest of public health and safety is not recent; indeed, attempts to control the activities of builders can be traced back to ancient times.[1] In England and Wales it was the fear of loss of life and property through fire that awakened the need to control the construction of buildings. As far back as the 12th century an ordnance requiring the construction of stone party walls in new buildings to restrict the spread of fire had been made, and this requirement later also applied to external walls.[2] Many business people thereafter constructed their properties using stone walls and tile or slate roofs to protect their stock from fire, but there were still many older timber framed buildings in close proximity. It was not until after the Great Fire of London in 1666, which destroyed nearly four-fifths of the city, that an Act was introduced to control the construction of new buildings in London.[3] The Act required all external walls to be of brick or stone, and introduced rules on foundations, wall thicknesses, timber and timber sizes and new chimneys. The rules gave closer attention to the problem of fire and for this reason required roofs, window frames and cellar floors to be made of oak which does not burn as rapidly as soft wood. The party walls were required to protrude above the roof surface to form a small parapet to restrict the spread of fire from one house to another, and larger houses had to have external balconies to facilitate the rescue of those who became trapped by fire. One important feature of the Act was the provision to appoint surveyors to see that the requirements of the Act were carried out. These enforcement powers were strengthened by the imposition of fines on persons contravening the requirements. Three persons were appointed as surveyors to enforce the requirements of the Act, but it appears that these three persons were not replaced as they left or died. Consequently, the requirements of the Act were not enforced.[4] The Act brought about some degree of standardization, and the requirement for minimum room height resulted in an even height to terraced housing. The rules for thickness of walls with defined widths of piers between windows provided not only a structurally sound wall, but also a balanced fenestration (see *Plate 1*). This type of house became popular with builders, who could estimate costs and contract much more easily, and also with owners, who found that a fireproof house could also be an attractive house.

The design was often copied in towns outside London, using the same rules as stated in the London Act, even though the towns in which they were built did not have such comprehensive laws.[5] The Act of 1667 remained in force until it was replaced by further Acts in 1772 relating to party wall construction,[6] and a more important Act of 1774 which provided a comprehensive approach to the classification of buildings, their size, location and fire resistance.[7] Principles of compartmentalization and isolation began to emerge, but important aspects such as drainage and ventilation were not included. Again, surveyors were to be appointed to administer the provisions of this Act. The need for enforcement had been recognized as essential if the provisions were to have any effect, a lesson that had been learnt from the poor enforcement of the 1667 Act.

Nevertheless, despite its building control system, London did not escape the ravages of cholera, typhoid, tuberculosis, and other diseases caused by insanitary conditions in the nineteenth century, and neither did it escape from the industrial and commercial pressures stemming from the Industrial Revolution. As a result, the provisions of the 1774 Act were found lacking in detail, especially in the areas of drainage and sanitary facilities, ventilation and damp proofing. Furthermore, the Act did not control the standard of building in areas abutting the cities of London and Westminster which would be greatly affected by an expanding metropolis. However, despite the problems which emerged from the administration of the 1774 Act, the experience of trying to establish a set of building regulations proved valuable in later efforts to extend Building Acts to the rest of the country.

The London Building Acts were the first in Britain to show how a town or city council could obtain and administer legislation that would control the construction of buildings within a city in the interests of safety and public health. National legislation did not exist at this time, and any other town council which considered that its town was threatened with the ravages of fire would also have to obtain a local Act giving them similar controls.

Serious fires occurred in the towns of Northampton (1675), Warwick (1693), Tiverton (1731), Blandford (1731), Wareham (1763) and Chudleigh (1808), where the extensive use of thatch as a roofing material encouraged the rapid spread of fire. The subsequent local Acts obtained by these towns were not in any way as extensive as the London Acts, being limited to banning the use of timber and thatch in the re-roofing works, instead requiring the use of lead, slate or tile.[8] This practice was used in Calais, France (occupied by the English until 1558), following an English regulation made under the Calais Paving Act of 1548,[9] but the principles of using legislation in England to control the construction of buildings in the interests of public safety was becoming established as accepted practice.

The Bristol Building Acts 1788–1840

The first city outside London to seek and obtain an Act for regulating buildings and party walls was the city of Bristol, a town also concerned with the effects of fire.[10] Bristol, a busy port which had expanded through trade and commerce, similarly harboured many timber framed buildings. Whilst the main market streets were up to 50 feet wide, with many others 35 feet wide or more, the less important streets, lanes and alleys ranged from six to eight feet in width, inadequate to resist the spread of fire between buildings. Much of the rebuilding in other towns in Southern England had been carried out in brickwork using the London Act 1667 as a guide.[11] Rather than allowing builders freedom of choice of materials in construction, in 1788 the Council of Bristol sought to impose standards by means of a Building Act. The Act of 1788 was concerned in the first place with fire prevention (see *Figure 1*) and contained 39 sections (see *Appendix 1*).

It was limited to the construction and alignment of external and party walls and chimneys, which were required to be of brick or stone and perpendicular, thus preventing the construction of jettied upper floor levels (see *Plate 2*). The administration of the Act was centred around the appointment of surveyors on short-term contracts who could be penalized and dismissed from office for neglect of duty (see *Figure 2*).

Builders were required to give notice of their intention to build and could be fined for failing to do so, or for failing to construct work in conformity with the requirements of the Act. This Act continued in existence until it was repealed and replaced by the Bristol Improvement Act of 1840.[12] In addition to the regulation of buildings, the new Act related also to street widening (including compensation and the purchase of houses and land), nuisances and their prohibition, moneys, mayoral duties and administration. The first 38 sections (see *Appendix 2*) related to building, and in repealing the previous Act it was recognized that contracts taken out before the new Act would continue and that moneys due from the former Act could be recovered under the new Act. This also applied to officers, who could continue in office until moved but were accountable for all their books, documents and other effects.

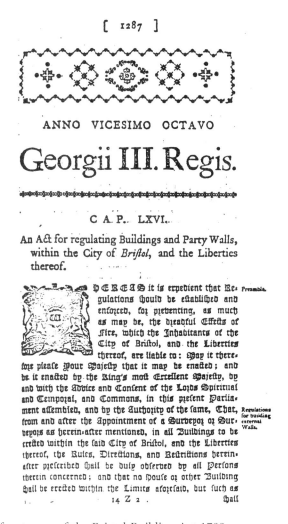

Figure 1: The front page of the Bristol Building Act 1788.

The Act provided for an improvement committee to be appointed, together with officers necessary to administer the provisions of the Act. The appointment of surveyors was a separate requirement, and these officers had to take a solemn oath which was similar to the oath of the 1788 Act. Although the surveyors were paid by the city corporation, they had the responsibility of collecting fees which were related to five classes of building.[13]

The technical requirements closely followed those specified in the London Building Acts and the fine for non-compliance was a maximum of £20.[14] This fine could also be applied to a surveyor who carried out his duties negligently. This was a good attempt to ensure an honest approach to the administration of the Act, but when misapplied could result in councillors

> XIX. And be it further enacted, That the Mayor, Aldermen, and Common Council of the said City of Bristol, in Common Council assembled, shall and may, yearly and every Year, nominate and appoint such and so many discreet Persons, skilled in the Art of Building, as the said Mayor, Aldermen, and Common Council shall think fit, to be for One Year the Surveyors to see the Rules, Directions, and Restrictions in this Act prescribed well and truly observed in and throughout the said City of Bristol, and the Liberties thereof, and shall and may appoint the several Districts which shall be under their respective Surveys, and from Time to Time, as they shall judge necessary, shall and may alter such Districts, or any of them; and it shall be lawful for the Mayor of the said City for the Time being, and he is hereby required, to administer to all the said Surveyors an Oath for the true and impartial Execution of their Office in that Behalf, which Oath shall be in the Form or to the Effect following; (that is to say),
>
> I A. B. being One of the Surveyors appointed in pursuance of an Act of Parliament, passed in the Twenty-eighth Year of the Reign of King *George* the Third, *for regulating Buildings and Party Walls within the City of Bristol, and the Liberties thereof*, do swear, That upon receiving Notice of any Building or Wall to be built, or other Builder's Work to be done within the District under my Inspection,
>
> Inspection, not being by Illness or otherwise lawfully prevented, I will diligently and faithfully survey the same, and to the utmost of my Abilities endeavour to cause the Rules, Directions, and Restrictions in the said Act prescribed to be strictly observed, and that without Favour or Affection, Prejudice or Malice.
>
> So help me G O D.

Figure 2: The appointment and oath of surveyors from the Bristol Building Act 1788.

with vested interests having influence over the way surveyors carried out their duties.

The Liverpool Building Acts 1802–1825

Liverpool, a town larger than Bristol, was also a thriving port enjoying the benefits of considerable and expanding trade with the Americas. It faced problems coping with a 100 per cent increase in population due to the arrival of Irish immigrants between 1801 and 1830, and this rate of expansion had led to the construction of a considerable number of poor quality houses using cheap and combustible materials and lacking sanitation. Civil engineer James Newlands,[15] the first engineer appointed by Liverpool Corporation, described conditions prevailing at the time – high population density, overcrowding, building over gardens and yards, lack of privacy, drainage and cleansing. The authorities were oblivious to the effects of these on public health, and were merely concerned that these conditions hindered trade and were an inconvenience to persons and carriages using the street. Therefore, whilst the symptoms of these problems resulted in improvement works, the sources were not tackled. Consequently, these were magnified by succeeding generations who, as Newlands argues, not only had to endure these conditions, but also the cost of remedying them. In 1788, the mayor and magistrates of Liverpool considered a report by the town's physicians drawn up by a Dr Currie, as to the unhealthy state of the town, and, in 1802, the Corporation of Liverpool applied to Parliament for an Improvement Bill. This bill would have had a significant impact on those persons causing, or profiting from, the unhealthy state. However, as Newlands put it, ' the interest of different individuals being affected by the Bill, the old cry of rights of property was as usual raised in defence of the wrongs of poverty, and inferior considerations triumphed over public good'[16] and not surprisingly, the bill failed.

Liverpool's interest in obtaining a Building Act was motivated more by sanitary reform than by safety from fire. However, the Act that was secured in 1825 had little of both, being extremely limited as to precautions against the spread of fire, and offering little in the way of better sanitation other than requiring water from buildings to be conveyed to drains and prohibiting smoke discharge from the front of buildings.[17]

The majority of these clauses related to requirements that could be found in the London and Bristol Building Acts, whilst the appointment and oath of surveyors was also very similar. The payment of surveyors in Liverpool would be by a fixed salary, whereas in London surveyors drew a fee relating to the class of building. The Liverpool Building Act of 1825 did not make any positive contribution to solving the insanitary conditions that existed in Liverpool, but nevertheless it was a start (see *Appendix 3*).

The role of local authorities

The initiative to tackle insanitary conditions lay with local authorities. The attitude of government was one of non-interference in what was considered a local matter, and it was up to town councils to improve their towns. Apart from the resistance that town councils would have received from persons having vested interests, the cost of securing a local Act was another deterrent and could vary between £2,000 and £12,000, depending on the special nature of the legislation.[18] The cholera epidemic of 1832 began to change attitudes towards local control as the disease did not limit its effect to any one town, and neither did it recognize or respect different classes of people.

Spread of disease

Cholera baffled the medical profession and confused town councils who were at a loss to discover the cause of the disease and the way it spread. Since the majority of deaths were in areas which suffered from overcrowding, poor housing, lack of sanitation, inadequate drainage, and poor water supplies, it was generally held that these conditions caused or contributed to the spread of disease. High death rates from typhoid, typhus, smallpox, scarlatina and other fevers were quite common and the death rate from tuberculosis was also high.[19] The problem was one of how to minimize the devastation in human terms.

It was not just disease causing illness and death that was of concern, it was also the conditions within buildings and towns that were alleged to have caused or contributed to these diseases. Living conditions for the poor sections of communities were far from good. The expanding industrial towns often lacked housing at economical rents to accommodate the increasing population,[20] and as a result houses were frequently overcrowded. Those who could afford to rent a house were attracted to the thousands of small houses being erected in and on the boundaries of many towns. This expansion was often encouraged by town councils, some of whom endeavoured to attract workers by means of advertisements.

Speculative building

With this demand for labour, the building industry was under considerable pressure to meet the accompanying need for houses and business premises. The situation was ripe for speculators, and since there was no control on where or what to develop, builders built the most profitable type of house in the most profitable positions they could acquire. Small terraced properties at high densities were built. These were often arranged in courts, usually open at one end, but not uncommonly closed at both ends. The enclosed courts were frequently unpaved and with no drainage; their orientation often meant that some dwellings in the court never had any sunlight and air circulation was severely restricted. In many northern towns, especially Leeds, Manchester, Bradford and Nottingham, back-to-back houses were erected, sometimes planned in court form. These houses had only one wall through which they could be ventilated and consequently it was impossible to obtain a through flow of air. Sanitary accommodation was provided in detached privies either in the court or at the ends of the terraces (see *Plates 3a* and *b*).

Cholera

As already noted, the lack of paving, drainage and sanitation, coupled with poor water supply and the high population densities caused by overcrowding and compact development, provided the perfect environment for the rapid spread of Asiatic cholera. People were beginning to realize that the conditions of urban life could kill. This was understood especially by those with financial and political control in towns where they and their families may have suffered illness or loss of life from endemic diseases. The death rate increased, especially amongst young children. In 1830 it was approximately 66 children per 1000 births, but it was also high amongst the adult population of the working classes, resulting in an average life expectancy in urban areas of between 15 and 19 years of age.[21]

The poor sanitary conditions, highlighted by high death rates and the devastation caused by cholera, were the prime forces in a desire to seek improvement in living and sanitary conditions. Dr Thomas Southwood-Smith's (one of the principal originators of the English public health system)[22] report on the prevalence of fever in the metropolis[23] was attached to the fifth annual report of the Poor Law Commissioners in 1839. In that report he considered that some causes of disease could be removed by sanitary measures in the form of building regulations.

Southwood-Smith was an anti-contagonist and believed that if cholera generated itself in putrid conditions in such places as India, similar conditions would promote the disease in England. He believed that fever could not be transmitted in pure air, and accordingly was an advocate of good ventilation in buildings.[24] However, Southwood-Smith also advocated some governmental involvement in securing building regulations. This was not only a move away from local control, but extended control from fire safety to health. The report was widely read and influenced many, including the Bishop of London who moved an inquiry into the conditions of the labouring classes in the House of Lords.[25] This inquiry was to be carried out by the Poor Law Commissioners.

The Health of Towns Select Committee and the Building Regulation Bills 1841–1842

The work and reports of the Poor Law commissioners tended to suggest that disease was proportional to the extent of insanitary conditions. This 'sanitarian' approach to the prevention of the spread of disease had the support of many, including R.J. Slaney,[26] a member of Parliament, who on the 4th February 1840 moved in the House of Commons that a select committee be set up to enquire into the causes of discontent of the working classes in populous districts, with a view to applying such remedies as Parliament could devise.[27]

In presenting his proposals, Slaney was concerned by the lack of legislative provision for the preservation of health and comfort in housing and considered that improvements could be achieved by means of legislative requirements and controls. Aware of the length of time that inquiries can take, he felt that a select committee would be able to act more quickly, so important was the subject. The House agreed to the proposal and fifteen members formed the committee with Slaney as chairman.

Evidence presented to the Committee

Thomas Cubitt

The committee sat for three months and took evidence from many people. Thomas Cubitt, a well-known and experienced builder in London, gave evidence as to the type of person who had caused such poor housing to be constructed in the first place.[28] The majority of such people were, according to Cubitt, 'a little shop-keeping class of person who as an investment would build such houses at low cost for rental. Few persons of capital made such an investment'. This statement emphasized the extent and complexity of the problem. New housing estates could more easily be designed and built by recognized builders to acceptable standards, but small backland and court type housing were the provinces of the small speculator and gave rise to the biggest nuisances. Cubitt added that he considered regulations controlling the construction and standards of dwellings would be beneficial but difficult to enforce. He highlighted another problem, where buildings built for another purpose were subsequently used for housing although unsuitable for that use, often lacking the open space at the front and rear so necessary for good light and ventilation. Cubitt considered back-to-back dwellings to be offensive. He pointed out the desirability of constructing party walls to resist the spread of fire and felt that special planning was needed so that masses of houses were not built together and the conversion of other buildings into houses placed under strict control. The widths of streets and drainage were also considered very important, in fact so important that Cubitt thought it necessary for public officers to provide and maintain maps of public sewers in each district.

George Smith

George Smith, District Surveyor for the South District of the City of London, in his evidence to the committee, confirmed from his experience of surveying and regulating buildings in Liverpool, Manchester and Bristol, that benefits would derive from a Building Act which would control ventilation, space about buildings and drainage.

Findings of the Committee

This evidence had considerable influence on the committee, who in introducing the report on the 17th June 1840, considered that the benefits derived from having a healthier town community would outweigh any benefits so far experienced.[29] The poorer parts of the community should by right be protected from the evils of unhealthy conditions caused by poor sanitary provisions and legislation was the only way this could be achieved. The report commented that, 'in the midst of what appears an opulent, spirited and flourishing community such a vast magnitude of our poor fellow subjects, the instruments by whose hands these riches were created, are condemned, through no fault of their own, to the evil so justly complained of, and placed in situations where it is almost impracticable to preserve health or decency of deportment'.[30] Pointing out that there was no Building Act to enforce the proper construction of dwellings for the working classes, and no drainage Act to enforce the effective drainage of buildings, the report asserted that the design, construction, amenities and siting of houses were left to the client and builder.

Recommendations of the report

The first recommendation contained in the report was for a general Building Act laying down regulations with respect to the construction of certain houses for dwellings of the working class. The committee was aware of the strong feelings that owners had over their 'property rights', and endeavoured not to impinge unduly on those rights, knowing full well that to do so would result in considerable opposition. It was considered that such regulations would not interfere with anyone's rights to manage their own property beyond what was necessary to protect the health of the community. The recommendations were intended to follow the legal maxim *sic utere tuo ut alienum non laedas* (so use your own property as not to injure your neighbour). This is still the basic doctrine of the law with regard to nuisance.

The regulations would restrict the use of cellars, the building of rows of houses in close courts built up at one end, and back-to-back houses which had no through ventilation. The space in front and to the rear of houses was to be proportional to the height of the buildings, there were to be underground drainage and sewers, and party wall construction for fire protection, but the preventive nature of these regulations would be such as not to restrict the discretion of the builder. Whilst these regulations would understandably increase building and development costs, the committee considered that increased cost incurred by complying with the regulations would not be significant, though it could result in a slight increase in rent. To offset anticipated objections and encourage public support, it was stated that an improvement in general health and environmental conditions would be worth the cost. Social benefits would also improve as it was recognized that poor housing was not attractive to live in. This approach was likely to gain public support, especially amongst those who needed improved housing standards, but the builders did not intend to fund those improvements out of their profit and their parliamentary lobby was strong and organized.

Sewage

Secondly, the committee recommended that there should be a general sewerage Act enforcing the construction of sewers for new buildings, the cost of construction being met by the builder and the cost of repairs being met by the rates. This alone would add to the cost of building and renting of houses, but there could be no denial that house drains connected to the sewer would produce healthier living conditions when the sewage was disposed of satisfactorily. The Act should provide for enforcing a connection between existing houses and the sewer, the cost being covered by the owner and the cost of repairs being met from the rate fund. Cesspools below the level of the main sewer should be prohibited. These proposals were quite radical in that they were advocating government involvement in matters mainly of a local nature but having national implications. This would provoke considerable objection but statutory action was necessary as London and Bristol had found out, and if local authorities would not tackle the problems, the government had to.

Recommendation for a Local Board of Health

This proposed building Act, if brought into being, would create a major change of principle in that the regulations would be made not only in the interests of safety but also health. Furthermore, the government would be instrumental in making rules and seeing that they were enforced on matters that had previously been local issues, often jealously guarded. Even the form of control was very centralized. The report recommended that in towns there should be a Local Board of Health, appointed by the town council or Board of Guardians who would report to a Central Board of Health or to the Secretary of State for the Home Department. In larger towns, an Inspector of Nuisances should be appointed to enforce the statutory provisions. To avoid the expense associated with obtaining a local Act, the report suggested that the proposed Acts could be adopted by towns with a local vote.

Adoption of the Building Act

Recognizing the possibility of reaction from towns objecting to the Act, it was proposed that only those towns wishing to have such powers adopt it; that is, the adoption of the Act was to be voluntary, not mandatory. Providing a discretionary clause was a weakness that could lead to the most insanitary of towns not having the Act merely because the town council did not see fit to adopt it. Indifferent control would not bring about improved sanitary conditions on a national scale to assist in combating the spread of disease in the way envisaged by Southwood-Smith. The measure recommended did not cover the entire problem of sanitary improvement and the report suggested that further consideration ought to be given to water supply, burial grounds, lodging houses, public open spaces and public bathing. This was widening the area of government control and influence, but it only reflected the extent of the social problems at that time.

Apart from passing private Acts for London, Liverpool and Bristol to regulate the construction of buildings, Parliament had little or no precedent in comprehending the contents of this report. The Health of Towns Select Committee recommendations were well-founded and of such an extent that when taken together with the other matters that needed further investigation it became clear that the field of sanitary reform was quite vast. So vast, in fact, that it was to take the next 34 years before legislation and administration could begin to deal effectively with the problem. The people who would benefit most from such reform were not in a position to vote either in the towns or in the country, and therefore could not influence Parliament in its decision other than by maintaining the high death and disease rates which provided statistical evidence in support of the recommendations. The growing knowledge of the problems, backed by statistical and scientific evidence, was such that they were elevated to a national scale. This implied that national action was the logical solution, as the state would then have the power to intervene and enforce the law.[31]

The Marquis of Normanby and the 1841 Building Regulation Bill

One person who supported the improvement of sanitary conditions in towns, and government interference was the Marquis of Normanby.[32] As the Principal Secretary of State for the Home Office, to whom the Poor Law commissioners reported, he had been made aware of the consequences of the sanitary conditions of the poor and was influenced by the commissioners' reports.

Normanby, also unwilling to await the report of the inquiry being undertaken by the Poor Law Commissioners, supported Slaney's report by introducing into the House of Lords in 1841 a bill for regulating buildings in large towns.[33] So keen was he to see that these measures were brought into law that he instructed the Poor Law commissioners to halt their inquiry. However, such was the indifference of government that the Prime Minister, Lord Melbourne, directed that this inquiry should continue.[34]

Provisions of the Bill

This bill was quite extensive in its requirements, including some 77 clauses (see *Appendix 4*). It was based on the London Building Act but with notable inclusions derived from the recommendations of the Health of Towns Select Committee. The bill provided for: the appointment of surveyors, in a similar manner to the London, Bristol and Liverpool Acts; inspection and enforcement of work; penalties; and the prevention of back-to-back houses fronting onto streets with no space at the rear. As previously mentioned, this form of construction prevented the floor areas of the house from being properly ventilated. Regulations were also proposed to control open areas around dwellings, the restriction of cellars for habitation where they lacked reasonable headroom, and ventilation and street widths. The building of court houses was also controlled. Since ventilation of such houses could be obstructed, totally enclosed courts would not be acceptable and such developments had to be open at one end and restricted in length. Chimneys and flues had to be constructed so as to properly extract smoke and prevent fire from spreading to the constructional timbers of the house. Wall thicknesses were specified to ensure structural stability, and party walls had to be imperforate to check the spread of fire between houses. Houses could not be extended so as to prejudice the standard of building established by the regulations. These 77 clauses extended the provisions of the Bristol, Liverpool and London Building Acts from structural requirements to prevent the spread of fire and collapse of buildings into matters of public health.[35]

Applicability of the Act

It was proposed that the Act should be applied to all municipal corporations, as defined in the Municipal Corporation Act of 1835[36], in England (including London), Wales, Scotland and Ireland, and that the provisions of the Act should be obligatory. Normanby's bill was passed by the House of Lords and introduced in the House of Commons on the 7th May 1841 when it was given a further reading and referred to committee.

Surveyors' fees

The committee included the provision for the payment of fees to the surveyor, in a similar manner to the London Acts, which would make the enforcement of the Act self-financing and not a burden on the ratepayer. These fees would be the surveyor's main income, but the Act did not appear to restrict the surveyor from undertaking other work that did not conflict with their statutory duties. Surveyors would be obliged to take an oath under the Act but this was nothing new and was taken from the Bristol and Liverpool Acts which extended the principle from the London Building Acts of 1667, 1772 and 1774. The Bill recognized the importance of adequate enforcement; without it the desired benefits would certainly not be achieved. The requirement to appoint surveyors, set fees for their services, and provide offices would establish nationally the office of surveyor which had previously been restricted to local Act provisions.

Reintroduction of the Bill

Despite the growing evidence that such a bill was needed, Lord Russell, the Prime Minister, abandoned it as there were other matters he considered to be of more concern to the House before the session terminated. Russell's government was replaced and the new government, not having been responsible for the formation of the Health of the Towns Select Committee, did not feel obligated to this bill.[37] Normanby, undeterred, re-introduced the bill, but unfortunately there was insufficient parliamentary time for it to be dealt with during that parliamentary session. Normanby once again re-introduced it in February 1842, noting that it had been passed by the House of Lords on two previous occasions.[38] The Building Regulation Bill had been modified only by the statement of fees and an amendment which provided for the surveying of alterations and additions.

The House of Lords passed the bill for the third time in 1842,[39] but Normanby was facing considerable opposition as it did not have government support. When the Building Regulation Bill was presented in the House of Commons it was again postponed after the first reading.[40] Town councils, Improvement Commissions and property owners had strongly objected to the proposals and as a result the bill was amended.[41] Some objectors emphasized the indifference and disorganized structure of local government and town councils discredited the Bill by stating that their towns already had building controls that were working satisfactorily and that the bill represented an intrusion into the rights of property owners. Improvement commissions agreed that existing controls were inadequate and that they should be given the powers to administer the bill. In some towns the opposite views were taken.

The main objection to the bill was the fear of increased costs. Normanby had been aware of this and was of the opinion that many speculators made exorbitant profits and it was those he was seeking to reduce. The bill itself increased costs as the system of enforcement by appointed surveyors was to be self-financing where builders would pay fees based on 2–3 per cent of the costs of building work whilst alterations and extensions to buildings would command a fee of only half that rate.[42] This was to increase even further in the London area, where fees could be paid for surveyors carrying out similar duties under the London Building Acts,[43] a duplication that could be avoided only by the repeal of the London Building Act. Profit margins on low cost speculative housing were frequently less than 10 per cent and the fees alone had a substantial impact on that profit margin. A further increase of cost would be incurred as a result of improved standards of construction, lower density of development due to street bye-laws, and the proposed abolition of back-to-back housing, which only made the projected profit margin lower. This was bound to produce extensive objection.

Objections to surveyors' efficiency

Objections as to the efficiency of building surveyors were also raised. For example, it was claimed that certificates issued by surveyors on completion of a building had fallen into disuse as the requirements of the Act were so minute that no surveyor could swear that they had all been complied with. But to expect a surveyor to check every minor detail was an ever-increasing task. The obligation to comply with building regulations rested with the owner and builders, not the surveyor whose role involved making periodic inspections, not constant supervision. The surveyors in Bristol and Liverpool were paid a salary and followed no other business, and this was felt less objectionable than being paid by fees, although fees paid would contribute towards their salaries. There was little objection to control being exercised by independent surveyors who operated under the London Building Acts, but builders did object to other builders who had been appointed to undertake a surveyor's responsibility and who still maintained a building business.

Extent of the Act

In some cases the Act did not go far enough. Preventing fire and restricting its spread had long been established, but it was also an important aspect of public safety that persons trapped by fire should be provided with means to escape. One lone architect pleaded this case. This was obviously a forward-looking proposal, but with the deletion of so many clauses relating to fire resistant construction, it was extremely unlikely to be considered.

The committee recognized that the proposals were incompatible with the London Building Act and in order to achieve an acceptable degree of harmonization a new bill should be constructed which consolidated the Building Regulation Bill with the Drainage Bill, the London Building Acts and all similar local Acts. This was a positive and constructive suggestion, likely to produce a satisfactory solution, but it was not developed further as the brief of the Select Committee was merely to take evidence and report. When the committee did report they made no recommendation and the report was not debated in the House.[44] However, the committee did amend the bill by reducing the original 77 clauses to 35 (see *Appendix 5*) and the bill was to apply to the whole of the United Kingdom.[45]

Retention of the fee system of surveyors

The office of surveyor, and the oath and fee system were to be retained, together with inspection and penalties for contraventions. The fee system was altered to permit authorities the discretion to pay surveyors by fees, or salary, or both. The lobby against fees secured a reduction from £3 10s for a first-rate house to a maximum of 10s for any class of house, a reduction in effect from 2–3 per cent to 0.3–0.5 per cent. At this level of fee it was more probable that local authorities would have to pay their surveyors a salary as the income from fees would be hardly sufficient to sustain their practice. Consequently, the intention of a self-financing Act was put to one side – a principle was sacrificed to speculative profit. If the industry had been able to police itself and absorb the cost it should have done so, otherwise it should have paid for the government to exercise these controls.

Speculative profit

The protection of speculative profit was clearly shown by the deletion of the proposal to prevent the building of back-to-back houses and closed court development, as the lobby to retain this profitable type of speculative building was extensive. It was argued that such cheap housing would be more suitable to meet the needs of the working classes at rents they could afford to pay. In addition, all the regulations on the construction of walls, chimneys, flues, timber near flues, chimney heights and the 15 sections regulating party wall constructions were withdrawn.

Enforcement of the Act

A clause was added allowing commissioners to enforce the Act in certain areas and granting Liverpool exemption from the Act. This strong opposition resulted in the bill's original clauses being so weakened that it could have little impact on preventing the construction of dwellings that had been considered to be objectionable to public health and safety.[46] Gauldie argues that the bill attacked the sanctity of private property, which was the same reason Newlands gave for the loss of the Liverpool Building Bill in 1802.[47] Slaney's committee had warned of this possibility when it referred to new regulations being framed to prevent injury to neighbouring property. The ownership of private property was a form of recognition in society, and to property owners, standing above the poorer classes and exploiting the use of their property by maximizing rents and minimizing investment, the thought of surveyors inspecting and enforcing construction standards, thereby increasing costs, was provocative and encouraged objection. This was undoubtedly a contributing factor, but Normanby had not encouraged support from the professional classes, architects, doctors, sanitarians, builders and developers which would have enabled him to produce statistical information to back the opinions expressed. Consequently, public opinion had not been swayed sufficiently to lead politicians to support the Bill.

Failure of the Bill

The weakened Bill, by trying to compromise the interests of both sides, invited attack, and business interests had the capability of influencing not only town councils but even the government.[48] Opposition to the Bill was sufficient to ensure that it did not receive a second reading in the Commons. Local control was considered to be better. The Bill had contained many of the London Act provisions, and according to Gauldie this similarity resulted in its being considered inferior to the Acts of Liverpool and Bristol and was another reason why it failed.[49] But this was not so. The Bristol and Liverpool Acts took many of their requirements from the London Building Act. If anything, it was the *superiority* of the London Act and its incompatibility to work alongside an inferior Act, particularly as it was not intended to repeal the London Act. It was the intrusion into what were considered local issues, for example, the specific requirements within the clauses of the bill which would restrict the use of local materials that caused builders and builders merchants trading in local materials to object. The fear of government dominance gave rise to supporting local measures, and certainly witnesses had submitted evidence to the committee that in their opinion local Acts were better. Gaskell adds that the adverse criticism the bill received from witnesses and the press was another contributory factor, which despite Normanby's parliamentary efforts, illustrates the lack of effort the supporters of the bill had made to explain their proposals.[50]

Despite all this criticism, property owners had little to fear from the bill. The provisions of the bill would not apply retrospectively and therefore existing properties would not have to be improved to the standards set out in the bill, a point not forcefully put over or even explained by Normanby. Certainly, new houses would cost more. In any case, building houses for the labouring classes was less profitable than other forms of housing [51] and it was the desire to maintain a steady flow of housing with good profits in building and in investment, which resulted in most of the fierce opposition to the bill. Those who would have been most affected by the bill shouted loudest, and the comments expressed by Newlands over the failure of the Liverpool Improvement Act of 1802 could equally apply to this bill.

The government, facing such objections and without positive recommendations from the Select Committee (who, as previously indicated, were not directed to provide any), could not proceed with the bill. It was finally postponed due to the fact that the report of the Poor Law commissioners on the sanitary condition of the labouring population of the United Kingdom would be in the hands of members by the end of the session. Matters relating to drainage and to building regulations could be considered together and it was the intention of the government to introduce a bill during the next session of Parliament which would embrace the whole subject. [52] Although the bill had been lost it was apparent that all levels of society were aware of the problems caused by insanitary conditions and by urban conditions that encouraged filth and pollution. The efforts of Normanby and his supporters mark the beginnings of a surge of public awareness and education in these problems.

The need for good sanitation and soundly built houses, highlighted by professional opinion, committee enquiries, reports and publicity, stimulated the search for constructive legislation to minimize the social effects, but these influences were offset by determined resistance from speculative builders, developers and other vested interests. Conflicts of interest were clearly beginning to emerge. The bill represented a sign that national action was needed to solve a national problem; attitudes of non-involvement in what were considered local issues would not provide a solution, local control was divided, often weak and easily influenced, but the opposition of town councils and Improvement commissioners gave a clear warning that local government wanted to retain the discretion to do as they thought necessary. The slimming down of the bill, especially the exclusion of the clause banning the erection of back-to-back housing and reduction in surveyors' fees, was an indication of how influential the speculative housebuilder was. Despite the opposition, the bill had its good points in that it sought to improve the standard of houses amongst the poorer classes and to bring about some uniformity of construction in materials, siting and design. In this respect the surveyor's role was not merely in relation to enforcement; it would also provide the basis for uniformity and the flexibility necessary for good administration. This point had not been made clear, and had the architects of the bill sought wider support from professional opinion and obtained a better press, the bill might well have been successful.[53]

Thus an excellent opportunity to establish the principle of one building Act for the United Kingdom was missed. It could have provided a uniform standard of control, bringing about equal benefits of improved public health and safety to all. Failure to act, due to extensive objections by vested interests, and a disorganized form of local government, resulted in the development of a form of building control dependent upon many local Acts which ultimately produced different systems of building control in England, Wales, Scotland, Northern Ireland and London.

CHAPTER 2
Local Improvement Acts and the Health of Towns

The previous chapter described how professional people, such as Southwood-Smith, Thomas Cubitt and George Smith, were able to inform and influence politicians about the need to introduce building regulations in the interest of public health and safety. It was these influences, sharpened by a broadening of social concern, which sought to control the construction of houses for the working classes amongst other public health issues. We turn next to the influence of Edwin Chadwick on building control.

Edwin Chadwick

Edwin Chadwick, as secretary to the Poor Law Commissioners, had the task of preparing a report commissioned by Lord Russell in 1839.[1] At first he shared Southwood-Smith's views that a Building Act could bring about sanitary improvements, but during the course of his investigations he began to change his views and opposed Normanby's Bill. Chadwick prompted the government to await his report, saying it would illustrate the problem and suggest the solutions more thoroughly than Normanby's Bill.[2] The report, presented in 1842, contained 450 pages of evidence, comment, recommendations and statistical appendices, and had taken just over two and a half years to complete.

Solutions for improving conditions

Chadwick's report set out the sanitary problems facing the labouring classes, putting forward a solution based on improving the infrastructure of towns. In doing so, he strongly criticized Building Act procedures and their use as a solution. The report cited numerous examples of poor construction, dampness, restricted natural light and ventilation, lack of sewers, drainage and water supply.

Of Sheffield the report said, 'there are parts of the town without drainage, the houses, which are private property, are built without any regard to sanitation or ventilation and constructed in a manner to ensure the greatest return at the least possible outlay'.[3] In rural areas, similar descriptions were given, for example, 'another cause of disease is to be found in the state of cottages. Many are built on the ground without flooring, or against a damp hill. Some neither have windows nor doors sufficient to keep out the weather or to let in the rays of the sun or supply the means of ventilation'.[4]

Mortality rates

Many of the descriptions of this time list common faults including dampness, poor ventilation, lack of sanitation, inadequate water supply and overcrowding. These conditions were considered to contribute to the high death rate amongst the poor classes. Mortality figures from mortuary registers of the metropolitan area of London for the year 1829 showed that of the 52 deaths recorded, 41 were only 25 years old or less and the average age of the 30 people who died of lung disease was 28 years. Mortality statistics were submitted from the towns and areas surveyed by the assistant commissioners, and Chadwick was able to use these figures to compare mortality rates with the known environmental condition of those areas. The collection of this type of information was important in the presentation and understanding of the effects of insanitary conditions and vividly helped to illustrate the underlying issues.

Table 2.1 Average age of death (in years)

	Manchester	Leeds	Liverpool	Rutland	Truro	Bath
Professional persons and gentry, including families	37	44	35	52	40	55
Tradesmen and families	20	27	22	41	33	37
Mechanics, labourers and their families	17	19	15	38	28	25

Whilst the figures in *Table 2.1* include a high proportion of children (for example, among the labouring classes in Manchester in 1840 the child death rate for under-fives was 1 in 1.75), they also indicate that the less congested of the rural areas provided a healthier environment. This was certainly a general view, but there were also examples of rural areas having a higher mortality rate than certain towns. The city of Bath, for instance, was described as an extremely healthy town for the majority of its inhabitants, comparable to many rural areas.

Costs

Any attempt to improve the health of the working classes by providing sewers, new water supplies, street cleaning and paving would cost money, which had to be obtained from public funds (for example, from taxes and rates), or through charitable bodies. Chadwick argued that the cost of improving the infrastructure of towns would be offset by a reduction in the cost of treating the sick, an increase of working hours and production due to the reduction of sickness amongst workers, and reduction in the cost of maintaining the poor, the sick, widows and their families.

Chadwick considered the expenditure of so much money to carry out remedial measures a sound investment that would have immediate effects of economy and public gain by reducing sickness in the worst areas by at least one third. The same conclusion was applicable to the cost of preventive measures directly or indirectly controlled by legislation in the construction of dwellings for the labouring classes. The cost would not necessarily fall on the taxpayer, but as an added cost to the property developer and speculator, who would doubtless increase the purchase or rental price of the property. Irrespective of the approach, someone had to pay the bill and Chadwick considered there would be fewer objections to his proposals if the burden fell on the taxpayer.

Proposals for Improvement

Whilst examples of unhealthy environments caused by poor buildings were obvious in almost every parish in England, Wales and Scotland as Chadwick's report had shown, examples of good buildings could also be found.

JC Loudon

John C. Loudon, having experience as a farm manager, developed an expertise in country dwellings and village development, and in his evidence to the commissioners, described how buildings could be improved.[5] He considered that the essential requisites of a comfortable labourer's cottage were that it should be adjoining a road and so oriented that the sun shone on every side throughout the year. It should preferably be detached, but not more than two cottages should be adjoined together, and situated in a plot with front and rear gardens, the total area being not less than one sixth of an acre. The plot size should be large enough so that the cesspool could be sited as far away as possible, not only from the dwelling, but also from any well providing drinking water. Where spring or well water was not available, a storage tank should be situated under the floor into which rainwater could be piped and then pumped up into the kitchen. For health reasons the kitchen should not open directly into the living room, and to minimize dampness the ground floor should be situated six inches to one foot above ground level. The privy should be sited away from the dwelling unless it was a water closet piped to the cesspool. The dwelling should have at least two storeys with the sleeping accommodation at first floor level. The staircase to the first floor should lead from a porch or hall so that in the event of a death the body could be removed whilst the family was in the front room. The standards specified by Loudon, in respect of ground floor and cesspool construction, would eventually form the basis of statutory bye-laws after 1858.

On density alone these proposals did not find favour among speculative builders in the expanding industrial towns, but were more suited to development in rural areas.

Captain Vetch

The evidence of Captain Vetch, an engineer with extensive knowledge of the infrastructure of towns, extended consideration of the relationship of internal environment to external environment, making reference to the need for good ventilation, drainage, sewage, and isolation from fire risk.[6] Regarding ventilation, he commented on the need for streets to be open and suggested turning blind alleys into thoroughfares, thus ensuring that noxious odours could be dispersed by currents of air. He considered it an absolute necessity that as towns became more and more crowded, drainage and sewerage should be provided, whilst towns which had the benefit of existing drainage and sewerage systems should not expand unless the system had been extended to accommodate the new development.

The structural and sanitary defects in houses illustrated by Chadwick and the specification put forward by Loudon could be controlled by a Building Act, as can be seen from the clauses in the Building Regulation Bill, but to do so would mean detailed specific clauses. This would not only add to the cost of housing, but also be considered interference in property rights, one of the reasons for the failure of Normanby's Bill. To avoid these problems and produce a solution that could be more acceptable, Chadwick chose to support the broader approach put forward in evidence by Captain Vetch.

Chadwick and the issue of building control

If Chadwick was to succeed in producing a solution that did not depend upon a Building Act, he first had to discredit belief in such an Act. This he proceeded to do by critically examining the problems experienced in administering the few Building Acts in England and Wales. The London Building Act took the brunt of that criticism, and he attacked its inflexibility by quoting some of its specific requirements. For example, 'the outer walls shall be constructed of well burnt bricks – and the mortar and cement shall be well compounded in the proportion of one part cement and three parts clean sharp sand'. In many parts of the country neither clean nor sharp sand was readily available and fine ash had to be used. This would be illegal, since no differing materials or construction methods could be used unless approved by Parliament. He recognized that changes from traditional timber framed building to masonry materials would bring conflict, and the benefits achieved were not worth the conflict they caused. This inflexible approach was too restricting to the building industry and caused bitterness, frustration and extra expense to many builders.[7]

Avoidance of Building Acts

Chadwick showed how unscrupulous builders avoided a Building Act by simply not building in areas that were subject to control. Mr Gutch, a district surveyor in the metropolis, stated that in his opinion speculators would construct dwellings outside the area controlled under the Metropolitan Building Act to avoid building to the standards of that Act. For example, New Kingston in Surrey, an area built by speculators outside the jurisdiction of the Act which encompassed Old Kingston, was noted for a higher fever rate than Old Kingston, which was well drained and healthy.[8]

A speculative development comprising forty to fifty fourth-rate dwellings constructed outside an area controlled by a Building Act, according to Gutch, would save the payment of a district surveyor's fee equivalent to the cost of one of those dwellings.[9] Developers were not only confronted with building surveyors' fees but also the fees and involvement of numerous other surveyors, such as commissioners of sewers, turnpike roads, surveyors of highways, paving, and bridges. Gutch believed that public benefit in terms of reduced cost and less interference to developers could well be achieved by combining the duties of many of these posts.

Administration of this Act was important, and whilst Chadwick recognized both the economics and skills necessary, it was not possible to combine many of those tasks because of the differing skills required.

Chadwick considered that any Building Act confined to a town or particular district would force unscrupulous builders to construct in areas which did not have building controls. These views had the support of Thomas Cubitt, who in his evidence stated that, 'anything in the nature of a Building Act that is not equally and skilfully administered will aggravate the evils intended to be remedied. To whatever districts regulations are confined the effect proved likely to follow will be that the builder of tenements that are in most need of regulation will be driven over the boundary and will run up his habitations before measure can be taken against him'.[10]

Lack of qualified surveyors

Chadwick criticized the lack of qualifications, skill and poor administration of surveyors appointed under the Building Acts. The Acts did not specify qualifications for appointment as surveyor, nor did the employer seek them. It was not uncommon for builders to be appointed who could, and often did, act unfairly against other builders who had no defence against such actions.[11] It was also alleged that some surveyors were hand in glove with builders to pass inferior work,[12] a practice that was to continue for many years.[13]

The clauses of the Act were complex enough to require skilful interpretation and application, but this was not often the case. In one large district of the metropolis it was reported that junior clerks of the district surveyor's office were examining building work for compliance under the Act.[14] This led Chadwick to comment that many local authority appointments should be filled by persons having special or scientific qualifications. Even where those qualifications were defined, persons were often appointed who did not have them and this resulted in incorrect administrative and technical applications, excessive costs and bad quality of service to the ratepayer. Chadwick thought that the committee procedure of local authorities protected such officers who had frequently failed in their own businesses prior to securing their council appointments.[15]

These views were entirely justified, given the necessity of having knowledgeable persons able to make technical assessments of building work to advise and establish compliance with the requirements of the Act. However, this argument was being used to destroy any support for a Building Act. Chadwick's disapproval continued when he added to the criticism that was expressed against the payment of fees during the debates on the Building Regulation Bill, by showing how expensive it was and how little it achieved. Fees payable under the Metropolitan Building Act varied between £3 10s and £1 per house. Chadwick estimated that if the annual rate of population increase in Great Britain (230,000) was accommodated in 59,000 new houses, the fee income could be between £80,000 and £100, 000 per annum, equal to the cost of all the sappers and miners in the Army plus the Corps of Engineers,[16] thus comparing the high charges for a poor unqualified professional service with the relatively low cost of a highly qualified and professional organization such as the Royal Corps of Engineers

In Leeds, the increase in houses per year was 855 and this would provide a fee income of £4 12s per day for building inspection work, estimated to take approximately three hours a day. This cost equated to the daily cost of a board of Royal Engineers officers comprising a colonel, lieutenant colonel, two captains, two first lieutenants and two second lieutenants.[17] This comparison did nothing to reflect the work of a good surveyor in private practice but merely emphasized the poor pay of the British army while not recognizing the private incomes that many of the officers enjoyed. Chadwick considered that the professional skill and expertise of officers of the Corps of Engineers were far in excess of those persons appointed as building surveyors under the Building Acts, and that if the services of men of independent position with the qualifications of engineers were secured, they could not fail to take notice of intentional and unintentional errors of building construction. The low standards among building surveyors reflected badly on the administration of the local Building Acts, even though the evidence suggested that the fee income could employ men of better skill and qualification, possibly retired Royal Engineers officers. If this was the intention it did not succeed. No Building Act was recommended and the question of fees did not appear again for another 132 years.

Chadwick and the issue of central control

Having described how a Building Act would be too specific, add to the cost of building, could be easily avoided, be expensive and poorly administered by its surveyors, Chadwick turned to his own solution, which was the improvement of the urban infrastructure. This would involve the improvement and installation of sewers, sewage disposal, water supply, roads and open spaces, work that required the skill of civil engineers and not building surveyors.

His attack on the local inadequacies of Building Act surveyors and the incompetence of local administrators was directed towards discrediting the increasing number of local Improvement Acts that were being passed. These included a few controls on building construction and the improvement of the infrastructure of towns. Chadwick seemed intent on destroying such Acts because he believed that the only way to eradicate many of the insanitary problems unearthed by his report was by an Act of Parliament constituting a central, as opposed to local, control, with himself at the helm.

Chadwick concluded that any form of Building Act should aim to control the incremental expansion of towns by ensuing adequate streets, drainage and open space, matters that would not increase the cost of housing. As everyone would benefit from such improvements, he thought it was likely to be a more popular recommendation, but this view was in advance of its time as the concept of town planning was not fully developed before 1909.[18]

Many of Chadwick's views were justified, but certainly not at the expense of the rest of England and Wales not having the benefit of Acts such as London, Bristol and Liverpool had. His blistering attack on the inadequacies, maladministration and cost of administering such Acts removed any hope of the matter being reconsidered by Parliament.[19]

Chadwick proposed that his recommendations could be brought about by an Act that provided a central Board of Health, to which local Boards of Health formed by town councils or Boards of Guardians would report. The mode of control was that put forward by Slaney's Health of Towns Select Committee in 1840. Thus, Chadwick simply removed the building regulation proposals, substituting his own proposals, a combination he felt had much political support.[20] However, his proposals for central control involving government interference and responsibility in matters still regarded as local would be certain to objection.

Chadwick's recommendations were not sufficiently conclusive to proceed with legislation. The report, however, could not be overlooked. So devastating were it contents that the government decided to set up a commission to enquire into the health of certain towns and report its findings to Parliament. The working of the commission would provide a breathing space for the government, who were pressured on one hand by the sanitarians and on the other by speculators and developers demanding that the *status quo* should be maintained.

Local Improvement Acts

The failure of Normanby's initiatives and the lack of government response to Chadwick's proposals meant that local authorities continued to improve their town environments in their own way. The regulation of building remained a local issue. Discretion as to how towns resolved their problems was one of the features of local self-government, allowing those in control to do as they pleased. Often their interests were not the interests of those who suffered from their actions. Those councils who wished to improve their towns could do so within the limitations of their Improvement Act, while others decided to do nothing. The city of Bristol improved their Building Act in 1840 (see p.3) and Liverpool did likewise in 1842 with a comprehensive Act of 131 sections, the first 92 dealing with buildings (see *Appendix 6*). Outer and party walls were to be constructed of non-combustible materials of specified thickness and openings in party walls were to be restricted. Chimney and flue construction, including heights and openings, were controlled and even sizes of timbers and mortar mixes were specified.[21] These requirements were taken from the London Building Acts and related to structural stability and fire resistance. However, the Act also included many matters relating to health such as ventilation, size of rooms, restriction on the use of cellars and the cleansing of drains, cesspits and privies. This was an extension of control in areas about which Chadwick had expressed concern. Although the provisions were not as extensive as Chadwick had proposed, it was a good example of how towns could take individual action without the need for general legislation. Towns were more easily subjected to local pressures, as in Bristol where the council, on amending their Building Act in 1847,[22] was seemingly influenced by Chadwick's criticism, amongst many others, on the imposition of fees. Consequently Section 15 of the Bristol Building Act of 1847 provided for a reduction, alteration or even abolition of fees.

Other towns followed, but their Improvement Acts were not as comprehensive in building control terms as those of Bristol and particularly Liverpool. Nevertheless, what was included tended to be based upon those Acts, thus making Parliamentary acceptance much easier.

Not all Acts were identical. In 1837 Newcastle-upon-Tyne secured an Improvement Act, similar to the Bristol Act, which controlled projections from the face of the buildings, thickness of walls, construction of chimneys and the siting of houses.[23] The Leeds Improvement Act of 1842 invested all the powers in the town council with which the Improvement Commission was merged, and was the first Act to require house drainage to be connected to a sewer or cesspool. Other controls related to the restriction of projections from buildings, widths of courts, alleys and openings into them.[24] Manchester was able as a result of its Improvement Act to restrict the erection of back-to-back houses with a requirement that an ashpit or privy must be provided in a yard attached to the premises but not in front of any house.[25] Leeds had a similar regulation but such was the pressure to build back-to-back houses there that the regulations were never enforced.[26] This is an example of how a local authority could be influenced not to enforce regulations.

Differences between local Acts

The differences emerging in the requirements of these Acts were mostly of details, as the broad principles remained those of the London, Bristol and Liverpool Acts. These differences were often sufficient to allow local materials, methods of construction and even house types to be used, as we have seen with the back-to-back housing in Leeds, and many other northern towns.

The mere proposal to introduce an Improvement Act frequently led to a boom in speculative building as builders sought to beat the increase in costs that the Act was feared to bring about.[27] The increase in construction costs would mean less investment, less building and lower profits. These fears also influenced many councils in how they enforced their Acts. It depended upon the extent of interest of, and advantage to, those in control or who exercised influence on the council; even the appointment of surveyors was subservient to the whims of councillors.⁽²⁸⁾ Such power and discretion varied. For example, in Sheffield, a surveyor was appointed who could neither read nor write, ⁽²⁹⁾ and therefore was hardly in a position to understand building regulations let alone enforce them.

These indifferent standards drew adverse comment over the ease or difficulty that builders experienced in building in various towns. The situation in Sheffield changed later following strong pressure from a group of artisan cutlers who forced the council to appoint a sufficiently competent and trained surveyor. ⁽³⁰⁾

Despite these relatively minor problems, it was readily accepted that legislation was needed to bring about improvement in property and town environments. The fact that the Acts were controlled locally offset the fear of central control, but the sum of all the Improvement Acts with their common approach in content and enforcement began to take on a national look.

Influence of the London Building Act 1844

Whilst towns in England and Wales were obtaining their Improvement Acts, thus enabling some control over building construction, a new Building Act was granted for London in August 1844. The Act applied to the greater part of the Metropolitan area and the technical requirements had also increased. The criticism made by Chadwick of the abilities of London Building Act surveyors had not gone unnoticed, and as a solution to that problem it was made a requirement that the surveyors appointed in the future should be qualified for the technicalities and responsibilities of the post. This important improvement resulted in a better and more professional administration and Normanby considered that with a little more thought the government could apply the Act to other parts of the country. This was easier said than done and the government was in no mood to force such an issue onto local government.

Instead, towns were encouraged to develop their own approaches to improvements, incorporating building control as they thought necessary. This enabled the government to give a lead as to specific improvement provisions whilst allowing local government discretion over their application, a nice balance that usually satisfied both parties. The Town Improvement Clauses Act introduced in 1847 comprised 216 sections dealing with paving, drainage, cleansing, lighting, party wall construction, street naming and numbering and general town improvement.⁽³¹⁾ It was a consolidating Act for Improvement Commissions and Town Councils of England and Wales. Some degree of control over the construction of buildings emerged from the Act as there were similarities between it and the Building Acts of London, Bristol and Liverpool. Surveyors appointed under the Act were required to make a declaration which was almost identical to the declarations made under those earlier Acts. The

Act required that party walls were to project above the roof and the roof covering was to be of non-combustible materials. The use of cellars for dwellings was also controlled and requirements were made with regard to paving and levels of new streets, street naming and numbering and the fixing of water downpipes to buildings. Ruinous and dangerous buildings could either be made safe by the owners or taken down by the commissioners, who were then empowered to recover the cost or sell the materials. Plans had to be submitted to ensure public buildings were provided with adequate ventilation. Where plans were not dealt with within 14 days the builder could proceed with the work. This was a form of deemed approval which in effect penalized inefficient councils by restricting their enforcement powers. Notice of building works had to be given to the surveyors who had to ensure that no new house was erected without drainage and that the level of the house was such that gravity drainage to the sewer could be achieved. Although the Act could have been improved, it was nevertheless a sign that Parliament was prepared to pass legislation of a public nature to be adopted at the discretion of the local authorities, appeasing both the general public and local influences. Thus, central government control was beginning to develop, bringing about a welcome degree of uniformity. The provisions of the Act, although not as comprehensive as the Bristol and Liverpool Acts, marked the beginning of building control for many towns. Nevertheless, the government did nothing about Chadwick's report for two years and when Normanby again pressed for action he was informed that the Health of Towns Commission had been formed and would soon report their findings.[32]

The Health of Towns Commission

The Health of Towns Commission was appointed on the 9th May 1843[33] with the Duke of Buccleuch as its chairman. Slaney, who had chaired the Health of Towns Select Committee in 1841, and had recommended a building regulation Act to apply in certain towns, was also a member of the Commission. Its task was to investigate the sanitary conditions of the poorer classes and recommend how the salubrity and safety of their dwellings could be improved by regulation and law. This involved a detailed study of 50 towns with high mortality rates and populations in total of over three million people.

The Commission Reports

The Commission presented two reports, the first a proposed Bill dated 27th June 1844, and the second an account of the enquiry and conclusions dated 3rd February 1845.[34]

The five divisions of the inquiry related to:

- drainage, including house, foul and surface water;
- paving of public streets, courts and alleys;
- street cleaning and removal of refuse;
- supply of water for public and private use; and
- the construction and ventilation of buildings.

The two reports and appendices highlighted the many problems that existed, with the second report containing recommendations as to the remedial measures necessary. The Commission was aware of the extent of the self-interest of builders and stated, 'Builders when unrestrained by law, construct houses upon such a defective scale and crowded together upon such small places as to render them insalubrious'.[35] The Commission recommended that town councils should be empowered to raise money to purchase property so as to open up streets, courts and alleys, to improve ventilation and increase the general convenience of traffic.

This suggestion opened up a wider role for local government involving redevelopment in addition to controlling new development. The proposals suggest that sizes of courts and alleyways should be proportional to the height of the buildings, but not less than 20 feet wide and open at each end to a height of at least 10 feet. The use of cellars for habitable purposes was to be restricted, unless they were of certain size, having a fireplace, opening windows, open space in front, foundations and proper drains. These proposals would, even though there were obvious benefits of more open space for ventilation, be objected to by developers because it would mean development to a lower density and consequently a lower profit. It has been suggested that the commission advocated a National Building Act [36] but whilst the Health of Towns Select Committee placed the regulation of building high on its priorities for action, it was quite clear the Commission did not. Instead, they claimed that building regulation affecting the structures of buildings was not only a general interference in details of structural stability and fire protection, it was also unnecessary.[37] Having discussed the need for detailed control on building, the Commission referred to the poor standard of surveyors appointed to administer local Improvement Acts, few of whom were professionally qualified. The Commission recognized the need to appoint persons of higher qualifications and that the annual appointment was unsatisfactory since it deterred qualified persons from applying. The Commission considered that a test of competency should be established similar to that undergone by surveyors appointed in London where they were examined and their appointment approved by the Secretary of State.[38]

Many of the views expressed by the chairman were similar to those that Chadwick had advocated in his report, and Chadwick had to ensure that the

Commission maintained this approach if his recommendations were to be adopted. This he was able to do. Although he was not a commissioner, he had been treated as a colleague and had been asked to assist in drafting a report on his recommendations. It is therefore not surprising to find the Commission confirmed many of Chadwick's recommendations and agreed in general with him about the remedial measures which should be taken.

A conservative attitude on this matter was well expressed. Slaney, who had chaired the Select Committee in 1840, and Cubitt, who had given evidence to that committee, were not able to reaffirm the principles of building regulations due to objections to the previous Building Regulation Bills, whilst Chadwick's report did nothing to enhance the prospect of a general Building Act. The lack of ability by the Commission to accept legislative interference in what seem to be private matters gave little hope that their report would be accepted.[39]

Thus, although the report resulted in a Health of Towns Bill in July 1845,[40] dealing with the improvement of sewerage and drainage, control over the water supply and promotion of the general health and convenience of the inhabitants, it was not proceeded with due to opposition prompted by the town councils. The latter were quite content with their own Improvement Acts and were suspicious of the government's intention, especially as the Bill included the Commission's recommendation of a central authority as originally proposed by Chadwick. The Bill was not to re-emerge again until 1847, by which time many more towns had obtained their own Improvement Acts.

The Health of Towns Bill 1847–1848

The Health of Towns Bill was presented on 30th March 1847.[41] The Bill received some support but in opposition it was argued that it would cut across many local Acts and raise constitutional problems in repealing them. Lord Morpeth, Commissioner of Woods and Forests in Lord John Russell's government, considered it an advantage if private bills were abolished, but those members who feared central control because it denied them their independence of political control and the benefits of patronage that existed in many towns resisted strongly.

Chadwick had advocated that the Bill should include London, but this provoked considerable opposition. Central control was not welcomed and consequently the Bill was withdrawn and re-introduced, excluding its application to London. The Bill, despite its opposition, and prompted by a further outbreak of cholera, eventually became the Public Health Act 1848.[42]

Nine years had elapsed since Lord John Russell wrote to the Poor Law Commission concerning the inquiry into the cause of disease amongst the labouring classes of England and Wales. The political battles that were fought, restricting the early introduction of legislation, were largely concerned with interference by the State in local affairs connected with public health. The move towards central control as a result of the Poor Law Act of 1834, and the provisions of elected councils with limited powers as provided by the Municipal Corporations Act of 1835 had made their mark in the restriction of the powers of the previous corporations. The city and metropolis of London fought hard not to be included in the Public Health Act (1848), preferring to control their own destiny. To this end, they had their own system of building control provided by the Metropolitan Building Act, which was administered by district surveyors.

Controls over building

The Public Health Act did not provide for building regulations relating to new building, as was proposed in the Building Regulation Bill or contained in local Improvement Acts, as the Health of Towns Commission had not supported the principle of such detailed building control. However, certain sections did contain some controls over the construction of dwelling houses. It became an offence to build over a sewer without consent, and maps of the sewers were to be provided by the council. New houses could not be built without adequate drains that discharged to a cesspool or other similar place or to a sewer within 100 feet of the property. As the provisions of the Act were not retrospective, existing houses could not be required to be provided with proper drainage, but new or rebuilt houses had to be provided with a WC or ashpit and these requirements could also be applied to existing houses. The choice of facility was the owner's and much depended on the availability of drainage and a public sewer within reasonable distance of the house.

This was a necessary power if any substantial progress was to be made in improving sanitary conditions, and it was not limited to residential property. Factories employing more than 20 persons could also be required to provide sanitary accommodation for both sexes. New cellars were not to be let as living accommodation unless they were at least seven feet in height with three feet of height above ground level extending the entire frontage. The window ventilation area was to be at least nine square feet and the cellar well drained and provided with a fireplace and chimney. This provision was similar to the proposal for the control of cellars in the Building Regulations Bill of 1841.

Section 53 of the Public Health Act 1848 required the builder or owner to give notice to the Board, at least 14 days before beginning to dig or lay foundations, giving details as to the level of the lower floor and cellar, with the situation and construction of cesspools and privies. A fine of £50 could be imposed if work started without the approval of the Board; however, it would be lawful to proceed if the Board did not notify the developer of its decision within 14 days of the receipt of the builder's notice.

Having adopted the Act, many of the provisions could be applied at the discretion of the local board. This discretionary element therefore allowed local boards to act as they pleased and consequently led to varying standards of administration and achievement. With the Public Health Act of 1848, England and Wales had been provided with the framework for both central and local administration responsible for public health. The Act was to continue in operation for five years.

Despite the encouragement given to town councils to develop their own building control and town improvement provisions, thus allowing them to maintain their independence and discretion of administration, the application of the Public Health Act and the establishment of a Board of Health were the beginning of government intervention and the imposition of central control on the way that local government conducted its affairs. The conflict of issues and interest between local and central government which emerged during the consideration of Normanby's Bill could only be widened by this action.

CHAPTER 3

The Local Government Act 1858 and Building Bye-laws

Reappearance of cholera

The reappearance of cholera in 1848 was a driving force for Parliament to complete the passage of the Public Health Act, given the devastating effects of the 1832 outbreak. However, the Act was too late to be of any assistance in preventing or restricting the catastrophic effects of the new outbreak of this disease, as the sanitary conditions in the towns and villages of England (including London) and Wales, had hardly changed since the last outbreak.

Formation of the Board of Health

Chadwick was unable to exercise any of the provisions of the new Public Health Act or the hurriedly produced cholera bill (called the Nuisances Removal Act) until the Board of Health had been formed and gazetted. Lord Morpeth was appointed president, Chadwick was the paid commissioner, and the third member was Lord Ashley.[1] Dr Southwood-Smith was appointed medical assistant, later to become the fourth commissioner, and the Board was gazetted on the 23rd September 1848. Three days later, cholera was reported in Sunderland, reaching its peak in January 1849 to fade away by April of that year. The outbreak was confined mainly to Scotland but in June 1849 it returned with tremendous effect in Manchester, Hull, Leeds, Liverpool and other towns. London too was severely affected. The Board was able to do very little to control the outbreak, although there was a serious attempt to clean up filthy areas.

Opposition to the Act

In many towns the Board met with non-co-operation, open hostility, and downright rejection of its involvement in councils' efforts to maintain their independence of action.[2] Whitstable in Kent and Newton Abbot in Devon were two towns where strong local opposition had developed.

In some towns, the Board had reason to believe that interested parties would even use misrepresentations and threats to raise opinion against the provisions of the Public Health Act. In Macclesfield, for example, the town clerk informed the Board that almost three-quarters of the signatures appended to a petition of objection could not be recognized as ratepayers. Many signatures were fictitious, repetitive, or those of non-residents. Despite this reaction, the Act was applied in 98 towns by 1852, whilst a further 132 had petitioned for it.[3] Even when a local board had been constituted however, there was no certainty that it would carry out its responsibilities. For example, the Bromyard (Herefordshire) local board did not elect a chairman, hold a meeting or take any other measure to implement the provisions of the Act, and after three months of inactivity it became disqualified, thus making the Act ineffectual.[4] At Selby (Yorkshire), interested parties won a local council election by unscrupulous methods with the prime intention of preventing the construction of works approved by the general board.[5] Complaints to the general board from the towns of Fareham, Tosham, Castle Ford and Worcester about the stupidity and inefficiency of local boards were met with the response that the general board had no power to enforce the provisions of the Act. It was because of this lack of power and the fact that much of the power vested in the local boards was discretionary that Chadwick and his colleagues considered it of little use to try to bring non-co-operative local boards into line or wave a writ of mandamus (writ issued by a higher court to a lower court) at them.

The weakness of the Act was that it tried to be a compromise between its supporters and opposition and as such was not an effective piece of legislation. It could only be effective where it had total local support. Above all, the town councils feared being governed by a central body and this principle seemed to be worth fighting over, even if it cost the lives of many through insanitary conditions. The fear of central control was such that following the fall of the government in 1852, the new president of the Board of Health, Sir William Molesworth, publicly announced that the Act would not be applied where the majority of ratepayers opposed it. With steady progress however, the Act had been applied for in 284 towns by 1854 and local boards had been elected in over 170 towns.[6] Nevertheless, sanitary conditions could not improve overnight even in areas which adopted the Act, and in those places which did not, sanitary conditions, if anything, became worse.

Opposition to Chadwick

The opponents of the Act had taken every opportunity to discredit the Public Health Board, and, in particular, Chadwick, who repeatedly found himself under attack. Toulmin-Smith[7] described the Act of 1848 as 'demoralising and mischievous in every aspect', stating that the authors of the Act had 'cunningly used words in utterly deceiving the public'.[8] He considered that the Act progressed towards central control by removing local freedoms and loosening the foundations of law and property. Local government he described as 'being a system of Government which has the greatest number of minds knowing the most, having the smallest interest, management and control over its subject matter'.[9] In many instances he was right, but, as we have already seen, there were many towns where central control was needed to ensure that benefits likely to be derived from public Acts were felt by the public for whom they were intended.

Critical attitudes towards Chadwick found much support in the House and Palmerston (then Prime Minister) realized that if the bill to maintain the Board of Health were to stand any chance of success, Chadwick must retire. Consequently Chadwick offered his resignation, followed by those of Lord Shaftesbury and Dr Southwood-Smith. The bill held and the workings of the Board continued under a reformed administration. Chadwick's bureaucratic and dogmatic attitudes were partly to blame for his downfall, but his determination to improve the sanitary conditions of the poor classes of society can only be applauded.

Chadwick's proposals for a General Building Bill

During his last months in office, Chadwick had been working on a General Building Bill.[10] He had previously favoured a Building Act, only to change his mind during the preparation of his report. The increasing trend for towns to seek Improvement Acts or adopt the Town Improvement Clauses Act showed a willingness to accept building controls as a way of obtaining a better urban environment and Chadwick, facing loss of office, was eagerly looking for a successful recipe in the field of public health.

Typically, Chadwick's views on desirable building standards were in advance of contemporary thinking. Despite the obvious need for controls on basic construction such as foundations, structural stability, fire resistance, ventilation and drainage, he advocated such matters as thermal insulation, double glazing, chimneys to gas appliances, damp proofing, siphonic WC pans and lining of lead pipes with a composition material to restrict lead poisoning.[11]

Dampness

The recognition of dampness as injurious to health was correct, but his proposals to minimize this involved the construction of land drains to lower the water table of a building site to below three feet from ground level. This was technically possible using open jointed clay pipes bedded in and surrounded by stone chippings, or simple French drains or stone chippings, but to produce a network of such drains throughout a dense development of working class housing would considerably add to the cost, even without considering the implications of disposing of the sub-surface water collected in the drains.

Floors

The proposal for floors to be of impermeable materials able to exclude ascending moisture and damp was a little simpler. Stone or brick floors permitted dampness to mix between the abutments and a more uniform floor was certainly desirable. This could be achieved by the use of concrete, a material gaining in popularity due to the increasing availability of Portland Cement from 1840. This material four inches thick placed on an equal thickness of compacted hard core would produce such a floor, but it would add to the cost. The use of suspended timber floors would also achieve this standard, but this type of floor was only found in more expensive forms of housing.

Water closets

The Public Health Act of 1848 required all new houses to be provided with a WC or ashpit. Chadwick now wanted a regulation requiring a siphonic WC. There were various types of WCs such as the long hopper closet, short hopper closet, valve closet, and, most common of all, being the cheapest, the pan closet. These closets did not function very satisfactorily, due to poor design and flushing arrangements. Chadwick recognized the ability of the siphonic action to pull away the waste, but this principle had not been established by any of the manufacturers. The first commercial siphonic pan did not appear until 1870,[12] and was not fully developed until 1900 when the siphonic 'Closet of the Century' appeared. To insist on a type of WC pan which was not available would have meant that the installation of an ordinary WC would have contravened the law and restricted the slow progress of sanitary improvement. Even if siphonic pans had been available, their cost would have prohibited use in working class houses.

Thermal insulation

Chadwick's proposals for thermal insulation were even more grandiose. Walls were to be non-conductors of heat, impermeable to water and washable inside and out. He called for the use of glazed bricks, which, although available, were completely out of the question on economic grounds. Had he advocated sound structural stability, the thickness of the walls would have needed to be at least nine inches thick, thus avoiding the construction of houses with external walls only four and a half inches thick. This in itself would resist the penetration of rain on all but exposed sites, together with improved thermal insulation. This form of requirement was more readily acceptable, as can be seen in the Building Acts of London, Bristol and Liverpool. The availability of bricks was increasing due to improved manufacturing methods and the growing number of local brickworks throughout the country trying to meet demand. Furthermore, the cost was not excessively increased after the abolition of the tax on bricks in 1850 while competition kept the cost low.

Windows

Chadwick continued with a proposal that windows should be non-conductors of heat and in cold weather equivalent to the non-conductive qualities of an outer wall. This was a call for double glazing, minimizing condensation, and whilst technically possible by the use of inner or outer secondary window frames, it would have quite easily doubled the cost of windows. The cost of glass was becoming cheaper due to the abolition of tax on it in 1845, and improved production techniques soon made the more expensive small pane crown glass redundant. The availability of larger panes of glass permitted less use of glazing bars, thus reducing the cost of windows but this would not have been sufficient to permit double glazing at an economical price. Window sizes had an important impact on ventilation standard. Chadwick's proposal that each living room should have an air flow equivalent to three air changes per hour was too specific, difficult to measure and enforce; a simple requirement relating to size of window opening relative to room size and so located as to provide a cross flow of air within a building would have been sufficient. The size of window could be increased without a significant increase in cost, as it was a simple matter of good design.

Gas

Gas came into use for lighting in houses from about 1840 with gas cookers starting to appear in the early 1850s, and gas water heaters coming into use in 1868.[13] Chadwick's proposal that all gas burners should be provided with a chimney to carry away the burnt gases was a good idea, as the early supplies of gas burnt extremely dirtily and added to the smoky atmosphere of a room, especially where open coal fires were situated. This proposal, although desirable, was difficult and expensive to achieve. Small metal pipes could have been used as flues supported by brackets and discharging to a chimney, but this was rather an unsightly arrangement within a house. However, this was unlikely to affect working class houses, as gas companies would not supply an area that could not afford its product. Domestic lighting was either by candle or oil lamps, and heating by means of coal or timber in open fireplaces and this was not to change for some time.

Lead piping

Many houses did not have a direct supply of water but in those that did the supply was conveyed by means of lead pipes. Chadwick's awareness of lead poisoning was the basis for his recommendation that lead pipes should be coated internally with a composition material to prevent this problem. Such pipes were produced, and the only two processes considered suitable were McDougal's patent where the internal coating was bituminous, and Schwartz's patent where the pipe was boiled in sulphide of lead, a substance insoluble in water.[14]

Failure of Chadwick's proposals

Good design, planning and simple sanitary appliances cost little but have a significant impact on the standard of habitation.[15] However, instead of proposing statutory standards that would be simple, effective and inexpensive, Chadwick's proposals, while sound and desirable, were not totally relevant to working class housing and were too expensive. Consequently, these proposals were ignored and when he left public office, the idea of a General Building Bill for the whole country left with him.

Local Government Bill 1858

The dogmatic and seemingly oppressive way in which the provisions of the Public Health Act were enforced and the control which Chadwick sought, although well intended, maintained the fears of centralization, and consequently opposition remained strong. So strong, in fact, that the government introduced a Local Government Bill in 1858 as an Act to amend the Public Health Act of 1848 and to make further provisions for the local government of towns and populous districts.

The bill had no opposition, as it was clearly stated that its object was to abolish the Board of Health, and this move was welcomed, especially by town councils. It also had the effect of streamlining local government by removing another administrative layer complete with its powers and officials. The Local Government Act of 1858 enabled every town in the country to adopt the powers of local government contained in the Act.[16]

Creation of the Local Government Act Department

With the passing of the Act and the Public Health Act of 1858, [17] local government powers became the responsibility of the Home Office, and a branch was created in that office known as the Local Government Act Department with responsibility for local bye-laws. At the same time the medical functions of the Board of Health were transferred to the Privy Council.

Perkin has described the loss of the Board as a triumph for the entrepreneurial ideal, the dominant theory of *laissez-faire* [18] and de-centralization, but he argues that one of the forces of decentralization was professional ideal and administrative practice.[19] Certainly persons with skills and knowledge of technical, medical or administrative matters were readily listened to, and their views influenced many, as we have seen with the witnesses appearing before committees and commissions. The collective weight of their argument was easy to accept and difficult to dispute. Because these professional skills were often lacking in local administration and because of the powerful influence of vested interest, Chadwick had suggested that these skills should be provided at central government level with the government taking responsibility. This approach was the basis of Chadwick's administration which might well have been tried. That this was a failure was not as a result of trying, but because of the poor structure of the Act with its adoptive powers. It would seem that a successful combination might come from local control, with central government providing professional guidance. This the Public Health Act of 1858 set out to achieve by the appointment of John Simon as Central Medical Officer.[20] The professional officers of the new Board of Health could appoint, liaise with and advise the officers of the newly created Local Government Act Department.

Weaknesses of the Local Government Act 1858

This Act provided town councils with the power to make building bye-laws not only in the interests of public safety but also for health. It followed the principle of allowing local control with central professional guidance, but its weakness was that it was adoptive. This was more to the liking of the anti-centralists. Toulmin-Smith described bye-laws as an acceptable form of law derived from the laws of the 'bye' or dwellers' union.[21] ('Bye' was an Anglo-Saxon word for settlement, sometimes also spelt as 'by'. It can be seen in place names such as Derby, Corby, Selby and Grimsby. 'Bye-law' therefore meant 'the law of the town or settlement'.)

Another weakness was that the Act did not apply to Scotland and Ireland, although separate building control systems were also to develop in these two countries. As a result, there are now, more than century later, three different building control systems in the United Kingdom.

The provisions of the Act applied to all cities, ports, corporate towns, chartered boroughs and all places that had adopted the 1848 Public Health Act.

The Town Improvement Clauses Act did not apply to many towns included under the new Act, which therefore opened up a larger area of England and Wales in which control of the construction of buildings could be applied. This did not repeal Improvement Acts and, as we shall see, controls by Improvement Acts and controls by bye-laws made under this Act would be administered concurrently. Those towns that had decided not to have important health issues administered by Chadwick and his board, or for other reasons, could adopt the Act by resolution of council. The control of sanitary administration, including the control of building construction, would now be administered by local councils without having to seek private Acts.

Many of the issues raised by the Building Regulation Bill and Town Improvement Clauses Act were now incorporated into this Act. These included space surrounding buildings, which could prevent the development of back-to-back houses, control over the occupation of cellars, regulation of streets, structural fire protection, demolition or repair of dilapidated buildings and the provision of sanitary accommodation and drainage. These matters, which were once fiercely resisted as interference with property rights, were now quite acceptable to councils who adopted them. The means by which these councils could control the construction of buildings was contained in Section 34 of the Act, which repealed Sections 53 and 72 of the Public Health Act of 1848, and enabled the making of building bye-laws in respect of:

1. the level, width and construction of new streets and provision of sewerage;
2. the structure of walls of new buildings for securing stability and prevention of fire;
3. space about buildings to secure a free circulation of air and with respect to ventilation of buildings;
4. drainage of buildings, WCs, privies, ashpits, cesspools;
5. closure of buildings or parts unfit for human habitation, and prohibition of use for habitation.

The bye-laws also provided for giving notice to the council and the deposit of plans and sections by persons intending to lay out streets or construct buildings. They provided also for the inspection of work by the council surveyor, giving them the power to require faulty work to be corrected or pulled down. The bye-laws could not, however, be applied to any building erected before the date of adoption by the council. As the framework of making bye-laws was limited to specific parts of buildings, matters concerning dampness, weather resistance, fire resistance other than walls, chimneys, roofs, and so on were not included. Therefore bye-laws could not be made on these important constructional elements as had been suggested in previous reports.

The most noticeable improvements likely to occur in working class houses would be in the provision of ventilation and space about buildings. This would provide better natural lighting, sunlight and air circulation which would bring about a better sense of well-being and a healthier environment. Requirements for structural stability, would, by requiring thicker walls, provide better resistance to rain penetration and improved thermal insulation. Dampness within new buildings still remained a problem, although it could easily have been solved by requiring a damp proof course in the wall and the provision of a solid or suspended timber floor.

Even these few improvements would be attractive to many councils wishing to improve housing conditions. Improvement Acts were costly to acquire, specific in their requirements and inflexible in approach, whilst bye-laws were adoptive and flexible in that they could more easily be changed, although their requirements were more specific. Indeed, they had to be specific as not all councils had the staff expertise to make professional judgements on technical performance and suitability.

Building requirements

Builders could comply with a specific requirement for a wall of a certain length, height and thickness more readily than with a statement that the wall should be constructed so as to support adequately the loads applied to it. Furthermore, specific standards were more readily translated in terms of cost, which was the real objection that speculative builders had. Builders constructing better class properties would have little or no difficulty as Improvement Act standards were achieved and frequently bettered. For those builders who did not comply with bye-laws, councils were given powers to enable them to enforce the requirements by issuing notices requiring faulty work to be removed, altered or pulled down. This task necessitated the employment of a person or persons having a suitable knowledge of building, in a similar manner to the administration of the Metropolitan Building Acts, but unlike those Acts, neither the office of surveyor nor the required professional standards were prescribed. No doubt the criticisms expressed by objectors to the Building Regulation Bill, evidence to the Poor Law Commission and Chadwick's opinions, as well as the problems that occurred due to the lack of technical expertise, were still in the minds of the architects of the Act. This was another example of anti-centralist policy in that town councils would not be pressured by law into appointing officers of any prescribed standards of technical education or professional expertise.

Development of the Local Government Act Department

In towns which had had surveyors appointed under their Improvement Acts, the further appointment of a surveyor to administer building bye-laws would appear superfluous. However, the lack of this requirement tended to strengthen the growth of central control as it allowed the Local Government Act Department to develop and maintain the professionalism needed to guide councils in these responsibilities. This role was to become very effective, as the department had to approve all bye-laws that local councils proposed to adopt. Unlike Improvement Acts, or the London Building Acts, bye-laws were not described in detail in the Local Government Act or its schedules, which at least ensured that members of Parliament would not argue over the technicalities or take political advantage of such minor matters. The Local Government Department could draft changes in the bye-laws at any time to meet changes in building technology and the desired standards of health and safety. A more flexible approach, if carefully managed, would be more responsive to any pressures applied to the system of control. Proposed bye-laws would be checked for relevance, and being based on the provision of the Act they would be enforceable. This mode of central control would tend to ensure that all bye-laws were so similar in content and requirement as to produce uniformity of building standards whenever they were applied and the department eventually produced a model form of bye-laws from which councils could frame their own (see *Appendix 7*).[22]

However, whilst it was possible to steer councils in the direction of the Act and the bye-law-making powers, there was no obligation for them to adopt the Act or make bye-laws. Section 34 of the Act stated that, 'Every Council may make byelaws'. This discretionary power was a serious weakness as having adopted bye-laws, councils were not obliged to enforce them. These provisions were in line with the anti-centralists' views as supporters of local self-government.

This discretionary form of control would also bring about a haphazard administration, providing situations whereby speculative builders would tend to build in areas of no control, as previous evidence showed (see p.24). The effects of building control in many areas would depend on the bureaucratic attitudes of the Local Government Act Department and the vested interests in town councils. The Act nevertheless enabled interested and eager councils to extend building control and develop sanitary improvements, setting an example to uncommitted councils and encouraging them to do likewise. The decision to place the administration of sanitary legislation, including building bye-laws, with councils rather than with a central independent body having been made, the foundations on which the current system of building control in England and Wales is still based were laid in 1858.

CHAPTER 4
The Growth of the Building Bye-law System

Model Bye-laws

The adoption and enforcement of building bye-laws were the responsibility of town councils, and many, especially in the large towns wishing to improve housing, eagerly accepted that responsibility. Bye-laws that councils wished to adopt first had to be approved by the Local Government Department, as discussed in *Chapter 3*. This was the only form of central control imposed on councils as far as building bye-laws were concerned, and ensured that bye-laws were in accordance with Section 34 of the Local Government Act of 1858. In adopting the model form of bye-laws prepared by the Local Government Department, which took account of similar controls in Building Acts, Town Improvement Clauses Acts and Metropolitan Building Acts, it had been hoped that councils would present some degree of uniformity, but this was not to be.

Local practices

Many towns retained their individuality, taking account of local practice in materials or construction methods, as for example in Sheffield. The model bye-law for preventing the spread of fire between houses required the party wall between houses to be constructed higher than the roof surface, forming a parapet wall. As it was not a local practice in Sheffield it was not adopted, but the roof covering of tiles or slates could be bedded in cement mortar on top of the party wall, forming a fire resisting structure between the two houses. Thus the aim of restricting the spread of fire had been met by two differing forms of construction, although the former was more expensive to construct than the latter.

Bye-laws that required the use of slate or tiles as a roof covering, and bricks or stone in the construction of walls to prevent the spread of fire, conflicted with the use of thatch and timber which was traditional in many parts of the country. No account had been taken of the fact that timber protected by plaster could offer some degree of fire resistance or that thatched roofs isolated from other buildings would not spread fire. Such omissions often caused builders additional and sometimes unnecessary expense.

Speculative building

When trying to meet the demand for low cost housing either to buy, or more commonly to rent, the speculative builder did not wish to shed any of his profit margins. Taxes on building materials already accounted for 30 per cent of the cost of a house[1] and any bye-law which increased the use of taxable material was itself considered a tax. High density development was quite profitable and requirements which resulted in a reduction of density were frowned on by speculative builders. The bye-law requirements for space about buildings did just that, preventing back-to-back housing, opening up court-type developments, ensuring adequate space for the circulation of air so as to remove foul smells and to ventilate the rooms of houses. Speculative builders were not motivated by social, aesthetic or philanthropic considerations but by likely development projects,[2] and where they could influence a council not to adopt or enforce bye-laws their interest could be maintained. For example, despite the eagerness of many towns to ban back-to-back housing by adopting open space bye-laws, this type of house continued to be built in Leeds until 1936 because the town councils did not exercise their discretion to adopt open space bye-laws (see *Plates 4a and b*). The density of development in houses per acre had serious implications for the purchase price or rental, so consequently the requirements for open space varied in many towns (see *Figure 3*), as did the distance that privies and WCs had to be located away from houses.

Councils, whilst using the same law, could establish a degree of individuality. This was often reflected in the pattern and style of growth of towns. The bye-law requiring a minimum width of street ensured that builders desirous of maintaining maximum density built narrow-fronted houses abutting the back of the footpath (see *Plate 5*). Later bye-laws required space in front of houses as well as at the rear, and this meant setting the houses back from the road, lowering the overall density and creating small front gardens (see *Plate 6*). Cellars and basements prepared for habitation were controlled in respect of size, room height and ventilation, often making their construction uneconomic.

Bye-laws were sometimes framed or not enforced so as to allow traditional forms of housing, often profitable to the builder and low in cost and rental, to continue to be built. Examples include the back-to-back type of house in Leeds, and also the long rows of single storey cottages with thin external walls fronting narrow streets built in Sunderland. Variations in sanitary improvements also occurred; for example, every new property erected in Sunderland had to be provided with a WC whilst in Leeds WCs could be shared, a practice that was to continue until 1912.

The Differing Standards of Rear Open Space required to Houses.

Name of Town.		Area of Open Space required	Distance across.
Bradford, Morley	1 Storey 2 Stories 3 Stories	150 square feet 180 do 225 do	10 feet 12 do 15 do
Bangor, Brighton, Barnsley, Derby, Doncaster, Dover, Grimsby, Leicester, Plymouth, Warwick	1 Storey 2 Stories 3 Stories Above 3 Stories	150 square feet 150 do 150 do 150 do	10 feet 15 do 20 do 25 do
Bolton	1 Storey 2 Stories 3 Stories	150 square feet 150 do 150 do	10 feet 12 do 15 do
Bradford, Nr. Manchester	1 Storey 2 Stories 3 Stories	80 square feet 80 do 80 do	10 feet 15 do 25 do
Cardiff		Four parts unbuilt upon to five parts built upon	
Coventry	1 Storey 2 Stories and above	Breadth of the building by Breadth of the building by	40 ft across 60 ft across
Darlington	2 or 3 Bedroomed houses Larger houses	Two thirds of the entire area of the ground floor One half of the entire area of the ground floor	
Sunderland		One third of the entire area of the ground on which the house shall stand	

Figure 3: The differing standards of rear open space required to houses in different towns. Extracted from the Bradford Report on the Building Bye-laws (Hole, 1866).

The effect of bye-laws on new technology

Bye-laws had little effect on the improvement of building technology; in many cases, they did not take account of aspects of current technology such as thermal insulation and the simple insertion of a damp proof course to check rising dampness in walls and floors. This applied also to sanitary appliances such as the WC. Model bye-laws did not require the WC to have smooth impervious surfaces with a cleansing action, or the drains to be of a certain size, laid to obtain self-cleansing velocity (see *Appendix 7*). The pan closet, described as a horrible device,[3] continued to be used for over a century and was still being made in 1891, although the Bramah valve closet, a more efficient and less objectionable WC, was by then available. Various improvements were to be marketed, such as the valve closet, the wash down closet, and the 'Hygienic Closet' with a flushing rim, all of which were connected to suitable traps. Bye-laws approved in 1875 still permitted the pan closet to be used, [4] but the Local Government Board condemned its use [5] and later bye-laws required WCs to be of non-absorbent material and to function cleanly.[6] Once technology had improved a material, product or mode of construction, bye-laws could be updated incorporating that improvement. Consequently, technological development was allowed to lead legislative requirements. However, where an improvement led to the modification of a bye-law, this could be used by many an intuitive manufacturer to restrict his competitors and improve his sales.

Sometimes bye-laws were so vague that they had little effect. For example,

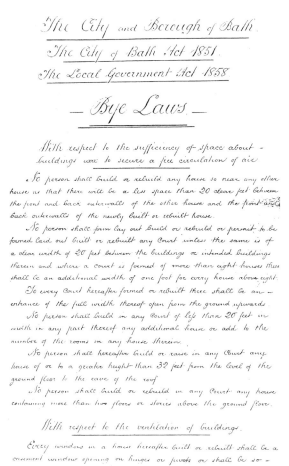

Figure 4: Bye-laws of the City of Bath 1866.

the city of Bath bye-law for ventilation openings in 1866 required the top part of a casement window to open for the full width of the window but failed to require a minimum size (see *Figure 4*); consequently any size, even though it would not provide adequate ventilation, was legally satisfactory. This was amended in 1868 to a standard based on the size of the room (see *Figure 5*).

Variations to bye-law requirements

Variations to bye-law requirements were often a result of pressure being applied to councils whereby councillors would ensure that bye-laws did not

Figure 5: Amendments to the City of Bath Bye-laws 1868.

cause too much conflict with speculative builders and developers and any changes in the bye-laws were incremental rather than radical. Gaskell argues that the form of bye-laws which most town councils followed were sometimes too specific whilst at other times they were too vague. This fact gave rise to problems of application which led many councils to turn again to private acts to control buildings. [7] But this was not the only reason. It was often found that the bye-law making powers were inadequate to control aspects of design and construction which in the interests of public health and safety they considered it necessary to control. Thus, for example, the town of Stockton secured an Act in 1869 which provided control over the construction of party walls, partition walls, level of ground floors, space about buildings not to be built on and the height of habitable rooms, together with the requirements to deposit plans, notice of building by the builder and inspection of work by the council.[8]

The St Helens Improvement Act 1869

In 1869, the town of St Helens obtained an Improvement Act, repealing a previous Act of 1855.[9] Section 141 of the new Act permitted the council to make bye-laws relating to new streets and buildings, and to the construction of foundations and walls, with a view to preventing fires. New buildings for public entertainment had to provide means of escape in case of fire or accident (see *Appendix 8*). (This provision was the first of its kind enabling a local authority to make bye-laws on this subject, a matter that was previously raised when Normanby's Bills were considered, see p.15). There was also provision for bye-laws to be made regarding the space about buildings, size of windows and ventilation as well as the drainage of buildings and the provision of WCs, privies, cesspools and ashpits. Provisions were also made for the thickness, material and construction of walls near ovens and furnaces, including furnaces not used for manufacturing.

Builders were required to deposit plans and give notice of building, whilst the council had powers to inspect work and enforce the bye-laws. Section 142 contained a provision that deposited plans would be deemed to have been approved if the council had neglected to notify the person who deposited the plans of their decision. This was an important measure since the council was penalized for inefficiency in that their powers of enforcement were taken away by the consent deemed to be given to those plans. It also avoided builders incurring increased costs where the passing of plans was unduly delayed. The provisions of this Act generally followed the bye-law-making powers of the Local Government Act of 1858, which the Corporation of St Helens eventually adopted in 1873.[10] The St Helens Act was a good example of how a town council could extend its powers of control over building. Means of escape in case of fire is a very important aspect of public safety as frequent disasters constantly remind us. This provoked demand for similar protective legislation, adding criticism to the indifference and seeking provision either by local action or by the imposition of central government.

Failure to improve uniformity of requirements

Whilst local Acts often extended the application of building control, they did little to improve uniformity of requirements. Further differences occurred when councils failed to adopt bye-laws and relied entirely on Improvement Acts to control buildings. This became evident in Liverpool, where Building Acts remained in existence as the sole means of control over buildings until 1864. The councils bordering on Liverpool had adopted building bye-laws under the Local Government Act 1858, enabling them to ban the construction of back-to-back houses, a restriction very popular in many towns. These powers were not available to Liverpool because they were not included in their Building Acts. Those desirous of seeking conformity with adjoining councils applied pressure on Liverpool to adopt similar powers and were successful when bye-laws were adopted in 1864. Despite this local initiative, the Building Acts remained in force and were applied alongside building bye-laws.

This duality of control existed in other towns. Leicester, for example, had six Improvement Acts with regulations controlling the construction of building, and in addition, had adopted building bye-laws for the construction of water closets. Town councils frequently differed as to their approach to building control, some wanting the best of both Improvement Acts and bye-laws. Understandably, many builders found the enforcement of both Improvement Acts and bye-laws very confusing and most objectionable. These objections were often put aside by councils, especially those that had adopted bye-laws and found them beneficial. The simple fact that these bye-laws prevented the construction of row upon row of back-to-back houses in many towns, ensuring in their place buildings with some open space, good ventilation, improved arrangements and sanitation was in itself a considerable improvement over previous developments. In addition, they ensured adequate stability and fire resistance.

Despite the continuance of Improvement Acts maintaining or extending their powers of control over buildings, councils continued with the system of bye-law control. The Local Government Act Department found itself constantly in demand by authorities seeking expert advice, and by 1871 some 1500 authorities had sought guidance on the framing of bye-laws.[11]

The gain in profits at the expense of better housing drew comment from James Hole, writing in 1866, who considered that:

'social or sanitary conditions do not sufficiently outweigh with the capitalist builder if they involve increased outlay without a corresponding return… the smaller the house the larger is his percentage profit, hence the space is contracted to the smallest unit. The largest number of cottages consist of a living room, one bed chamber, and a closet called a bedroom, the small capitalist builder who owns it, and maybe a score of these cottage tenements, is often as ignorant as the tenant is himself of the vital necessity of light and pure air. If by ingenuity he can cram a cottage or two more on the land, all this increases his percentage profit and he will only be too glad to do it and if there are no municipal regulations enforced he will do it. If by a little contrivance he can let off the cellar as a separate dwelling he increases his profits.'[12]

The majority of these speculative builders would take advantage of any weaknesses in the law. Pridgin-Teale,[13] through his excellent illustrations, described how they would construct insanitary housing by taking advantage of specific bye-laws that were not comprehensive in their requirement, by using cheap and shoddy materials and deceiving local authority surveyors. He described the installation of sanitary appliances such as WCs, sinks, baths, basins, without traps or with traps that were easily siphoned off by the flow of water in the pipes and the action of other appliances on the same system. He pointed out that the terminals of ventilation pipes to drains were often situated in close proximity to windows. He deplored the use of 'seconds' pipes by many speculative builders, often resulting in fractures and leaks within, under, or in close proximity to buildings. The lack of damp proof courses to walls and the ground floor resulted in obnoxious air being transmitted into the building. Drains were often laid with adverse falls, with no bedding, or joints which readily leaked, and became blocked, while cesspools were situated in close proximity to wells polluting the water. Drains leading towards, but not actually connected to the sewer were common, and Pridgin-Teale describes an easy ploy by builders not wishing the local authority surveyor to inspect the drain. They would merely arrange for an inspection at a time inconvenient for the surveyor to inspect. Then, if an inspection was not carried out, they would cover the drains over.

However, amongst all his criticisms, Pridgin-Teale wrote favourably of the building bye-laws in Leeds, stating that they had prevented many a bad drainage situation from occurring. On one bye-law concerning the building of dwellings on sites which had previously been used as refuse tips, he concluded that, 'such provisions will surely be impossible in the future thanks to the new building bye-laws of our town of Leeds' (see *Figure 6*).[14] This particular bye-law became incorporated as part of the Public Health (Amend-

Figure 6: 'Terrace of the future on refuse of the past' (Pridgin-Teale, 1878).

ment) Act of 1890,[15] where Section 25 banned the construction of buildings on any ground which had been filled with faecal, animal or vegetable matter, unless previously rendered innocuous.

Pridgin-Teale's observations, comments and recommendations were very practical and relevant to the situation as he saw it. He highlighted how easy it was for sanitary defects to be caused either through bad design, poor workmanship or deliberately. He also investigated rural housing conditions where he found many faults relating to the construction of country cottages, disposal of refuse and water supply.[16] Damp sites, lack of damp proof courses, porous ground floors, leaking roofs, lack of or incorrectly assembled rainwater, foul and waste water systems were common faults. Pridgin-Teale produced recommendations for improvement, often by simple and inexpensive remedies (see *Figures 7a and b*). He concluded that many of the defects resulted from not complying with bye-laws or Act requirements. He accepted that sanitary authorities were not speedy or efficient in enforcing the bye-laws and sought to offset this inefficiency by suggesting that everyone should make an effort to improve their houses and so contribute to their own and others' health.

Need for a central body

Hole considered that one should look to town councils to remedy bye-law requirements and enforce the many Acts passed by the government. Whilst a solution lay in that direction, the motivating forces of vested interests

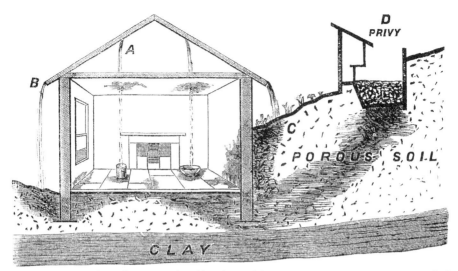

FIG. 1.—Cottage, damp from A, roof leaking into ceiling; B, unguttered eaves; C, soil against outer wall, wet with soakings from garden and privy midden; D, privy midden above level of ground floor.

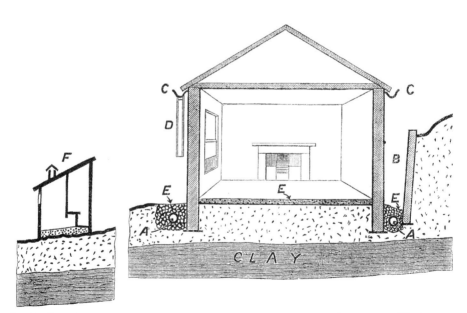

FIG. 2.—Remedies applied to fig. 1. A, drain surrounded by rubble; B, air-space round the house; C, rain gutter; D, fall pipe; E, concrete surface; F, privy removed to lower level.

Figures 7a and b: Illustrations showing the simple constructional and siting improvements that could be made to cottages which did not significantly add to the cost of the dwelling.

frequently brought about a lack of control, or indifferent control with little benefit to speculative builder and public alike. Hole remarked that local self-government, in many cases, meant local mis-government, and there was a need for a central body to force the councils to carry out their duty.[17]

Sir John Simon, a medical officer, after many years of public service also concluded that a strong central control was needed. He was very concerned about the difficulty of attaining a balance between the inexorable pressure of the commercial screw towards starvation wages and the establishment by Parliament of laws relating to public health, including the wholesomeness of buildings. On the laws relating to dwellings, Simon was extremely critical of all local authorities, including town councils, describing them as inefficient, even corrupt. He claimed that the beneficiaries of the law had consequently not received the protection the law had intended for them and he pointed out that these injustices had caused unnecessary exposure of the public to diseases which an efficient and effective administration should prevent:

> *'I refer to the quantities of disease and death brought upon the public through the almost unbounded facility that exists for abuses and dishonesties in the house trade and by the frequency with which jerry-built and other unfit houses having in them latent malconstructions, dangerous to health are let for hire to persons who have not knowledge enough to protect themselves against harm.'*[18]

This was an indictment against local authorities justified by all the evidence Simon had accumulated over the years. As we have seen, both Simon and Hole considered that councils should be under some form of central control to see that these powers were fairly and honestly carried out, and to do this every town should have medical and health officers. Moreover, a general Building Act regulating widths of streets, prohibiting back-to-back houses and cellar dwellings and controlling the construction of houses should be introduced. This was a move back towards Acts and regulations but centrally applied, as opposed to local authority adopted.

Most of these powers were already on the statute book, but because they were discretionary powers, councils could avoid their adoption and enforcement. These views, nevertheless, represented quite the opposite of the policies advocated by Toulmin-Smith in 1851 which were widely supported. Interference with the rights of property was still objected to at local level and councils, committees, councillors, and officers frequently considered they were acting correctly in refusing or restricting any action which had the slightest connection with the rights of property. These attitudes were bound to result in very indifferent application of Local Improvement Acts and building bye-laws. Simon and Hole spoke clearly for all who advocated that government action and municipal interference were not only necessary, but the only means by which better housing could be brought about. Local control with central guidance was, by virtue of the Public Health Act and Local Government Act of 1858, beginning to emerge as a better alternative to local Act administration, despite the forceful opposition of vested interests.

Development of philanthropic housing

A form of housing development that seemed not to need local control or central guidance was the design and construction of houses for industrialists. They not only recognized the values of good housing for their employees but also had the economic power to provide them. This approach had started prior to 1782 with a few houses, often in terrace form, but in that year Richard Arkwright started to develop New Lanark in Scotland. The village was completed in the early 1800s by Robert Owen, and by 1816 housed 2,297 people.[19] A smaller project was begun at Belper in Derbyshire in 1792, but it was not until the mid-nineteenth century that villages for industrial workers were constructed on a wider scale.

The first was begun in 1847 by Colonel Ackroyd at Copley, Yorkshire and was eventually completed in 1853. This development comprised back-to-back houses, school, library and workers' canteen. Ackroydon, near Shipley, followed in 1859; Saltaire, near Bradford, developed between 1850 and 1870 by Sir Titus Salt, comprised 850 houses, 45 almshouses, a church, institute, public baths, shops, hospital and park. All the houses were well-constructed with sanitary facilities, and development on this scale could take advantage of proper planning allowing for good road layout and open space much in the manner that Chadwick had envisaged in 1842 (see p.26). Port Sunlight, in Cheshire, is a good example of this type of development, commenced in 1888 and completed in the late 1920s. Here the houses were either semi-detached or built in groups of four to six, separated by open space and having open-fronted gardens onto curved streets so that houses and landscape merged together. This avoided the monotonous gridiron urban layout that characterized bye-law housing during this period. Bourneville, on the outskirts of Birmingham, was built by the Cadbury brothers and was begun in 1893 on some 120 acres. The housing was made available to people who were not employees of Cadbury. One thousand houses had been built by 1912, and 3,500 by 1955.

Establishment of Garden Cities

However, not all development was carried out with this approach to good planning, construction and sanitation, but whilst many a speculative builder battled against the enforcement of building bye-laws, Ebenezer Howard continued the theme of planned development and transferred this idea from a philanthropic approach to one of self-support. In 1903 he established the first Garden City Limited and proceeded to develop Letchworth Garden City in Hertfordshire, followed in 1920 with Welwyn Garden City. The philanthropic and garden city developments were planned and built by those who wanted to have a better standard of housing, village and town layout, and felt that their objectives would be achieved by adopting sound principles of town planning. Consequently, with this motivation, building bye-laws were considered unnecessary as the standards imposed would not only be achieved but often bettered. The gradual improvement brought about by the housing ideals of philanthropic housing and the imposition of bye-law requirements raised the level of speculative housebuilding so that the skilled workman was able to find a house that was safe and sanitary to rent or to buy.

Housing demand

Despite these different approaches to housing for the working classes, the problem of sufficient stock remained unsolved. By the turn of the century, some 100, 000 houses were estimated to be necessary to meet the demand for decent housing [20]. Market forces always had a controlling influence over speculative builders and consequently their output varied – they only built when the market had the buyers for their products. Estate and industrial philanthropic developers built to suit their own needs and not the wider needs of the poorer classes.[21] Commercial philanthropy seemed to lose sight of its initial objectives and moved in the direction which favoured the vested interests of the capitalists.[22] Both groups found that building controls were to be avoided because they increased costs by requiring specific construction. They also reduced the number of houses they could build by requiring space standards, interfering with the choice of materials and form of construction, and were frequently irrelevant.

The speculators sought to lobby councils, influence the political control of bye-laws and prevent their enforcement. The philanthropists tended to seek exemption from bye-law control contending that the standard of housing produced under their schemes was better than the standards imposed by bye-laws. Local authorities, who eventually took over the mantle of the philanthropic developer, continued, as we shall see, with the theme of exemption, whilst the speculator sought avoidance.

The adoption of building bye-laws and the retention of Local Improvement Acts were certainly creating a division between local and central control. This was not surprising, especially amongst towns which were leaders in the creation of legislation to improve the construction of buildings, but even Liverpool, a founder member, had to adopt bye-laws to bring about some uniformity in the Merseyside area. There was a need to reduce these differences. Town councils were politically strong and the system of control by local Act was difficult for central government to influence and control.

Both systems had weaknesses in that the standards imposed were specific. This did not provide the flexibility needed to permit other materials to be used that would still meet the intentions of the regulations. At the same time they lacked sufficient detail to prevent unscrupulous builders from taking advantage of inadequate bye-laws. Thus, two major issues were beginning to emerge from the introduction of bye-laws.

Public Health Act 1866

This haphazard approach by councils was also repeated by the government who, at the threat of a further outbreak of cholera, introduced the Public Health Act of 1866.[23] This Act amended the Sewage Utilisation Act of 1865, enabling the formation of special drainage districts and providing for better house drainage. Dwelling houses without a drain could be required to be connected to a sewer if within 100 feet of one; if not, a cesspool or some other adequate place was to be provided. In addition, earth closets could be constructed instead of water closets and every dwelling house, new or rebuilt, was required to have a water closet, earth closet or privy. The powers contained in this Act would be available to every sewer authority. The basis of this legislation is still operative today, but these provisions only added to the existing problem in that they created one more authority. It was a reflection of the faith that central government had in the ability of existing authorities to enforce the powers they already had. The second part of the Public Health Act of 1866 dealt with nuisances and introduced into local government a very important responsibility that would ultimately be shown as very relevant to building control over one hundred years later.[24] That was 'a duty' to administer the provisions of the Act for the benefit of persons for whom it was intended. This Act expressly declared that it was the duty of councils to provide for the proper inspection of their districts to locate nuisances and to remove them. Those that did not carry out that 'duty' could be forced to do so by the Secretary of State and the courts, a further encroachment of central control.

The 1866 Act did not contain all that Simon had wished for on the subject of building regulation.[25] This Act was typical of the piecemeal way that sanitary problems were being dealt with – another authority to administer the work of another Act. The growing number of Acts involving sanitary improvements, with their attendant authorities, resulted in an unco-ordinated approach. There was a need to streamline the whole approach to sanitary improvement not only in what was required but also in how it was to be achieved, with defined roles for local and central government. This had not gone unnoticed.

Interested associations involved in medical and sanitary matters followed the work of Simon and his department and the views expressed by others. Wherever and whenever these associations could prod the government into action, they did so. It was such agitation by the British Medical Association and the Social Science Association that led Disraeli's government to appoint a Royal Commission to investigate the administration of sanitary matters (the Royal Sanitary Commission).[26] This agitation resulted from the growing public interest in health and safety. An informed public was now demanding improved legislation, consolidation of existing legislation, conversion of permissive powers to compulsory powers and the rationalization of local government to ensure proper administration and enforcement and effective central direction and administration.

A change in attitude was occurring by 1868 from that which had forced the disbanding of the Board of Health in 1854 and 1858. Public opinion was now more receptive to any changes that a Royal Commission might propose. It was becoming accepted that government interference in these matters was increasingly necessary.

The Royal Sanitary Commission (RSC)

A change of government resulted in the reappointment of the Royal Sanitary Commission (RSC) in 1868. Its terms of reference were to investigate the operation and administration of sanitary law, the constitution and areas of health authorities, and the certification of deaths in England and Wales.[27] (Scotland, Ireland, and the whole of London were not included in the areas to be investigated.) Among the many matters that the Royal Sanitary Commission was instructed to inquire into were the laws relating to sewerage, drainage, water supply, control of building and the administration of these laws. Reference to building bye-laws could include experience in areas other than England and Wales, but the terms of reference of the Commission would not permit it to recommend a single building control system for the whole of the United Kingdom, simply because Scotland, Ireland, and London were outside the area of investigation. If a building control system were to be recommended, then it should be modelled closely on the London system to unify the two separate systems that had developed in England and Wales.

The Commission, under the chairmanship of Charles Adderley,[28] was appointed in April 1869. Evidence given before August 1869 was presented as a first report, with the second and final report being presented in 1871. This, comprising some 386 pages, consisted of report, analysis and minutes of evidence. It reviewed the existing sanitary laws, presented and analysed the evidence of 101 witnesses, and proceeded to recommend the amendment of law and restructuring of administration considered necessary to establish effective benefits for the population of England and Wales. The report, as far as the control of building is concerned, was very influential in that the basis of building control in England and Wales today conforms to the recommendations established in the 1871 report. The ineffectiveness of the existing legislation, due to the multiplicity of Acts and authorities, was readily recognized.[29]

From the Parliamentary Select Committee on the Health of Towns in 1840, Chadwick's report of 1842 and the Royal Commission on the State of Large Towns and Populous Districts, had stemmed some 19 Acts between 1848 and 1870,[30] many prompted by outbreaks or fear of, cholera, typhoid and typhus. All the Acts dealt with some aspect of sanitary importance and were administered by some 700 district or borough, urban and rural councils, boards, and/or commissions. The power to make building bye-laws was adoptive and of those authorities which did adopt and make bye-laws it appears that most were large ones where long-standing problems of high density and low quality buildings were causes of sanitary defects and disease.

Monetary loss because of public ill health was estimated at many millions of pounds per annum due to the increase of expenditure and the decrease in work both by the sick and by those looking after them.[31] Employers were affected by loss of production and lower profits, and the Commission recognized the economic importance of effective sanitary legislation. The essentials named included:

1. The supply of wholesome and sufficient water for drinking and washing.
2. The prevention of the pollution of water.
3. The provision of sewerage and utilization of sewage.
4. The regulation of streets, highways and new buildings.
5. The healthiness of dwellings.
6. The removal of nuisances, refuse and consumption of smoke.
7. The inspection of food.
8. The suppression of causes of disease and regulations in case of epidemics.
9. The provision for the burial of the dead without injury to the living.
10. The regulation of markets etc., public lighting of towns, etc.
11. The registration of death and sickness.

This list was not given in any defined order of priorities, but as a list of preferences the regulation of new buildings is placed high on it.

The administration of these necessities was, and still is, of extreme importance, and the Commission stressed the importance of the established principle of local self-government:

> '*Local administration, under central superintendance is a distinguishing feature of our Government. The theory was that Local Authorities should assume the widest possible responsibilities and that public expenditure should be chiefly controlled by those who contribute to it. Whatever concerns the whole nation must be dealt with nationally, while whatever concerns only a district must be dealt with by the district.*'[32]

Whilst the disadvantages of local administration were recognized, including the smallness of units, parochial attitudes and the administration of conflicting and disconnected laws, the Commission nevertheless recommended that local administration should be simplified, strengthened and set in motion. Local authorities that had adopted the Public Health Act of 1848 and the Local Government Act of 1858, had only experienced central supervision of building control matters since 1858. The principle had not been firmly established, thus strengthening the hold that central government had over how local authorities conducted themselves.

The regulation of new buildings was clearly a local matter, as could be seen from those authorities which had sought local Acts or had made bye-laws under the Local Government Act of 1858, and were making an attempt to enforce them. The Commission did not wish to add or detract from those who sought the sanctity of private property. The national drive was to ensure that all authorities had building bye-laws of a uniform nature.

Many of the 101 witnesses who gave evidence to the Commission on the subject of building bye-laws and their administration mentioned the limitations of the system which brought about a lack of uniformity and incomplete control. Towns which had building bye-laws were able to point out the beneficial results in comparison to other areas which did not adopt and make bye-laws. The supervision required in the enforcement was considered by builders to be interference. This resulted for example in Bradford Borough having to relax their bye-laws for a time and for Oldham to modify theirs.[33] Uncertainty about validity was the main problem. Bye-laws had in many cases been found to be *ultra vires*, that is, beyond their power, and some courts had strained this rule against local boards. For this reason alone, some councils did not enforce bye-laws. Evidence was given that bye-laws should be either a part of statute, or receive Parliamentary approval, or that when they were sanctioned by the Secretary of State they should have the effect of law. Simon, in his evidence, stated that the central authority should have the power to make bye-laws for any place where the council refused to make them and this the Commission accepted.[34] However, the use of bye-laws as a vehicle to achieve the desired standard of health and safety was not fully realized; Gauldie argues that bye-laws were framed to protect property and not ensure health and comfort.[35] Certainly, the opposition to building bye-laws had limited their effectiveness and local control.

The Commission recommended that building bye-laws should remain as the instrument of control and that local authorities were, despite criticism, best placed to administer them. This was hardly surprising since the Commission had stressed the importance of local self-government. The chaos of authorities, and areas which the Commission was prominently aware of, played a significant part in the recommendations. In urban areas it was recommended that a single authority, the town council, should exist. In rural areas, the Poor Law Union was to be the area and the Board of Guardians the authority. These authorities were to administer all matters of public health, thus reducing the existing multiplicity of councils, boards and commissioners. To oversee the workings of the local authorities, the creation of a new central sanitary authority was recommended. The partial and optional application of sanitary law was considered to be no longer admissible and it was considered that the superintendance given by the central authority must be made more effective.[36] The grip of central control would thus be tightened.

Rural districts

Rural districts did not have the same powers as town and urban authorities, but the Commission considered that they should have the power to make and administer building bye-laws. This proposal had a significant impact in that it extended building control from those councils who previously had the power to make building bye-laws to the areas controlled by the proposed new Rural and Urban District Councils. Thus all these local authorities could take an active interest in securing the construction of better houses. However, there would be some differences in the way that control would be administered. In rural areas the deposit of plans was not considered necessary; neither should these authorities have the power to pull down non-conforming work, although they could prosecute for a fine. Such a recommendation would only add to the criticism of bye-laws administration since local authorities would be expected to require the bye-law standard to be attained whilst being deprived of the power of effective enforcement. If the courts were sympathetic to the developer, local authorities would not even try to enforce, as had been described in evidence to the Commission. This was an example of a compromise to allow the law to appease those who sought its protection while at the same time limiting its effectiveness to appease those who would be affected by its enforcement.

The Commission recommended the widening of bye-law making powers by including the damp proofing of ground floors in addition to walls, the drainage of building sites and the provision of earth closets. A further recommendation referred to providing satisfactory means of ingress and egress in all buildings used for public assembly. This important aspect of public safety was at last recognized, but its implications were far reaching in that it could be applied to existing buildings as well as new constructions. This was the first step towards retrospective action and this principle was not to be easily accepted.

The enforcement of these matters was an important measure. Smaller authorities would not have the resources, either financial or staff, to ensure effective enforcement, but as the Act provided authorities with discretion to act or not, small authorities would not act any less efficiently than some of the larger authorities. Effective powers of enforcement were needed otherwise bye-laws became meaningless, but to be enforceable they had to be clear and precise. John Liddle, M.O.H. for Whitechapel, gave evidence to the RSC in which he referred to a paper he had presented to the Association of Medical Officers of Health, in which he pointed out how the powers of the Metropolitan Building Act could be avoided. He described the case of a builder who had constructed two houses on a site which had open space at the rear of 100 square feet, the amount required for one house only by the Act. The builder was summoned to appear before the magistrates, but prior to his appearance, he constructed a hole in the party wall and stated that the house was one house and not two. The court accepted his argument and he was not prosecuted. Clearly, the hole was effectively closed at a later date.

The Act only applied to new buildings, and Liddle gave a further example of how the Act could be avoided by carrying out alteration work to a new building. He referred to a builder who had taken down the front and rear walls and rebuilt them, then removed the roof and rebuilt, but at the same time building over the rear open space originally required by the Act for the circulation of air.[37] Such was the ingenuity of unscrupulous builders who frequently complained that they could not understand bye-laws, or were not aware of them. But these examples show that some of them understood only too well, and highlighted the inadequacy of badly structured regulations.

The Commission was unable to give full consideration to effective building control simply because it was not able to enquire into the control of building in London. Not that such an enquiry was needed, but it would have allowed the Commission to make a comparison between the two systems. Thus a second opportunity to unite the building control system of London with that of England and Wales had been missed. Nevertheless, the Commission was keen to improve the current system which had functioned in some places extremely well. To maintain the same system meant *status quo*, the presence of central authority, the growing position of the professional, the emergence of the government administrator, prompting and cajoling the government into accepting professional solutions to the problems they were facing. To maintain the building bye-law system meant the strengthening of the Local Government Department and the Commission's recommendations followed this pattern.

A Period of Consolidation 1871–1875

The report of the RSC was accepted in full by Gladstone's government in 1871. The Conservatives in opposition, led by Disraeli, also supported the report, having in the first instance set up the Commission in 1868. Three important Acts came from the report, the Local Government Board Act (1871), the Public Health Act (1872), and the Public Health Act (1875). In addition, a further Public Health Act was introduced in 1874, which although relevant to building bye-law control, was almost immediately repealed by the Act of 1875.

Public knowledge on the subject of public health and safety had advanced rapidly in the previous decade, aided by associations which had been to produce a better understanding of the problems and the way to tackle them. The benefits of sanitary legislation, although limited in both content and application, had changed social attitudes and made them more responsive. The exponents of *laissez-faire* policy had a difficult task to destroy, delay or amend bills based on the recommendations of the RSC. The very nature of the task set for the Commission resulted in both a continuance and consolidation of sanitary law and enforcement.

Local Government Board Act 1871

The first Act emanating from the Commission's report was the Local Government Board Act of 1871.[38] This Act created a Local Government Board to replace the Local Government Act Department, in which the consolidated central functions would be placed. This was the means by which central control would be enlarged and strengthened. The bill became law on 18th August 1871. The new board consolidated the staff from the Poor Law Board, General Register Office, Local Government Act Office and some of the staff on the Medical Department of the Privy Council. The Act did not pass without comment, and the anti-centralists and sanitarians were still active and forceful in obtaining a delay in the government's proposals.[39]

The Public Health Act 1872

The second Act, the Public Health Act of 1872,[40] created the basis for local sanitary organization of the urban and rural districts to complement the existing borough councils. The structure, necessary to administer sanitary legislation including building bye-laws, was now beginning to take shape. The objections to the Local Government Bill in 1871 had produced a cautious approach to the introduction of the changes needed. Lord Stanstead, the minister responsible for the Local Government Board, did not fully appreciate the opportunities that existed for the speedy introduction of all the Commission's recommendations. The incremental approach allowed constant agitation by anti-sanitarians and anti-centralists to oppose the piecemeal proposals. Stanstead's weak leadership was the opposite of what the Commission had envisaged in an effective central authority.

Public Health Bill 1873

A Public Health Bill, introduced in 1873 to amend the Public Health Act of 1872, had followed a previous bill for the consolidation of the sanitary law. At the same time, the government had sent a digest to all local authorities giving details of all the existing Acts and suggesting amendments as an interim measure before proceeding with an Act to consolidate all existing legislation.[41] Consolidation of building requirements into a separate building Act would have aided understanding and enforcement. and this would have met the demands of those who still advocated a separate building Act. Such a demand came in March 1872, during a debate on the Fires Bill, based on the report of the Fire Protection Committee of 1867.[42] The Committee stated that although it was not possible to prevent fires, it was possible to insist on buildings being reconstructed so that, should a fire occur, the risk to life could be reduced to a minimum. A new Building Act should make it compulsory to require the floor between a shop and dwelling to have adequate fire resistance, similarly for larger shops with living accommodation over. Satisfactory ingress and egress should be provided to all public buildings, a matter that the RSC had previously recommended, while stairways, passageways and corridors were to be constructed of fire resisting materials. The report commented on an increase in the number of fires due mainly to the increase in smokers and the use of matches. Reference was made to a previous suggestion for a tax on matches and the discussion in the House centred on this matter, whilst the technicalities of the fire resistance of building structures faded away as did the bill and any hope of a Building Act.

Sanitary Laws Amendment Bill 1874

The new Conservative government was obliged to implement the recommendations of the RSC. Slater-Booth, the new Local Government Minister, introduced the Sanitary Laws Amendment Bill in June 1874.[43] The bill was to amend and extend the existing sanitary laws and included a proposal to broaden the scope of building bye-laws both in content and administration. The Board of Guardians and the Rural Sanitary Authority were to become one and the same and the new Rural Authorities were to be allowed to make building bye-laws for their areas. These bye-laws had to be available for public inspection before and after they were approved by the Local Government Board (LGB), allowing for objection in the first instance and awareness in the second. This was the first legislative move to introduce building controls in rural areas. Building bye-laws were extended to control foundations, rainwater gutters, downpipes and roofs. The RSC had not recommended the inclusion of roofs although the roof of a building clearly plays a major part in keeping it dry, and if a building catches fire, its roof can spread the fire either by radiation or the convection of burning embers. It seems surprising therefore that the standard of roof construction had not been included before, although many borough councils had these provisions in their Improvement Acts. Similarly, foundations and rainwater pipes were not RSC recommendations, but both have a great influence on the health and safety of occupants of buildings.[44]

The Sanitary Laws Amendment Act became law in July 1874, and although insignificant in comparison to some preceding Sanitary Acts, was very important in building control matters. Not only were the powers to make bye-laws enlarged to cover important parts of building structure, but enforcement functions and costs of remedial works were defined. Most significant were the powers for rural districts to make bye-laws. Thus, for the first time, buildings could be controlled throughout the whole of England and Wales. However, this Act did not become effective, for no sooner was the ink dry than the provisions were repealed by the Public Health Act of 1875.[45]

The Public Health Act 1875

Disraeli had one more commitment to fulfil after his agreement in 1866 to enquire into, and where necessary, amend, the sanitary laws of England and Wales. This was to consolidate the many sanitary Acts, and the bill for consolidation was introduced on the 11th February 1875[46] by the president of the LGB, George Slater-Booth. In referring to the need for consolidation, Slater-Booth spoke of the possibility of removing the permissive nature of the previous Acts. The bill would be the most important measure the House would deal with during that session, and the consolidation of 29 statutes was welcomed by sanitary reformers and lawyers. What was not mentioned was the danger that the defects of previous Acts would be repeated. It was unlikely that these defects would be overcome as the government had no intention of introducing new sanitary legislation.[47]

During the committee stage, Stanstead, the previous president of the LGB, considered that many urban and rural areas were not capable of fulfilling the duties set out in the bill. He thought that it was not possible to make the country healthy by Act of Parliament but only by the willing and intelligent application of local authorities.[48] The criticism of local authorities previously expressed by Simon and other witnesses to the RSC and by Hole tended to support these views. Certainly those authorities who wished to maintain the privileged position of local self-government would find great difficulty in accepting an Act which provided agency characteristics with central direction and control. The principle would be enough to alienate those authorities from the benefits of the Act which became law on the 11th August 1875. The Act did not apply to Scotland, Ireland or the metropolis, but it confirmed both mandatory and discretionary powers of local authorities in England and Wales. Simon considered that the provisions were not as forceful as he would have liked. The 'duty' to enforce the law did not apply to the discretionary matters unless local authorities adopted the powers, and if those powers permitted a discretion of operations the exact extent of 'duty' would be difficult to define. Only borough and urban authorities were permitted discretionary powers to make bye-laws. Rural authorities no longer had that power, as the powers of the Sanitary Laws Amendment Act of 1874 had been repealed. This discretion enabled many local authorities not to adopt bye-laws, particularly those who had not done so previously, and consequently building construction continued to be controlled in a haphazard, inconsistent and unco-ordinated way.

The technical content of bye-laws was enlarged to apply to the structure of walls, foundations, roofs and chimneys of new buildings for securing stability, the prevention of fire and for the purposes of health, space about buildings, drainage, water closets, earth closets, privies, ashpits and cesspools.[49] Further bye-laws required builders to give notice and deposit plans, and local authorities had the power to inspect the work and enforce the required standards.[50] These new powers could not be applied to buildings retrospectively, so the insanitary condition of existing houses would have to be dealt with by other legislative means.[51]

The powers to make bye-laws did not cover all the matters considered important by the RSC; for example, dampness in walls, floors and building sites were not included. The provisions for securing adequate ingress and egress in public buildings had also been omitted. As these matters had not been included in any previous Public Health Act, they consequently could not be included as a consolidating measure. However, powers to enable local authorities to deal with dangerous and dilapidated buildings, previously included in the Town Improvement Clauses Act 1847, became incorporated into the new Act.[52] Enforcement powers were improved but they were still worded in such a way that inefficient authorities might fail to work within a legal framework. Thus, a deceitful builder and inefficient local authority together potentially could result in the perpetuation of jerry building.

The mandatory parts of the Act, where authorities had no discretion, were to ensure that all buildings were constructed with adequate drainage connected to a sewer providing it was within 100 feet. When this was not possible, drainage to a cesspool had to be provided.[53] Building over a sewer was prohibited unless the authorities agreed, and new houses had to be provided with satisfactory sanitary accommodation.[54] The provision of mandatory and discretionary powers did little to help the uniformity of application and enforcement, which was one of the principal aims of the sanitary reformers and administrators. However, central control had been strengthened and given the skills and encouragement; the Act was a step in the right direction.

The Act of 1875 has been described as a great Act [55] and in terms of consolidation and amendment it *was* great, but this was due to the excellent foundation provided by the report of the RSC and to the untiring efforts of sanitary reformers, supported by Simon and the dogmatic Chadwick before him. Consolidation was necessary due to the incremental approach to sanitary improvement, enabling a review of the old laws, ironing out the difficulties experienced in their administration and making necessary amendments. A consolidated Act emphasizes the importance the government attaches to its contents, but no Act is good if it cannot be properly administered, and the importance of the 1871 and 1872 Acts in providing more effective control and local administration should not be overlooked.

As for the control of building, the 1875 Act did not provide any significant advancement. The factors that gave rise to indifferent control were allowed to remain, and were of major concern to the building industry, property speculators and even central government. Despite this, local authorities could still exercise discretion not to adopt bye-laws. They could seek, and often obtain, modification of model bye-laws, they could seek, obtain and administer Improvement Acts, and they had freedom as to the quality and quantity of staff resources used to administer this Act. Despite the strengthening of central control this was insufficient to remedy these problems, and even the restructuring of local government would not improve the administration where vested interests could still influence and possibly dominate local administration. The 1875 Act did not provide legislative controls on all the issues raised by the RSC, but nevertheless was an incremental step in the growth of the building control system. Further legislation was still needed to ensure that buildings were constructed that would not be prejudicial to public health and safety.

CHAPTER 5
Bye-laws and the Anti-bye-law Lobby

The restructuring of central and local government administration together with the consolidation of public health law gave greater central control of the building control system. It also provided a new impetus to local authorities to update existing bye-laws, or to adopt new ones based on the wider areas of control provided by the 1875 Act. As we saw in *Chapter 4*, these improvements, necessary and welcome as they were, did not overcome the inherent defects in the system, namely the discretion to adopt bye-laws, the specific nature of these bye-laws and their application and enforcement. These defects would continue and it is interesting to look at both the way that resistance continued to build up against the bye-law system and the means that were sought to maintain a balance of control and acceptable building standards.

Introduction of a model set of building bye-laws

A positive contribution to the uniformity of bye-law requirements had been the introduction of a model code by the Local Government Act Department (see p.45). This move was reinforced by the new Local Government Board (LGB) who, with some assistance from The Royal Institute of British Architects (RIBA), produced a model set of building bye-laws. Local authorities were encouraged to adopt these model bye-laws either to amend existing ones, or preferably, to replace them completely, and a circular to this effect was issued by the LGB on 25th July 1877.

The model set contained 94 bye-laws on the same principle as earlier ones, providing guidance on the preparation of bye-laws for LGB approval. These bye-laws described requirements for widths and gradients of new streets, including footpaths, and prohibited the erection of buildings on sites filled with offensive materials. Oversite concrete was required to be six inches thick or alternatively a layer of asphalt was to be used. Foundations and wall sizes were taken from the London Building Acts, while the space required about buildings was set at 24 feet at the front, to the centre of the road, and 150 square feet at the rear. The requirement for open space at the front was in addition to street width required by street bye-laws and this resulted in many houses having small front gardens. For example, where street bye-laws required an 18 feet wide road with two six foot footpaths, buildings would have to be 30 feet apart but the open space bye-law required 48 feet between houses, thus leaving a nine feet long front garden to each house. The depth of rear open space varied according to the height and width of the house, and the space was to remain clear apart from small structures such as porches, WCs and steps. Habitable rooms had to have a window of a size equal to one tenth of the floor area, and half the window had to open. Rooms without a fireplace had to have a ventilation shaft of an area not less than 100 square inches. Damp sites had to be drained by subsoil drainage and no drains were permitted to pass under a building without being suitably protected (by being covered with concrete for example), and with ventilation provision at both ends. Water closets had to be placed against an external wall with permanent ventilation being provided by means of an air brick and an openable window of a minimum size of two foot by one foot. These requirements, together with many others, made the model bye-laws a comprehensive working document which, although specific, was informative. It provided speculative builders with a code of basic building construction which, if closely followed, would enable them to construct sound houses of a reasonable standard.

The model was also helpful to local authorities, enabling them to set bye-laws comparable with neighbouring authorities, and producing standardization of requirements which would ultimately assist in standardizing building materials and components. It was inevitable that the bye-laws would clash with some traditional materials and construction methods and we have seen examples of how authorities were pressured into seeking variations to allow the use of local materials and methods to continue despite the risk to health and safety (see p.45). The model bye-laws presented an alternative to a National Building Act, and, if widely adopted and enforced with some degree of uniformity and professional skill, they could easily have had a national effect. A major advantage was the relative ease with which bye-laws could be altered, either at the request of the local authority, the recommendation of the LGB, or due to technological change or political pressure. Local Acts did not have this ease of change but this did not prevent local authorities from continuing to seek and enforce their own Improvement Acts. Liverpool, despite adopting building bye-laws, continued with this form of control and secured a new Building Act in 1882. In doing so, the council took the opportunity of ensuring that some sections were compatible with the model bye-laws. This helped to reduce any criticism that could be made about indifferent standards, but more importantly it provided Liverpool with almost the same powers, but without the controlling interference of the LGB.

Nevertheless, old bye-laws remained. The town of Barnstaple in Devon adopted bye-laws for the first time in 1875, based on the provisions of the 1858 Act, which consequently became out-moded when the new model was produced by the LGB (see *Appendix 9*). Despite the 1875 Act and the new model bye-laws, different bye-laws, Improvement Acts and enforcement standards continued, much to the annoyance of builders and sanitary reformers alike. Criticisms of these differences were reinforced during the evidence presented to the Royal Commission on Housing of the Working Classes in 1885.[1] The Commission took evidence from 188 witnesses amongst whom was the ever forward-looking Edwin Chadwick. On this occasion, Chadwick, who had developed an interest in the wider uses to which concrete could be put, advocated that the technology of house construction could be improved considerably by the use of concrete, even to the extent of building complete houses with it.

New Technology
Cements

The use of Portland cement had increased the strength and consequent desirability of concrete quite considerably. So named because its grey colour resembles Portland stone, this cement is made by calcining a mixture of chalk and clay, giving a mix of about 60 per cent lime, 22 per cent soluble silica and 12 per cent alumina plus small amounts of oxide or iron and magnesia. Mixed with sand and stone aggregate, and hydrated by water, a good strong concrete is produced. Likewise, its use with sand as a mortar increases the strength of brickwork allowing it to carry greater loads. It has a tensile strength, when mixed neat with water, of 400 pounds per square inch after seven days, and 500 pounds per square inch after 28 days, compared with 202 and 183 of Roman cement and 298 of Medina cement. (Roman cement was made from calcining nodules found in London clay and Medina cement from the septaria found in Hampshire and the Isle of Wight.) When mixed with sand, the strength would fall, but the Portland cement mixture would still be about 15 times stronger than other cements.[2] Lime cements were even weaker and had the problem of not setting in damp soil. Consequently, they had little value other than for simple hardcore and were frequently used as a matter of custom. Awareness of the weaknesses and limitations of the traditional use of weak lime concrete, or the slightly stronger Roman cement concrete, had left a nervous acceptance of the use of Portland cement since its introduction around 1840. Concrete was mainly used for making foundations and with the use of weaker cements it was necessary for the base of the wall to comprise brickwork footing. This spread the load of the wall over almost the whole width of the concrete in case the wall loading compressed, crushed or sheared the concrete. Whilst Portland concrete was strong enough to support the wall without footings, bye-laws were still being made permitting the use of non-Portland cement concrete, and consequently retaining the requirement to construct costly brick footings. The conservative and traditional attitudes of the building industry contributed to the retention of this bye-law but the advantages of Portland cement concrete both constructionally and economically took some time to be accepted and it was not until 1912 that model bye-laws allowed the use of cement concrete of sufficient thickness to replace the need for footings on a nine inch wall. The year 1928 saw the removal of the need for footings to all domestic walls and an indication that the Minister of Health would be likely to agree a similar modification for all walls if anyone proposed it. Despite these provisions the bye-laws retained the clauses permitting the use of lime concrete and footings to walls.[3]

The use of Portland cement did not stimulate an instant change in the bye-laws. Firstly there had to be time for the new material to prove itself. Failure would most likely result in a bye-law restricting its use, but in this case the cautiousness of the building industry and its conservative approach to changes in traditional methods meant that there was insufficient political pressure to force a change and insufficient scientific testing and assessment of this material to encourage change.

The use of concrete at upper floor levels

Concrete technology had not been limited to its use in foundations. The extra strength that Portland cement provided enabled concrete to be used not only for the ground floors of industrial buildings but also at floor levels above ground floor. The compatibility of concrete and steel to work together and maintain a working bond was generally recognized, allowing strong floors to be constructed. This permitted heavy machinery to be used on upper floor levels, resulting in larger and taller buildings and for the industrialist meant increased production with corresponding returns. Another important quality was that the alkali in the cement would protect the steel from corroding while the concrete around the steel gave a fire resistance. Consequently, the use of steel framework floors with concrete infill soon became recognized as a fireproof construction. However, not all the designs were fireproof. In some the steel work was totally or partly exposed, allowing the steel to move under the high temperatures that could arise from industrial or warehouse fires, permitting unacceptable deflections and total or partial collapse. Despite the advantages of good concrete and steel design, no bye-laws were made as to the stability of an industrial floor or its ability not to collapse in the event of a fire, as the provisions of the 1875 Act did not permit this. The bye-laws concerned themselves with the ability of external walls to carry loads, and of walls and roofs to resist the effects of a fire. However, little concern or attention was given to the safety of people in and around the building.

Further developments in the use of concrete continued to take place, including the reinforcement of concrete by the use of small diameter steel bars. This would accommodate the tensile loads allowing the concrete to maintain its integrity by accommodating compressive loads. A Newcastle-upon-Tyne builder, William Wilkinson, patented a system using discarded wire rope from a colliery hoist draped through the concrete floor and inserted hollow clay pipes at mid-span to reduce the weight of concrete. This method was used in practice and was found to work quite satisfactorily.[4] A twisted metal bar was developed in America in 1884 which improved the bond between concrete and steel. A Frenchman, François Hennebique, was also working on the development of reinforced concrete. His method of resisting the tension developed in the concrete by turning up the ends of the reinforcing bars was patented in 1892. He designed the first reinforced concrete building to be erected in Britain. This was Weavers Mill at Quay Parade, Swansea, a six-storey building with a 14 foot cantilevered part over the loading bay. The building was completed in 1897 and remained in use until 1966, a good example of the developing building technology of the late Victorians. The building was demolished in the early 1980s to make way for a supermarket.

Reinforced concrete was used for the structural frame of Britain's first skyscraper, a 167 feet high building topped with a clock tower, overall height 310 feet. This was the Royal Liver Building in Liverpool, designed by Louis Gustave Mouchel, Hennebique's representative in Britain.[5] This was an example of the changes taking place in building technology. It was not a cheap alternative to the traditional forms of construction, but provided another way of producing larger buildings capable of supporting greater loads over bigger spans. This was necessary to achieve the floor areas required to accommodate the ever-increasing use of machinery within factory buildings and the more economical use of labour, materials and land.

Bye-laws were not able to control this type of building, and the 1875 Act did not provide for it. Reinforced concrete is a material which requires careful design and good workmanship if failure is to be prevented, yet no minimum working stresses had been defined to be used in steel and concrete so as to avoid structural failure. Of course, failure was the last thing in the minds of those designers and builders who wanted to impress developers and local authorities with the virtues of this new material. Consequently, the possibility of failure was somewhat remote but it does show how the lack of accommodating legislation restricts the use of new materials and methods of construction.

The construction of a house using concrete throughout in Paris in 1862 was the type of housing development that stimulated Chadwick to advocate its use in housing.[6] To exploit concrete for this advantage Chadwick suggested the formation of building companies.[7] However, industry was not as sure as Chadwick, and although progress was made in the prefabrication of concrete products, industrialized concrete houses were a long way off. The point had been made that to take economic advantage of new materials and methods, bye-laws should be flexible, provided health and safety aims were met. But as long as bye-laws retained an approach to the protection of property and were reactive in their development and inflexible in their application, they were unlikely to be helpful in the acceptance of new ways of constructing buildings which met the needs of their occupiers. This situation could have been improved by the way local authorities undertook their responsibilities, but the attitudes of many received a lot of criticism.

Outside of London, it was alleged that there were instances where town councils were dominated by the interests of builders and property speculators who were opposed to the introduction of bye-laws or indeed any restrictions on speculative property development.[8] In other towns, influenced but not so dominated by vested interests, bye-laws were less strictly enforced than they should have been.[9] Thus, while speculators and jerry-builders[10] were the main causes of the construction of inadequate houses, the non-enforcement of bye-laws resulted in defective sanitary arrangements, drainage and poorly-constructed buildings.

Role of the surveyor

These attitudes paralleled the effectiveness of bye-laws. Witnesses considered that in some towns bye-laws were too stringent[11] while in others they were found to be adequate in controlling materials and open space.[12] However, the effectiveness also depended on the way bye-laws were enforced and this was largely the role of the surveyor.

In Birmingham bye-laws were reported as satisfactory in that they had stopped jerry building by requiring the inspection of buildings under construction. At least five inspections of each building were carried out by local authority surveyors before being passed.[13] Surveyors employed to enforce bye-laws were extremely active, but evidence suggests that in many towns the amount of building work subject to control was beyond their staff resources to inspect. Many surveyors were found incompetent and were dismissed. Surveyors in London were considered to be more competent than those working in the provinces, but in many authorities surveyors had to work against local influences, such as the previously-mentioned vested interests, and this restricted their performance.

The variety of building standards and indifference to the enforcement of bye-laws was the chief consequence of the existing laws being permissive rather than compulsory, a view previously expressed by Simon and emphasized by Chadwick and other witnesses.[14] This suggested that central government should carry out the enforcement of Acts and bye-laws. On the other hand, if all the Acts and regulations were enforced by local authorities, most problems arising from bad sanitation would be removed, but the difficulty was that provincial authorities exhibited considerable apathy about enforcing the law.

The Local Government Board

These criticisms could not and did not go unnoticed. The expanding role of the Local Government Board, in advising not only on bye-laws but on housing and many other sanitary aspects, was also an expanding bureaucracy. It was no longer simply advising ministers on technical matters and sanitation, it was also the administration. Consequently, administrators began to control the higher levels of government departments. Simon had found that direct access to the Minister, to which he was still entitled, was now restricted, as was his other work, by the constant intervention of John Lambert, the first permanent secretary to the Local Government Board. Lambert had quickly created a bureaucratic environment within the Board which would not respond to Simon's demands. Consequently, he became disillusioned with his role and this finally led to his retirement in 1876 at the age of 59.

After Simon, the responsibility for public health and safety passed from the sanitarians to the administrators. The technical expert was relegated to a secondary role, an unfortunate situation that has continued to the present day. Such was the growth of central control over local authority matters that administrators had taken the role of directors, assessing needs and seeking solutions from technical officers and other interested organizations. In building control matters, this meant determining the areas where bye-laws would be of assistance, framing the technical solutions into bye-laws that could be administered and recommending them to local authorities for their adoption. Despite this approach, Simon considered that the law was framed in such a manner that it enabled local authorities unlimited licence to inflict insanitary conditions with impunity. The discretionary provisions of the Public Health Acts, of which building bye-laws was one, allowed acts of wilful neglect which caused injury or endangered public health, and for which compensation should be paid.

The Public Health (Amendment) Act 1890

The Local Government Board, taking note of the observations expressed in the report of the Royal Commission on Housing of the Working Classes also took into consideration the recommendations of the RSC which were not enacted in the 1875 Act. This resulted not in any simplification of that Act, but a further consolidation which incorporated local Improvement Act provisions. The advantage was that many other towns could use improved bye-law-making, and other building control powers, without the expense of seeking private Acts. It also enabled a reduction in the proliferation of Improvement Acts minimizing variety and indifference of control, yet at the same time strengthening the role of central government.

The Public Health (Amendment) Act 1890[15] extended bye-law-making powers to include the construction of floors, hearths, staircases, height of habitable rooms, paving to adjoining buildings, open space in connection with dwelling houses and the provision of sufficient water for flushing of water closets. Local authorities could now prevent alterations to buildings which had previously been erected, in accordance with the bye-laws. This covered the loophole which had been highlighted by Liddle in his evidence to the RSC (see p.63).

In addition, the findings of the House of Commons Select Committee on Fire Protection 1867 had not been overlooked. The Fires Bill (1872) which had renewed concern on emergency provisions in public buildings, previously expressed by the RSC, had prompted the inclusion of the St Helens Act provisions requiring satisfactory ingress, egress, passageways and gangways in public buildings as Section 36 of the 1890 Act. There were 28 model bye-laws prepared by the Local Government Board (see *Appendix 10*) that could be adopted as a result of this Act.[16] These related to secondary means of access for removal of refuse; sizes and spans of timber in floors and roofs, including roof battens for laying and fixing tiles, sizes and spans of timbers for floors of public and warehouse buildings, the size of floorboards and the provision of bridging or strutting the joists. Staircase standards for domestic, public and warehouse buildings were described (for example, the standard for domestic staircases was eight inch tread, nine inch rise, one and a quarter inch strings, one inch thick treads, three-quarters of an inch nosing and the provision of a handrail). The heights of rooms in roof spaces could now be required at nine feet over two thirds of the area of the room measured at a height of five feet above floor level, whilst in other rooms the room height could be eight feet. These bye-laws now covered matters of detail, timber sizes in particular, increased room heights and staircases. All these requirements would add to the cost of house construction, especially in areas not used to such control. Although the additional requirements were considered necessary, the specific detailing of structures to small dimensions less than an inch did not provide any room for flexible judgements in control terms, and consequently resistance to them was bound to arise. These model bye-laws were again orientated towards traditional forms of building construction. They did not attempt to control steel and reinforced concrete, although bye-law-making powers for such control now existed.

Adoption of bye-laws in rural areas

Between 1860 and 1882 some 1000 urban and 600 rural authorities had adopted some of the bye-laws. Not all of these authorities had adopted the 1877 model bye-laws; many retained the bye-laws made under the 1858 Act. Others had no bye-laws at all; this was most common in rural areas which had limited powers of adoption and those that did not use those powers were most difficult to persuade.[17] Those that did caused the reaction expressed in objections to the RSC.[18] Rural authorities adopted bye-laws that were structured for urban situations and seemed to act rather erroneously when applying them to rural development. The growth of this type of bye-law in rural areas resulted in landowners fighting back against what were seen as restrictive and inappropriate controls.

The application of building bye-laws to urban style development could be appreciated but did not seem so appropriate when applied to isolated and sporadic development. One surveyor, JL Green, in his book about country cottages, expressed resentment and objection to bye-laws in rural areas.[19] He aptly described the construction, layout and sanitation of country cottages which had been built on the large estates of such landowners as the Dukes of Bedford, Westminster, Rutland and many others. In 1850, the cost of building estate houses was between £160 and £200, which were rented at about 1s 2d per week. The cost of repair was £20 to £30 per annum. From these figures, it was clear that the net return was not profitable. It was alleged that to comply with bye-law standards construction costs would rise and this was strongly objected to. These costs compared with speculative housing costs in Leeds and Halifax of between £150 and £200,[20] whilst back-to-back housing cost about £110,[21] which was also the average price of a terraced house in London.[22] These prices included the cost of the land, and furthermore, the volume of speculative building could attract the discount cost of bulk buying which added to the profit margins.

Whilst Green took account of the economies of estate development, he concluded that due to good construction and sanitation of estate cottages building rural housing to the standard required by bye-laws was in many instances unnecessary and in the public interest, undesirable.[23] His views cannot entirely be substantiated. Thus, whilst the better cottages on the Duke of Bedford's estate, constructed before the introduction of bye-laws, remain to offer good and attractive housing, many of the cottages, some of which can be seen in the village of Ridgmont near Woburn in Bedfordshire, were built to bye-law standards (see *Plate 7*). These houses, having nine-inch thick brick walls, tile roofs and basic sanitation were structurally capable of modernization in the 1960s and are still providing good housing. This would not have been the case if the walls had been only four and a half inches thick, as advocated by Green. Such are the long-term economic benefits of good housing standards to which building bye-laws contributed.

There was a similarity between philanthropic industrial developers and paternalistic estate owners. Daunton points out that providing better housing would lead to a more contented and more productive workforce, without affecting the basic relationship of capitalist production. It was a development in social responsibility in an advancing industrial economy, as was the introduction of building bye-laws.[24] This should have resulted in some degree of harmony instead of resistance, but the objections to both cost and compulsion were widespread. Previously it had been the industrial, commercial and property speculators of the urban areas who had been challenged with bye-law control. The jerry building and property speculation by landowners and farmers, although previously questioned, had not been effectively challenged. This had now changed.

R. MacDonald-Lucas, a chartered architect practising in the Southampton area, experienced great 'frustration' in obtaining approval of plans which he deposited with the South Stoneham Rural District Council. This frustration and anger led to a series of articles in the *Southampton Observer and Hampshire News*.[25] Lucas took the same line as Green, criticizing the bye-laws for their inability to cover traditional construction and to take into account new technologies. The use of concrete, apart from foundations and reinforced concrete, was not recognized by the bye-laws and those relating to brick or stone walls ruled out the use of timber frames.[26] The problem, as we have seen, with the bye-laws was that they were specific in their requirements rather than relating to functional or performance standards that could be interpreted and applied. Specific bye-laws were easy to apply, but performance standards and functional requirements required a higher level of skill to enforce and this was an area where Lucas was extremely forceful in his views.

Lucas, like Chadwick before him, chose also to discredit the standard of surveyor appointed to enforce bye-laws. In his experience with South Stoneham RDC, the 'evil' of the system was the surveyor, an 'official required by the 1875 Acts, who approved the plans and who in some cases combined the qualifications of a coster with the authority of a censor'.[27] Lucas considered that bye-laws should contain a rule that the person holding the appointment of district surveyor should be competent to understand plans and be conversant with ordinary methods of construction.

Lucas' alternative proposals

Whilst citing building bye-laws as a curse and supporting those who advocated their total removal, Lucas recognized the need for a form of control that resisted the onslaught of jerry-builders. Therefore, he put forward an alternative form of control as a schedule of instructions to intending builders, written as far as possible, in plain English. Lucas felt that every person involved in the building trade should be in possession of a copy, and that the district surveyor of the local authority should be able to give advice when required. It would be up to the builder's discretion whether they accepted or ignored the advice upon which they would proceed to build, and subject to reasonable inspection, be left alone by the district surveyor until the building had been completed. Before occupation, the surveyor would inspect and display on the property a certificate of merit or demerit. The certificate of merit would be renewable every five years and where defects occurred, be noted on the demerit certificate. This would be read by purchasers, tenants and mortgagees who would form their own judgement as to the relevance and importance of these defects. Only if a property was unsafe, presumably capable of collapse, was it to be demolished or remain empty. In addition, Lucas suggested that builders should have a right of appeal if they held differing views from those of the district surveyor whose judgement should be final in cases where the appellant was judged wrong. According to Lucas, the surveyor would have to be a qualified person, a requirement which would weed out many persons holding such office, no doubt including the then surveyor of South Stoneham R.D.C.

Lucas' criticism added further weight to the views previously expressed about the professional standard of surveyors appointed to enforce building bye-laws. His proposal, however, would not prevent a building being erected contrary to the interests of health and safety, which was the purpose of the building bye-laws. The discretion he proposed the builder should have was far too wide, as any builder could, at their discretion, knowingly erect faulty work with the cost of correcting that work, including any demolition cost, ultimately falling on the owner. The architect, builder and developer would have long since gone from the site.

Lucas' articles were attacked as ineffective and incapable of being administered by law.[28] They provided no legal basis for enforcement or indeed inspection, and consequently the whole scheme for offering some degree of public protection on health and safety would fall to the ground. The basis of the proposals was nothing more than a gentleman's agreement. Lucas staunchly defended his proposals, but his desire to remove building bye-laws, especially in rural areas, was well known. He was a member of a delegation to the President of the Local Government Board in November 1904 when a proposal for the abolition of building bye-laws in rural areas was put forward. The President of the Board, Mr Walter Long, made it clear that building bye-laws were a necessity and that the proposal could not be entertained. The delegation, who were members of the Building By-laws Reform Association, were not subdued by this rejection and the campaign continued with the aim of securing a change in the form of building bye-laws in rural areas. The Association used the term 'by' as opposed to 'bye', a different spelling with the same meaning, the origin of which has already been discussed (see p.41). In 1902, Sir William Chance, a founder of the Association, reflected that he had heard it said that the only reform the Association had achieved was the deletion of the 'e' from the word 'bye', although, as we shall see, the Association did not even achieve that.[29]

Application of bye-laws in rural areas

A considerable number of objections to the bye-laws stemmed from the fact that rural authorities, who were able to adopt bye-laws as a right due to the provisions of the Local Government Act of 1894, were offered the Urban Model Bye-laws by the Local Government Board as a basis. The fact that these rural areas had no previous form of building control seemed a curse to many builders and some architects.[30] The Building By-laws Reform Association considered that to seek the abolition of bye-laws would be a waste of time and effort and that their energies would be better spent seeking amendments and alterations so as to provide a more elastic approach in administration and to remove the injustices and hardship that bye-law enforcement inevitably inflicted.[31]

This approach would require bye-laws to be more functional than specific, thus allowing interpretation of their requirements. However, this would require a more professional standard of administration, an approach which would not be welcomed by the Local Government Board, as it would mean a lowering of the demand for their services in the advice that they gave to local authorities. The Board had responded to the criticism of onerous bye-laws in rural areas and their solution had been to prepare a series of model bye-laws for use in rural areas (see *Appendix 11*). These were available for adoption by local authorities in 1902 but very few chose to.

The agitation by the Reform Association against bye-laws in rural areas led the Local Government Board to issue a circular to rural authorities in January 1906, informing them of the objections that had been received concerning the adoption and enforcement of bye-laws intended for use in urban areas.[32] The circular encouraged the adoption of model bye-laws for use in rural areas.

The 106 rural authorities (and parts of another 32) who adopted these bye-laws seemed to be enforcing them satisfactorily. Rural areas which had urban characteristics could be dealt with separately if such areas could be defined. The Board could not enforce or insist, but only *recommend* rural authorities to review their position and where desirable adopt the rural model. The Board assisted by providing the appropriate forms to enable the revision of bye-laws and to supply information if required. The contents of the rural model were limited to the structure of walls and foundations of new buildings for purposes of health; space about buildings to secure a free circulation of air; the ventilation and drainage of buildings; water closets; earth closets; privies; ashpits and cesspools. There were also powers to close buildings unfit for human habitation and to enforce the observance of the bye-laws by requiring notices and plans.[33] These demands were less than the bye-laws could have made under the Local Government Act of 1858, which also included provision to make bye-laws in respect of the stability of buildings and prevention of fires. The latter was now excluded from the rural model, and with the omission of the principle of safety the trend of expanding building bye-law control was reversed.

These provisions reflect the concern of the Local Government Board and the introduction of rural bye-laws was their way of maintaining control over the system. What it showed was the easy way in which bye-laws could be updated or changed in response to pressure, but we have previously seen it was a more flexible approach than local Acts, many of which were still in force. The problem was getting local authorities to respond to the need for change.

The Reform Association considered the rural model in detail and recommended alterations to many of the bye-laws. These recommendations were accepted by the Local Government Board and incorporated into a new rural model.[34] This co-operation was much appreciated and the chairman of the Association gave credit to the Board for making every effort to persuade local authorities to adopt the new code. The Association considered that in many respects their work had been done for them, but, as many rural authorities were reluctant to adopt the new model, although it contained less demanding requirements, legislation was still necessary to effect the change. The Association proceeded to draft a bill and model code of bye-laws which was introduced as a Private Members Bill into the House of Lords by Lord Hylton on the 1st March 1905.[35] The Bill, known as the Public Health Acts (Building Bye-laws) Bill, was intended to amend the Public Health Acts with respect to building bye-laws in rural districts in England and Wales, excluding London.

The Association recognized that the administration of the London Building Act of 1894 was carried out without much complaint[36] and that larger towns and urban areas needed a more comprehensive set of bye-laws, but in rural areas there was not the need to have such extensive control. Accordingly, the bill was small, containing only five clauses dealing with:

1. The application and extent of the Act;
2. Exemption of certain buildings;
3. Alterations to exempted buildings;
4. Power of Local Government Board to extend the provisions;
5. Procedure of persons aggrieved by the bye-laws.

Isolated buildings

The exemptions proposed in respect of isolated buildings were complete apart from bye-laws relating to drainage and sanitary conveniences. A block plan would have to be approved, but above ground the builder would be free to build as he pleased provided he did nothing contrary to public health regulations. The isolation of properties would ensure the benefit of not overcrowding dwellings and provide labourers and artisans with good space for gardens. Alterations and extensions would be subject to the submission of plans and approval. This included alterations to boundaries so as to decrease the area below that permitted as an exemption, and where this occurred, the exemption would cease to exist. The bill could be extended into urban and borough areas on application by the local authority or by one tenth of the ratepayers of the district – such orders could also be revoked by the same procedure. This was one way in which the Reform Association sought a reduction of bye-law control in urban areas. The appeal system was included so as to allow aggrieved persons to appeal through the courts.

Lucas, who was involved in the preparation of both the bill and the bye-laws, was able to incorporate many ideas which had been expressed in his articles, although the end product was somewhat tempered from his previous radical solutions. It was considered desirable that some bye-laws should be applied in all areas, but keeping the bill small was one way of minimizing objections and getting approval. Lack of Parliamentary time meant that there was no chance of the bill becoming law during 1905. However, the Lords passed the Bill.[37]

Undeterred, Hylton reintroduced the bill in March the following year. In his introduction he said that the bill sought to encourage the construction of suitable detached and semi-detached houses of cottage type for the working classes, freeing them from the onerous and tyrannical conditions imposed by bye-laws which were intended for the crowded streets of cities.[38] Hylton added that the bill would permit the use of materials other than brick, and would overcome the reduction of room sizes proportionate to window sizes. He did not state the alternative solution, namely, an increase in window size to provide better ventilation, or point out that it didn't seem to be objectionable for roofs and walls to let in rain, going on to add that the bill would not permit the construction of cheap and nasty houses. As the bill related only to detached and semi-detached houses, jerry-builders would not so easily be able to take advantage as their developments were invariably terraced houses on small plots. Hylton stated that local authorities who had adopted the 1877 model bye-laws would overcome the majority of problems if they had adopted the 1901 rural model, but many authorities were not keen to do so as it was alleged that it would be unfair to previous developers and owners of property to permit the construction of cheaper houses. Hylton concluded that the aim of the bill was to permit more houses to be constructed, which itself was advantageous.[39] Earl Carrington, in reply, said that the government was in sympathy with the bill but, as it applied to England and Wales, it included the cities of Manchester, Leicester and other large towns, which was not the purpose of the bill and should therefore be restricted to rural districts or urban districts with the approval of the local government board. Whilst the bill would encourage the building of houses nothing should be done which would diminish the safeguards against insanitary conditions and the erection of bad houses. The bill completed its third reading without further amendments and was passed to the House of Commons, where it was introduced on the 5th November 1906, but did not proceed to a second reading.[40] The government's support was one of sympathy and Carrington's statement to the Lords seemed only half-hearted support, exercising caution in relaxing any standards. Eventually, when opposition came from the powerful Urban and Rural District Councils Association the bill was dropped.

This action obviously upset the By-laws Reform Association, but they at once proceeded to re-negotiate the contents of the bill with the Urban and Rural Districts Councils Associations. A new draft was agreed but the reluctance of the Reform Association fully to support the modified bill led to its not being proceeded with.[41]

In response to the argument for less bye-law control, or even complete exemption, the Local Government Board saw an opportunity to increase their control of the system by supporting views put forward by the Rural Housing and Sanitary Association. This resulted in a section being included in the Housing and Town Planning Act of 1909, which provided the Local Government Board with the power to revoke bye-laws which impeded the building of cottages, but not houses. Also, where the authorities did not make new bye-laws, the Board could make them and insist on their enforcement by the local authorities. The Reform Association was doubtful of the value of this provision in that it was unlikely to be used. Aware that its influence was fading, the Association was dissolved in 1912 when the British Constitutional Association assumed charge of the bill, with the arrangements being made by the chairman of the Reform Association who was a member of the Constitutional Association. The action taken by the Reform Association reflected the views of many developers and represented a serious political threat, backed with some technical support, to the government's policy of securing a reasonable degree of health and safety measures in new houses. The need for relevant bye-laws, flexibly and skilfully applied, had been emphasized and had not gone unnoticed by the government.

Public Health (Amendment) Act 1907

The activities of the By-law Reform Association motivated the government to prepare and pass the Public Health Amendment Act of 1907.[42] The government recognized that much of the agitation was caused by local authorities not updating their bye-laws to the current model, and particularly in rural areas by not disposing of the urban model in favour of the rural or intermediate models, despite the advice contained in the 1906 circular. The Local Government Board had amended the model bye-laws since their restructuring in 1877, issuing further models of the urban series in 1899, and the first rural model in 1901 (see *Appendix 11*). The Board recast the urban and rural models in 1903 and issued an intermediate model in 1905, the latter for use by rural areas within which were villages of urban character where more structural fire resistance was necessary.

To overcome the objections to enforcement of outdated bye-laws it was essential to remove the validity of previously approved plans and require a further deposit of plans to which the new updated bye-laws, hopefully adopted by all councils, would be applied. It was not unusual for some authorities to maintain old bye-laws to use as a lever to obtain other concessions which they could not legally demand.[43] Other authorities would not adopt new bye-laws as it was considered that this would give an unfair economic advantage to a builder constructing to the new bye-laws compared to buildings being constructed to meet the old bye-laws. The advantage to the builder was that under the urban code a density of 40–50 houses per acre could be developed, while under the intermediate model it was 50–60 per acre and 60–70 per acre under the rural model.[44] Thus the more rural models adopted, the more profitable development was likely to be.

The Act set out to ensure that the latest set of model bye-laws adopted by any authority would be the ones enforced. Provisions were made for plans deposited for more than three years and not acted on to be of no effect, and this was to be stated on all approved plans. Deposited plans and details could now be retained by local authorities.

The heights of chimneys relative to buildings and chimney stacks for steam engines, breweries and industrial buildings could now be controlled.[45] Yards adjacent to buildings could be required to be paved. Temporary buildings, which had not previously been the subject of control, were covered by a new section to the Act.[46] Plans had to be deposited and conditions could be attached to the approval of these plans relating to sanitary arrangements, ingress, egress and fire protection. Plans had to be considered within one month of deposit and where this did not happen local authorities could not use their powers to remove buildings which did not comply with conditions. Provisions were also made for authorities to repair or enclose dangerous places which abutted public places.[47] Whilst these powers did not add to the bye-laws of local authorities, they did extend the control that rural districts had on the safety of buildings both new and old.

The Act not only added to existing bye-law-making powers, it also included provisions contained in local Improvement Acts. The Local Government Board had previously used this procedure in 1890, not only to strengthen their control of the system but to make these provisions available to other towns that had not sought such powers by means of an Improvement Act. It also encouraged councils to repeal their Improvement Acts in favour of public Acts, producing more uniformity over the control system. The action of government control in the late Victorian era has been described as being expanding, bureaucratic, centralized and incrementalist, and this Act, like the 1890 Act, was an example of that trend.[48]

The continuance of objections to bye-laws

The consolidatory trends of the 1907 Act did not prevent the continuance of objections against the content and enforcement of building bye-laws. These emerged during the debate on the Housing and Town Planning Bill 1909[49] when Mr Walter Guinness, in support of the principles of the By-law Reform Association, moved that the statutory obligation enabling the Local Government Board to revoke bye-laws should be dispensed with. He gave instances of bye-laws requiring higher costs, such as a requirement for a nine-inch thick separating wall between dwellings where he considered a four and a half inch wall to be adequate, and the rear open space in Croydon being required to be 500 square feet, while it was only 150 square feet in Edmonton. These were differences between building bye-laws and the London Building Acts. Guinness added that among the 140 local authorities in the Greater London area, bye-laws varied enormously, adding to the cost of construction and confusion to both architect and builders.[50] He proposed that the clause should be amended to permit local authorities to dispense with bye-laws where the Local Government Board thought necessary.

Guinness's proposals were not supported by Mr Burns, President of the Local Government Board who said that the principle of the objection was that of relief for the London County Council which had built outside of its area and had come into conflict with building bye-laws. The London County Council was asking, through Guinness, that the Local Government Board dispense with all bye-laws in the areas that the London County Council was encroaching upon. Burns, a member of the Fire Brigade Committee of London for 18 years, considered it 'reproducing evil in a worse form' to ask for four and a half inch thick walls and not to penetrate the roof space and roof surface. He went on to add that by building on land which was cheaper than in central London, the London County Council had no right to require people to live in cheaper property. Furthermore, a four and a half inch wall did not provide adequate sound insulation and there was a need for people to relax in peace. Burns considered that the present system of bye-laws was satisfactory and concluded that if London was an example of good building they should not adopt such low standards.[51] This outburst against the imposition of standards by bye-laws illustrated that even local authorities could adopt the attitudes of development speculators in their need to construct low cost housing. It is therefore not surprising to see why many did not adopt or update their bye-laws.

Housing of the Working Classes Bill

The ramifications of the Reform Association's efforts lingered on and gained strength through the advocates of unrestricted building who sought abolition of building control. This manifested itself in a number of bills being presented to the House between 1911 and 1914 under the guise of the Housing of the Working Classes Bill. These bills had a philanthropic intention to improve the housing of the working classes, but they also had as an underlying purpose the abolition of a substantial part of model building bye-laws. The first bill was introduced on the 7th December 1911 and its supporters were hoping to follow the success of the Education (Administrative Provisions) Act 1911.[52] This Act exempted the Board of Education from the application of a bye-law control by local authorities. The Secretary to the Board of Education, Mr C.P. Trevelyn, referred to a departmental committee report which stated that the construction of educational buildings would be reduced by not constructing to bye-law standards, particularly in areas where antiquated bye-laws were in existence. Despite objections, Trevelyn was adamant that there would be no local authority interference. He stated that cost was all-important and there was a need to override local building bye-laws.[53] It was agreed that local authorities would always be consulted prior to plans being approved by the Board of Education and that they could insist on matters of sanitation.

This Act reflects the growing dominance that central authority was exerting over the building control system. The government, finding itself an injured party by the inadequacy of out-dated bye-laws and indifferent local authority control, cast itself free of these problems by placing the control within the Board of Education, where it has remained ever since. The sponsors of the Housing of the Working Classes Bill saw the problem of bye-laws as one of cost; cheaper houses would mean more being built and more people in the working classes being housed. Guinness again commented on the unreasonableness of bye-laws and argued that the Garden City movement had shown how absurd they were. He considered bye-laws were ineffective against jerry builders and impeded, harassed and hampered the public-spirited reformer. These arguments, although attractive, were unsubstantiated and did not win the day. When the vote was taken, the bill was dismissed.

The sponsors proceeded to re-introduce the bill on 6th August 1912.[54] The aim of the new bill was to encourage the private ownership of dwellings and businesses amongst the working classes, and the provision as to the relaxation of bye-laws was included in respect of ordinary housing schemes. The bill went to a Standing Committee where Burns objected to many clauses, although he was prepared to agree an alteration which referred to local authority schemes only. This was an extension of the relaxation or dispensation principles established by the Education (Administrative Provisions) Act of 1911 and was a concession the sponsors of the bill eagerly accepted. However, in their eagerness they proposed amendments to give exemption to housing schemes approved by government departments and to private schemes if certified by a local authority. Burns objected to these further proposals and the bill proceeded no further.[55]

In the meantime, the Local Government Board was trying desperately to get local authorities to update and change their bye-laws as without these changes central authority would continue to be challenged. A further circular from the Local Government Board reminded authorities of the need to update their bye-laws so as to accommodate changes in construction methods and materials, permitting the use of composite construction such as steel, reinforced concrete, timber framing, slate and tile hanging on panelled walls with an infill of incombustible material.[56] The circular also reminded rural authorities of the rural model which avoided the restrictive nature of urban bye-laws on small houses. The Local Government Board also offered their assistance to those authorities who wished to revise their bye-laws.

Model bye-laws, despite this plea, were not amended to control or provide guidance on the structural use of steel or reinforced concrete as a frame, part frame or component use. They were amended so as to prevent local authorities from insisting that all walls should be of load-bearing brickwork in accordance with bye-law requirements on thickness relative to height rations. This would permit the use of composite construction, but in doing so it applied no control over the load-bearing elements if not of brickwork. This indicated a lack of scientific guidance of an independent nature and quality that the Local Government Board could readily accept as being unbiased and suitable to include within a bye-law. Local authorities did not have these resources and were not in a position to prompt the Board into suggesting the content of a format of new bye-laws to control those new aspects of building technology. Consequently, the circular was only limited in its aim. Nevertheless, any improvement in reducing the restrictiveness of bye-laws without affecting health or safety was a step in the right direction. The extent of urban bye-laws can be seen by reference to *Appendix 12*. Response to the circular would take time and time was not on the side of these who sought to abolish bye-law control. The anti-bye-law attitudes remained when the bill was again submitted on March 13th 1913.[57]

Resubmission of the Bill

This time the bill sought better application and enforcement of the Housing of the Working Classes and to amend the Small Dwellings Acquisition Act of 1899. Central to the bill was the reduction of construction costs in working class housing and this could be achieved by overriding the requirements of any building bye-laws. Burns was prepared to support the useful parts of the bill for administrative reasons but could not support the entire bill because of its financial aspects and it was mainly for this reason the bill was defeated.

In pursuance of this objective, the sponsors re-introduced the bill yet again on the 13th February 1914, when at the second meeting the new president of the Local Government Board, Mr Herbert Samuel, said that the relaxation of the bye-laws required the Board to go into the merits of every case throughout the country, a task the Board could not undertake.[58] He went on to say:

> '...further I agree with the Honourable Member who introduced the bill that it is desirable to remove or restructure the byelaws which hamper public utilities, societies, and others in building houses in various locations. In spite of the Local Government Board and the exhortations to the Local Authorities, many Authorities are far too rigid and in many cases enforce obsolete byelaws. We must be careful not to allow, in the name of town planning, jerry building to re-appear. The whole question is one of great complexity and my Right Honourable Friend, the Parliamentary Secretary of the Local Government Board, has accepted the duty to act as Chairman of a Departmental Committee which I am setting up to go into the whole question of local byelaws and after consideration of all interests concerned to make proposals for legislative and administrative action.'[59]

The Local Government Board did not want to lose any of its controls over local authorities, or influence over the growing importance of sanitary improvement. Their growing bureaucratic approach needed more, not less, control. A strong central authority was the only way to force many local authorities into some form of positive action on these issues. The Board had sufficient influence to ensure the government retained its position in this respect. However, such extensive bad building and insanitary problems existed in both town and rural areas that it would have been unwise and socially unacceptable for the government to abdicate its responsibilities. It therefore set up a committee. The objections raised by the anti-bye-law lobby were now to be considered by the Departmental Committee. This provided a further chance to get their views accepted, but on this occasion the evidence would be put forward by those who supported the principle of building bye-laws. The growth of bye-laws since 1875 both in content and application was necessary to curtail the development of houses that could seriously affect public health and safety. The result was generally quite successful as the majority of houses erected at the end of the nineteenth century exceeded the minimum bye-law standard.[60] The various standards applied by the Urban, Rural and a mixture of the two, known as the Intermediate Model Byelaws, together with Improvement Act and Public Health Act requirements were confusing, onerous, conflicting and indifferent. Consequently the extent of objection was not surprising. The Local Government Board, having developed its bureaucratic control over the system did not intend to lose its grip and recognized the need to continue bye-law control. It needed to take the heat out of the arguments being made and place the matter once again firmly under their control and this could be achieved through the workings of the Departmental Committee. Although prompted by the Local Government Board, the government was correct in deferring to a Departmental Committee where structured and informative argument could take place. The steady hand of government was needed, otherwise there would have been a breakdown of control resulting in building control reverting to a Local Improvement Act system, which, although good in some areas, would not have been extensive enough to have been in the national interest. The Local Government Board provided a lead to which many local authorities responded, although unfortunately many did not, causing an imbalance in the system. It was this area of local government response that was problematic – the discretionary role was critical.

Chapter 6
Committees, Commissions and Circulars

The Parliamentary battles for the reduction, or where possible, the abolition, of building bye-laws, were over by 1914. Those who supported the Housing of the Working Classes Bill had lost. The government had conveniently, but rightly, referred the matter to a committee where there was less political meandering and more critical argument. Above all, the growing Civil Service had influence and therefore some control over the proceedings. Building control was never a compelling subject to stir emotions or public concern, or even to command Parliamentary time, but by debating the issues in committees or commissions, there was a likelihood of improvement in the system. In this chapter this growing trend will be examined to determine the influence of the committee on the type and change of bye-laws, legislative changes and the extent of central control over the system.

The Departmental Committee on Building Bye-laws

Supporters of the Housing of the Working Classes Bill were appointed to the Departmental Committee on Building Bye-laws by Herbert Samuel, President of the LGB. Sir Randolph Baker sat during the 1914 sittings, but due to war service was replaced by Colonel Sir A. Griffith Boscowan. The committee, formed on the 30th April 1914, was chaired by the Right Honourable J. Herbert-Lawes MP, Parliamentary Secretary to the LGB. The committee secretary was Mr KMC Shelley of the LGB.[1] The outbreak of war in August 1914 seriously delayed the work of the committee and with other duties being placed on members it became impracticable to continue. By the end of the Parliamentary session of 1914, the committee had held nine meetings and interviewed 14 witnesses.

Their brief was limited to 'consideration of the control at present exercised in England and Wales over the erection of buildings and the construction of streets by means of byelaws and local regulation and their effect on building and development and to make recommendations'.[2] It did not include London and therefore a comparison between bye-laws and the London Building Acts could not be made. This in effect prevented any recommendations to merge the London system with that of England and Wales. In the prevailing mood any such suggestion would have been strongly resisted. Neither could the committee investigate the effects of building control on public health and safety, to the extent of determining whether or not the bye-laws were achieving their aim of improvements in those areas. This surely should have been the main intent of bye-laws, yet it was avoided because the problem that led to the enquiry was their effect on building and development, rather than health and safety issues. This raised questions such as whether the bye-laws were inadequate in rejecting old building methods and traditional materials, or restrictive of new methods and materials and whether this increased the cost of building whilst reducing profits. The latter question particularly concerned those specializing in the development of working class houses and the growing trend of development based on new town planning principles that had emerged from the philanthropic and Garden City developments. This was the nub of the inquiry.

Prior to the end of the war, on the 29th October 1917, Mr W. Hayes-Fisher, the then president of the LGB reconstituted the committee. A further 24 meetings were held, interviewing 35 witnesses. By the time the committee finished its work on 20th March 1918, the report was completed and was presented to the president of the LGB on 13th November 1918. It comprised some 49 pages, appendices and a supporting document of minutes of evidence from the interviews of the witnesses.

Despite the considerable Parliamentary support for the removal of building bye-laws, evidence given to the committee did not substantiate that view. Chance, who had done much to inspire and lead the anti-bye-laws campaign, agreed that there was a continuing need for building bye-laws but that they should be so constructed and administered as to avoid causing unnecessary injustice and hardship. These views were in general supported by representatives of The Royal Institute of British Architects (RIBA) and of The National Federation of Building Trades Employers (NFBTE). Both bodies agreed that the control of building by a public authority was necessary in the interests of public health and safety and that the bye-law system with LGB approval was the best; it was the subject matter and specific nature of the bye-laws which were at fault. The representatives of the Rural District Councils Association (RDCA) and of the Urban District Councils Association (UDCA) agreed that bye-laws were necessary, so much so that they took great exception to authorities who had not adopted bye-laws or taken adequate measures to ensure proper administration and enforcement.

National Federation of Building Trades Employers (NFBTE)

The evidence given by the representatives of NFBTE was, however, divided. Two were in agreement on the principle of bye-laws but Williams, a builder from South Wales, maintained total opposition and stated that fewer bye-laws meant less interference, especially by the officials who appeared to have uncontrolled powers of administration. Good builders in their own interests would build to a good standard, he added, and bye-laws were unnecessary.[3] The majority of complaints brought to the attention of the committee had little relevance to bye-law control. The report states, 'it has been brought to our attention that the majority of complaints made in the press against byelaws are in general terms and that it is seldom that the complaints descend to detail and give instances showing exactly what the difficulties are. The same tendency has been apparent in much of the evidence before us. There has been a great deal of generalisation to the effect that byelaws are, or may be, unduly restrictive but such facts as have been adduced in support of the allegation have not always been borne out by the complainant'.[4] Nevertheless, the committee recognized there was grievance, though some 70 per cent of the complaints made had nothing to do with bye-laws but referred to the control by regulation in local Acts, statutes and discretionary control. It was clear that the differences had to be resolved and this could be achieved either by accepting that there would be no control or alternatively by introducing one common set of rules.

The Royal Institute of British Architects (RIBA)

Supporting the principle of control by the local Acts, Pick, a witness on behalf of RIBA, had had experience with the regulations made under local Acts in Leicester. He contended that such control was better and should not be done away with by an unusual system of bye-laws, quoting examples of buildings being more expensive to construct outside Leicester due to bye-laws requiring greater thickness of wall construction.[5]

The presentation of other evidence

FW Platt, a building surveyor who was not representing any organization, had submitted evidence based on his many years of experience as a building surveyor with Salford Corporation. He explained that Salford had not been hampered by building bye-laws, as the town had four local Acts controlling building. The first Act, dating from 1862, was followed by Acts of 1870, 1871 and 1875 which remained in operation until 1899. Admittedly, these Acts related only to housing and there was no control over public or warehouse-type buildings, many of which subsequently became the subject of dangerous building notices because of dilapidation or their inability to sustain the loads to which they were subjected. As a result, regulations had been introduced in 1901 extending control over this type of building, but even then wall thickness was limited to nine inches with party walls of only four and a half inches. Similarly, regulations relating to drainage controlled only the size and direction of flow, and not the joints. Consequently, it became possible and even permissible to construct drainage with leaky joints. This highlighted the weakness of specific requirements in that if they were not specific enough the aim was frequently missed. The irregularities were partly removed when Salford adopted bye-laws in 1899. The operation of these bye-laws provided some elasticity of administration and ease of updating which, in Platt's opinion, was not only better than control by local Acts but was welcomed by builders.[6] Platt's experience had shown him that bye-laws were not an imposition and in the main prevented jerry building and in this alone they were successful.[7] *The Builder*, however, considered that 'jerry builders were not such a problem and actually contributed to economic building. It was stated that the jerry builder has never been accused of jeopardising the safety of his structures, on the contrary, he has reduced the science to a fine art besides appreciating the values of standardisation'.[8] Whilst there may be some truth in this opinion, jerry-builders have very little understanding and feeling for the principles of the science of building. In any case, each building should not be an extension of research into the limits of structural stability or sanitation.

The committee considered that control by local Acts was too rigid as this could be changed only by Parliament. Builders had little knowledge of the regulations that could be applied and the discretionary powers enabled updating in an indifferent way, causing inconvenience and indignation. Bye-laws, on the other hand, had to be made public and were readily available to the builder, making his task much easier. Whilst there were benefits in both systems, the committee came to the conclusion that bye-laws should be the standard method of control, and all matters controlled by other methods should be transferred to the bye-law system.[9] This recommendation was a means of simplifying control, making the system and its requirements uniform, but in doing so it was placing the overall control firmly in the hands of central government. Despite local authorities being deprived of independent control, there was no other place for national control other than through the LGB. The problems expressed were national problems and therefore could only be dealt with nationally.

The system of control had now been established; the problem was not one of form but of content. Dolton, the principal officer in the legal department of the LGB, gave the committee a very thorough explanation of the bye-law system and its development since 1858. When questioned on the outcry against bye-laws, he explained that although there had been some complaints, it could not be described as an 'outcry'. He stated that the majority of these complaints were against old bye-laws which tended to be more restrictive than the latest model bye-laws, and that where these were adopted the complaints lessened.

The cost of construction could be raised by overdemanding bye-laws. Bye-laws had restricted the use of four and a half inch thick walls, which were not only inadequate in strength but also in weather resistance, lacking thermal and sound insulation. The 11-inch thick cavity wall was becoming popular even in low cost housing, and permitted by many authorities. However, in Cardiff the bye-laws required a nine inch outer skin and a four and a half inch inner skin, thus increasing the cost of cavity wall construction by approximately one third without any good reason. Similarly, many authorities still required the party wall between houses to be taken up above the roof despite a model bye-law permitting a non-combustible roof covering to be taken over the top of the wall and bedded in cement mortar. Worsley, an architect at the LGB, sought not to increase the responsibility of the LGB, and advocated that it was better not to have a bye-law than one that caused problems.

These views may at first sight seem pathetic but what was being made clear was that bye-laws based on specific requirements were becoming quickly outdated by the introduction of new materials and building technology and it would be a never-ending job for the LGB to keep updating. What was needed was a form of bye-law that stated a functional or performance standard and allowed the local authority and the builder to interpret the details of meeting that requirement. This form of bye-laws was suggested by Professor Pite, a RIBA member, who, in his evidence on behalf of RIBA, considered that a simple code which stated the principles to be achieved rather than one specifying the details of how to achieve them was desirable. He thought the code should be universal, thus eliminating the varying bye-laws that existed and illustrated the idea by pointing out that the laws of gravity worked the same in Dover as in Birmingham, so there was no reason why bye-laws on structural stability should vary.[10] H.W. Fovarque, representing the AMC, remarked that the same principle applied to fundamental health conditions.[11]

Both Pite and Platt recognized that differing traditional building materials and methods existed throughout the country. The functional bye-law would accommodate these variations although Platt's approach tended to be more specific than Pite's.[12] However, if the committee agreed to Pite's suggestions, there was a strong possibility of increasingly wide variations of interpretations by local authorities, giving rise to the difficulties already complained of.

Methods of updating

The committee did not feel that the evidence in favour of one uniform code throughout the country was conclusive, but a reasonable solution could be achieved by ensuring that the LGB did not permit local authorities to adopt bye-laws which varied significantly from the model bye-laws. The LGB had made some efforts to achieve a wider adoption of current models, but having done so it was necessary to keep up-to-date. The committee considered the methods of updating, first by alteration of Section 44 of the Housing and Town Planning Act of 1909, thus providing the Board with stronger powers; secondly by permitting a builder to build in accordance with the current model in districts that had not adopted that model; and thirdly, by discarding all bye-laws at a certain date, making it necessary to adopt new and up-to-date bye-laws. The first method was discarded as the Act only related to houses and it was necessary to extend the powers to all buildings, whilst the second method would deter local authorities from keeping their bye-laws up-to-date. Therefore, the third method was agreed whereby all bye-laws would lapse after a period of ten years. Using this procedure, many, though not all, bye-laws would inevitably change in content, but more importantly would develop into a 'national code'.[13]

As we have seen with the emergence and growing use of steel, concrete and reinforced concrete, buildings were becoming larger and more open, taller, supporting greater loads, containing more combustible material and requiring greater fire resistance. This was the result of growing industrial and commercial development, and had an impact on health and safety issues as well as satisfying the need for good housing. The committee failed to appreciate the rate of change that was occurring with building technology. To limit the review, change and adaptation of new bye-laws to a ten-year cycle would be inadequate. The same problems would keep re-emerging. A more frequent review was needed, together with powers for the central government to require local authorities to adopt new bye-laws and repeal the old.

Enforcement of bye-laws by surveyors

The enforcement of outdated bye-laws by surveyors who carried out their duties diligently only added to this problem. Many objections were made concerning the skills of surveyors, generally reflecting the low standard encountered and the indiscriminate use of their powers. To avoid most of these problems a capable professional should have been employed as a surveyor.[14] This would have been very appropriate if bye-laws were functional, allowing the surveyor the discretion to interpret the adequacy of the construction, but bye-laws were specific, often defining a dimension as a measure of adequacy and it did not require a high level of skill to do that. Gaskell refers to the problems of supervision and inspection frustrating the operation of the bye-laws,[15] which was certainly reflected in the objections expressed to the committee, but the effectiveness of bye-laws can be frustrated by the lack of supervision as much as by diligent inflexible inspection and enforcement. The need for good inspection and enforcement was made clear by the committee in that a duty to the housebuilder existed and the authority had this responsibility, although often ignored. As many as 170 rural districts still had not adopted any building bye-laws (about one in four of the total), an unsatisfactory situation which encouraged builders to develop in these areas away from the imposition of control.[16]

The committee avoided the objections relating to the skills of the surveyors, as this was not seen as a matter for their concern but more as an internal matter for local authorities. Consequently, their attention turned to the way the responsibilities were administered by pointing out that the reasons why a plan was rejected must be stated, quoting the bye-law or section of the Act which was contravened. They also added that objections that could have been raised on the original plan should not be raised on resubmitted plans. The existing rights by either party to resolve their differences in the courts were thought to be adequate, but in addition the offices of the LGB would be available to determine the issues.[17] These proposals would ease the frustrations experienced by builders, and the availability of the LGB to determine issues could prove a more convenient, quicker and more sympathetic way to solve bye-law problems.

It was not uncommon to find that in many areas builders acted as they pleased, and many local authorities 'winked' at contraventions of the letter of the law provided the spirit of it was met. The latter was more in keeping with Pite's philosophy. The committee steered away from the idea of a system which allowed the surveyor discretion, as evidence suggested that such discretion would be fraught with problems of rivalry, jealousy and favouritism, and that some surveyors could not be trusted. The committee recommended increasing powers of central government to enable the LGB to appoint county councils to enforce the bye-laws when district councils had defaulted from their duties. This was a similar procedure to their powers in respect of defaulting boroughs in London.[18] It might be considered reasonable for local authorities not to enforce certain matters of a minor nature, but more serious matters should be enforced. There was no moral or legal right to take the irregular course of non-enforcement, particularly if the authority derived benefit from non-enforcement.[19] However, the law as it stood did not compel a local authority to enforce its bye-laws if it chose not to. Whilst the LGB had certain powers to require enforcement of the Public Health Acts there was no power compelling the Board to do so. The authorities had a free hand. The committee recommended that the county council or any ratepayer or inhabitant of the district could take action for a breach of bye-laws if the local authority had been requested to take action and refused to do so. The costs would be borne by the defaulting authority if the action was successful.[20] This was an unacceptable situation for Local Building Bye-law authorities.

Reaction to the report

Although central government was the main beneficiary in the policy of exemption, the committee did not wish to see this policy expanded and it was suggested that wherever possible the exemptions already granted should be withdrawn.[21] It is clear that the recommendations of the committee were not revolutionary. Rather, they retained the *status quo* of control, based on Parliamentary legislation with a central body available for advice to both central and local government, but with increasing directive control over borough, urban and rural authorities who would retain the power to adopt and enforce building bye-laws. The recommendations did not resolve the problems of building control, which were handed back to Parliament from whence they came.

The editor of *The Builder* expressed his disappointment with the report, stating:

> 'whilst acknowledging the contentious work undertaken we must express ourselves disappointed with the conclusions. We are faced with a new situation and by no means a temporary one in which every incentive should be given to building and builders should be relieved of as many burdens, especially litigious burdens, as possible and we fear that the very cautious recommendations, if adopted, will take years to carry out'.[22]

The rate of change was slow – it had taken 16 years to report on many of the issues brought into the open by the forceful approach of the Reform Association, and it was not surprising to find that it would be another 16 years before these reforms were brought into being.

Having been faced with the possibility of building control, the LGB had not only re-established the basis of building control, but had, through willing witnesses, strengthened the system. The work of the committee was needed not only to clear the air in response to the allegations made against the system, but also to establish strengths and weaknesses. It was clear that bad building had to be prevented.

The workings of the committee had established beyond any doubt that legislative control was necessary, particularly where speculative working-class housing was concerned. The construction of structurally weak, insanitary properties with poor fire resistance qualities was to be avoided, but a philanthropic approach was not the solution to the problem. Furthermore, local authorities having taken over the role of the philanthropist as the providers of working-class housing were expected to set a high standard. Central authority maintained an air of mistrust over the ability of local authorities, many of whom could not be relied upon because of the influence of vested interests.

Consequently, they took the opportunity of securing tighter control over their central role in bye-law-making, giving directions and professional advice to local authorities. The proposal that all local Acts should be abolished in favour of a central bye-law system would strengthen the grip of central authority. Independent action by local authorities was limited to their discretionary powers of adoption and enforcement. A centralized system had the benefit of providing a uniform approach to requirements, on which economies of standardization could be built, while many technological advances could be incorporated into model bye-laws and so become more widely acceptable. This approach would have provided some degree of flexibility and allowed innovations and commercial application, but the opportunity should have been taken at the same time to remove discretionary powers and to make the adoption and enforcement of building bye-laws compulsory. This would have aided the introduction of up-to-date bye-laws and the repeal of private Improvement Acts, or at least those parts with a building control element. It would have been a spur to local authorities to accept their responsibilities, which might have resulted in a more professional attitude towards the administration of building control.

Building bye-law reform was not seen to be such a priority in 1918 as it was in 1914; four years of war had changed the nation's financial position. Industries, especially munitions, had expanded to meet the war effort. This had meant full employment, but rationing and lower wages had kept the demand of everyday consumables low. On the other hand, demand for housing was high. Private house building had stopped by the end of the 1914 and by 1919, in the region of 610,000 houses were needed. Despite the tremendous loss of young men due to active service, the demand for both public and private housing remained high. The committee had recognized this demand, but had quite rightly not advocated a lowering of standards or controls merely to meet demand, or an attractive purchase price to the buyer and high profit element for the speculator. Such a recommendation would have been likely to result in the continuation of slum development. The solutions offered by the committee would iron out most of the problems raised, but Parliamentary time for further legislation on the lines recommended by the committee was limited, if not completely unavailable, due to many other more pressing matters after the war.

The Housing (Building Construction) Committee

The housing problem was extensively discussed by the Housing (Building Construction) Committee which had been set up by the President of the LGB, Mr W. Hayes-Fisher on 26th July 1917. The brief of this committee was to 'consider questions of building construction in connection with the provision of dwellings for the working classes in England and Wales and to report on the methods of securing economy and despatch in the provision of such dwellings'.[23] Sir John Tudor-Walters[24] was the chairman, Mr E. Leonard of the LGB was the secretary and there were nine other members including one other MP, two civil engineers and one architect.

Construction after the war

House construction during the war had been very limited and had failed to make much inroad into the need for working class houses. Furthermore, returning soldiers had been promised 'homes fit for heroes'. Houses constructed to bye-law standards were fit for habitation, but the problem was not only one of quality, it was also one of quantity. Local authorities had taken on the role as providers of housing and this role was slowly beginning to develop. Before the war, they had provided one per cent of all new housing but a considerable contribution was needed to meet the national housing needs. Any control that restricted the output of housing or unnecessarily increased the costs would not be accepted, and it was not surprising to find that building bye-laws were considered to be restrictive. The Housing (Building Construction) Committee were aware of the workings of the Departmental Committee but felt it necessary to report that many witnesses had satisfactory solutions to the building bye-law problems.[25]

This evidence had not been sought by the Housing Committee but so strong were the views of the witnesses, it was felt that they should be reported. Witnesses were often not clear as to whether their objections related to bye-laws, regulations made under Improvement Acts, or other requirements made under Public Health or Local Acts; they were all condemned together as being restrictive and uneconomic. It was contended that statutory control had restricted progress in new forms of construction, and that was one reason why construction in England lagged behind in the use of concrete and reinforced concrete. Old-fashioned methods and traditional materials had been adhered to by many a builder who could not be bothered to seek approval for new methods and materials not recognized in the local bye-laws. Witnesses claimed that bye-laws actually helped to maintain old-fashioned, undesirable forms of development, although this could not be said about many towns and cities where bye-laws were enforced to prevent the erection of terrace upon terrace of unhealthy back-to-back houses. Neither was it true in many rural areas where pressure had already been exerted to amend building bye-laws to permit older and more traditional forms of construction, other than brick and stone, such as timber frame construction and thatched roofs. However, the maintenance of old bye-laws did restrict the use of cavity walls, a form of construction that offered better thermal insulation and weather resistance for basically the same constructional costs. Also, the use of Portland cement concrete as a complete foundation on brick footings to the base of the wall was still insisted upon. Despite some variation, many authorities had bye-laws which required the party wall to project beyond the roof covering producing problems of weather resistance of the parapet and roof. Differing requirements for structural timbers, staircases, open space and ventilation were other matters that had a restrictive influence. Most of these problems could be resolved, as we have already seen, by the use of up-to-date bye-laws. The rigidity of the bye-laws system was recognized by the committee and their report called for a more flexible approach to amending bye-laws which would allow greater freedom in the use of new materials and methods.

Reference was made to relaxing powers provided in Scotland by Section 39 of the Burgh Police Act (Scotland) 1902, but it was felt that bye-laws should be so framed as to be quickly amended. Such an approach had been undertaken by the LGB, but as we have seen, local authorities were slow to respond. It would seem that the committee was calling for a functional or performance standard as Pite had advocated to the Departmental Committee, but this did not have the support of the LGB partly because it would limit their role as professional advisors to government and local government. It could also result in many local authorities having to improve the quality of their surveyors in order that acceptable levels of professional judgement could be given to the interpretation of bye-law requirements.

As building materials were likely to be in short supply after the war, economic use of them was essential. However, the bye-laws were to ensure that buildings, particularly dwellings, were erected to provide safe and healthy occupation and any amendment to them should not result in standards not meeting that aim. Timber was a good example, as unscrupulous builders would often use undersize timber, which when slightly overloaded would slowly deflect. However, by the time the defect was noticed, the builders would be outside their contractual obligations and would not be obliged to correct their faulty work.

Dispute resolution

The report suggested that disputes over interpretation or application of bye-laws should be resolved by application to local housing commissioners which the committee recommended to be appointed. Unlike the Departmental Committee report, this report considered that it was desirable that bye-laws should be relaxed in areas which were developed in accordance with town planning schemes prepared under the Housing and Town Planning Act 1909. However, due to the various stages that the schemes had to pass under the provisions of that Act, this would produce an unacceptable delay. The committee had given this matter much consideration as they had concluded that buildings for the working classes could not be economically or expeditiously provided under the existing system of rigid bye-laws and statutes. The report recommended that during the emergency period after the war, and until suitable alternative legislation had been enacted, the Local Government Board should be given the power to exempt from bye-laws, statues and regulations any housing scheme for which plans and specifications had been approved. This approach suggested that until the building bye-law system had been radically altered and its requirements easily applied, exemption from bye-law control should be granted to those who wanted it. The proposal to extend exemption was based on frustration and the desire to avoid unnecessary bureaucratic interference, but as we have seen, the Departmental Committee brushed the proposal aside and firmly established that exemption should not be granted to anyone. The suggestion that the LGB should assess local authority proposals and grant relaxation was also not supported, as the LGB did not have adequate staff resources.

Specification of good practice

The report went on to consider in great detail the construction of dwellings including siting and design, and specifications for good practice were drawn up. The Committee took the opportunity to draw attention to suitable alterations to model bye-laws. It was recognized that standard design with minimal environmental standards such as room sizes, kitchens, sanitation, outbuildings and drainage, could be constructed more quickly and cheaply where components such as doors, windows, bricks, floors and roofs were made to standard sizes thus minimizing variations on site which were expensive to achieve. The Committee was assisted by the Department of Scientific and Industrial Research (DSIR), established in 1916, and part of their work was the investigation of building materials. The Engineering Standards Committee, formed in 1901 and later to become the British Standards Institution (BSI) in 1919, also assisted. With the help of these bodies and the evidence submitted, the Committee was able to draw up a construction manual.[26]

Differences between the two committees

Had the brief given to the Departmental Committee allowed investigation into the content and application of bye-laws, it might have been possible for the committee to work closely with the DSIR and Engineering Standards Committee. Building bye-laws could have been analysed for their requirements against the materials and technology available, thus producing a better set of model bye-laws more in the nature of a constructional specification. This would have permitted a better balance between the working of the two committees whereby the respective constructional specifications could have been adopted into one. This would have avoided the Housing Construction Committee recommending exemption as a policy of avoiding increased costs associated with obsolete bye-laws. As it was, the Departmental Committee was mainly a committee to which objectors could vent their frustrations and the real issues such as content, interpretation and application were not effectively dealt with. As for aiding the construction industry in achieving better standards, the Housing Construction Committee, by the issue of the manual, was the more successful committee.

How could the reports of these two committees be implemented to provide better and more economical housing and an improved, yet effective building control system? Whilst one committee recommended relaxation of building bye-laws on approved housing schemes, the other recommended the maintenance and improvement of controlling standards on all buildings. The latter was designed to minimize jerry building whilst the former could well produce the opposite effect. In its desire to make up the shortfall in housing needs, and to seek full employment, the government did not seek improvements in a system that had been criticized as being restrictive even when such improvements could have been beneficial; it seemed better to relax restrictions and build. The president of the LGB made this clear. When asked if he intended to act on the recommendations of the Departmental Committee, he replied that he could not promise any legislation on the lines of the Committee's report. When similarly questioned on the Housing Committee report he stated that it was being fully considered with a view to introducing a Housing Bill.[27] What was needed was for the LGB, which was responsible for both housing and building bye-laws, to unify the standards set out in the Housing Committee's report with current model bye-laws and to produce a new model. It would then be necessary to make local authorities adopt a new model, and at the same time take the opportunity to repeal all local Building Acts and introduce a system of relaxing bye-laws standards to suit certain circumstances. This was an alternative to functional bye-laws and could have been acceptable to the LGB. The principle of relaxation of bye-laws affecting local authority housing schemes, introduced by the 1909 Act, was retained in the Housing Bill of 1919[28] and extended to cover any house scheme of a public utility or Housing Trust. In introducing the Bill, the President of the LGB said that it was essential to remove any unnecessary impediments in the emergency programme of house building. Even aesthetics had been 'thrown out of the window', the construction of houses being considered more important than their design, 'when thousands of people, many of whom had fought for their country needed a roof over their head. It was the Government's duty

Plates

Plate 1:   Terrace of early 19th century town houses, Southernhay, Exeter.
Plate 2:   Jettied housing, St Mary's Exeter
Plates 3a & b: Back-to-back housing, Thornville Row, Thornville Place, and Thornville Street, Leeds
Plates 4a & b: Back-to-back housing, Norman Row and Norman View, Leeds
Plate 5:   Pre-1912 housing, Jubilee Road, Exeter
Plate 6:   Post-1912 housing, First Avenue, Exeter
Plate 7:   Rural estate housing, Duke of Bedford's Estate, Ridgmont, Bedfordshire
Plate 8:   Early bye-law housing, Normanby Road, Exeter
Plates 9a & b: Pre-fabricated buildings
Plate 10:   Modern lightweight industrial/commercial building
Plate 11:   The challenge for modern building regulations

Plate 1: Terrace of early 19th century town houses, now used as offices, built in the Georgian style, Southernhay, Exeter, Devon. Note the regularity of the structural fenestration.

Plate 2: Houses at Stepcote Hill, St Marys, Exeter, showing jettied upper floors.

Plate 3a: Back-to-back housing, Thornville Row and Thornville Place, Leeds.

Plate 3b: Thornville Street, Leeds. Back-to-back housing in blocks of eight, four each side. Note space between blocks for location of privy. These properties have been modernized and have internal sanitary facilities.

Plate 4a: Norman Row, Leeds. Back-to-back housing built 1890–1907 with bye-law approval. At a density of 30–40 per acre, each house comprised a scullery, living room, two bedrooms, an attic with semi-basement of cellar and WC, and 15 foot forecourt. These houses were modernized in the 1970s.

Plate 4b: Norman View, Leeds. Back-to-back housing erected in the late 1920s and up to 1935–36. Bye-law approval was given for the construction of long unbroken terraces with small front gardens. The development had the requisite street layout approval. Each house has a scullery, living room, two bedrooms, and a bathroom with WC.

Plate 5: Housing at Jubilee Road, Exeter. Erected pre-1912, and showing the bye-law requirement for separating walls to be taken up above the roof covering.

Plate 6: Housing at First Avenue, Exeter. Built in the 1920s, it shows the non-combustible roofs taken over the top of the separating wall which was fire stopped between the slate and top of the wall.

Plate 7: Housing constructed in 1911 on the Duke of Bedford's estate in the village of Ridgmont, Bedfordshire.

Plate 8: Early bye-law housing at Normanby Road, Exeter, showing the separating wall being taken above the roof covering. The 1877 model series did not require front open space, hence the house abuts the back of the footpath.

Plate 9a: One of the four main types of 'prefabs', the Unico-Seco prefabricated single-storey house. Built in South London at the end of WWII, it remained in occupation until 1978, and is now on display at the Imperial War Museum, Duxford, Cambridgeshire.

Plate 9b: Prefabricated bungalow, Walton Road, Shirehampton, Bristol.

Plate 10: Modern lightweight industrial/commercial building, the development of which is more suitable to the flexibility of the 'functional' regulation.

Plate 11: The challenge for modern building regulations – the juxtaposition of the old and the new in this city centre development in Plymouth.

to provide houses, after that it could be discussed whether they were aesthetically pleasing or not'.[29]

The Housing Acts of 1923 and 1925

Controls were seen as a restriction and this attitude persisted with the introduction of the Housing Acts of 1923[30] and 1925.[31] The relaxation powers were strengthened further by enabling the Minister to require a relaxation of bye-laws on any building erected within a borough, urban or rural district. Where the local authority refused to do so, the Minister had the power to revoke old bye-laws and apply new ones. These powers provided further pressure to update bye-laws, or face possible embarrassment in having the Minister do it. The Conservative Government seemed to favour up-to-date bye-laws as being an equitable way of ensuring uniform and necessary standards that did not restrict economic construction. During the debate on the Housing Bill in 1919, it was stated that the consolidation of the building standards imposed by the Acts of 1875, 1890 and 1907 should be done quickly. The action taken by the LGB to update bye-laws was also questioned, and it was feared that many local authorities would not adopt bye-laws unless driven to it. Many were afraid of any increase in construction costs, while in other cases there was a lack of healthy public opinion, thus allowing vested interests to dominate. It was alleged that the only way to keep a local authority up to the mark was to have a strong driving pressure from central authority.[32] From 1919, it was the role of the Ministry of Health to prompt and push, but it was a paramount principle that the discretionary powers of local government were not to be touched by Parliament or its agents. This did little to prevent jerry building since builders and speculators who benefited from such freedoms would complain of any restrictions applied to them even when developing in areas that had no bye-laws.

As we have seen, the problem derived from the indifferent use of discretionary powers. The majority of authorities adopted bye-laws, but there were still many who did not. In South Wales, 104 authorities had not adopted bye-laws and the government had no intention of forcing them to do so.[33] Even a request to those with bye-laws to update met with little response, and 72 per cent did not reply to the ministerial circular. Experience showed that local authorities were not acting in a responsible manner. The government appeared to deflect the responsibility, allowing many authorities to become scapegoats for criticisms of the building control system. Many of the large boroughs that retained their Improvement and Building Acts jealously guarded their independence. The anti-centralists were still active, even though local authorities had an ever-increasing social role. The application of regulations and bye-laws still caused much confusion and dissent, and simplification was long overdue, although the Ministry of Health kept trying with varying degrees of success. When the Minister was questioned on the subject in 1931, he replied that:

> 'outside of London few areas exist which have not procured a modification of their own Acts so as to follow a more flexible method. I am always prepared to assist Local Authorities in adopting the more modern or convenient method'.[34]

Once again, 'discretionary power' was upheld, even though the discretion was at times detrimental to the building industry in its constant pursuit of economical building.

The recommendations of the Departmental Committee remained to be implemented and would have reduced many of the problems. The government did not use the Public Health Act of 1925 to bring this about, but relied on its policies of exemption and the efforts of the Ministry of Health in encouraging the adoption of its latest bye-laws. The government was firmly set on this course of action, and seemed to be leaving the private sector of housing to deal with its problems as best it could.

A firmer control had to be put on local authorities if the government wished to produce a building control system of some uniformity equally administered by all concerned. The lack of interest and general inability to adopt or update the bye-laws was again emphasized in evidence to the Royal Commission on Fire Brigades and Fire Prevention in 1923.[35] Just over three years had elapsed since the Departmental Committee had reported, and a further opportunity existed to review the technical content of the bye-law system and its administrative effectiveness. Nevertheless, only structural fire resistance was considered. Evidence submitted to the Commission showed that of the urban districts in England and Wales (including boroughs), numbering some 1,460, at least 50 had not adopted any bye-law whatsoever.[36] In 60 authorities bye-laws made under the original Act of 1858 were still in force and in many authorities bye-laws of similar antiquity were enforced.[37] Prior to 1901, rural areas often adopted the full model bye-laws which were urban in content and, despite the LGB circulars of 1906 and 1912, of the 600 rural authorities, 200 had bye-laws substantially of the urban type in all or part of their districts, between 40 and 50 had adopted the intermediate type, 250 the rural model, leaving some 150 without any at all.[38] (For a description of the Rural and Urban Model Byelaws, see *Appendices 11* and *12*.) These figures show clearly the pattern of local authority response and apathy to their building control responsibilities and reveal the considerable task the LGB had in trying to establish the responsibility and uniformity the system badly needed. The consistent flow of this type of revealing evidence led the Commission to concur with the Departmental Committee that the existing statutes should be consolidated and procedures simplified. Bye-laws should be brought up-to-date, especially in the case of smaller urban districts; this would ensure the precautions against fire were adequate and up-to-date, while at the same time their procedure would remove unnecessary obstacles to the construction of dwellings at reasonable cost. It was felt that matters of fire prevention should be dealt with by statute rather than bye-law, which seemed to take a leaf out of the London Building Acts. Where this was not possible, then the procedure of updating laws at least every ten years as suggested by the Departmental Committee would be considered as an acceptable alternative. The differing content of bye-laws was again shown to be a problem, not only economically but also constructionally in the way it was necessary to meet the requirements of the bye-laws. An example quoted by the committee, referred to previously (p.100), was that separating walls were required to extend above the roof surface so as to effect complete fire separation. Many authorities had retained this bye-law although some enlightened councils had withdrawn it. The city of Exeter had such a bye-law until 1912, after which it was discarded in favour of walls up to the underside of the roof covering, simply by adopting the latest model bye-law (see *Plate 8*).

In Birmingham, where this requirement did not exist, it had been found that in two-storey dwellings, acceptable fire separation was obtained by taking the separating wall up to the underside of the roof covering which was bedded in cement mortar on top of the walls. It was due to such councils taking the lead that model bye-laws were structured to meet the latest form of construction. Reducing construction costs reached its limits when the Commission considered that bye-laws on the construction of fire resisting hearths, which had been dropped from the latest model issued by the Ministry of Health, should be reintroduced in all future models. Hearths had been a part of buildings for centuries, and not to have a bye-law which limited the use of combustible material in or close to hearths was somewhat ludicrous.

Timber buildings

Inconsistencies were also causing problems with timber buildings. In some areas there was no control at all, while in others, particularly rural areas, bye-laws existed that required all walls to be constructed of brick or other fire resisting material. Timber frame buildings were quite common in rural areas, being erected for low-income families as they were cheap to construct and timber was readily available, so exception was taken where restrictions limited or prevented their construction. It was considered that there should be a more comprehensive and uniform approach to this problem and that such buildings should be properly isolated. Where this isolation was not available, party walls were to be constructed with an adequate degree of fire resistance.

The resentment about restrictive control on timber buildings mainly affected development in rural areas, but in the borough of Brighton (East Sussex), a bye-law had existed since 1886 which permitted the construction of timber buildings provided they did not exceed a terrace of three. The timbers were to have an infill of brick and a backing of brickwork not less than four and a half inches thick, and the buildings were to be isolated from other buildings by at least 15 feet.[39] These provisions did not find their way into the Exeter bye-laws until 1912, some 26 years later. (For a brief summary of the 1912 model bye-laws, see *Appendix 12*.) The extent of this delay is another example of how the discretionary powers of local authorities could be applied, thus frustrating the actions of builders or central government seeking some uniformity in bye-laws.

Public buildings

Shops, cinemas, hotels, theatres, churches, schools, hospitals, libraries and other public buildings also needed controls for safe use by the general public. Whilst there was firm control over cinemas in London, due to the Metropolitan Management and Building Act of 1878, and licences were required for music and dancing in London and Middlesex, such control was virtually non-existent in 1923 in the rest of England and Wales. The Commission recommended that for buildings used for entertainment, a code be drawn up, based on the London County Council model, to give guidance to local authorities, and that either the Home Office or the Ministry of Health should issue a set of guidance regulations setting out the standard means of escape from hotels. These should be enforceable in a similar way to the Lowestoft Corporation Act and the Ramsgate Corporation Act, both of which already catered for flats, restaurants and taverns. These proposals were weak, as it was hardly worth suggesting that codes or regulations be drawn up merely to guide local authorities or theatre owners on satisfactory means of escape in case of fire. In the majority of instances such standards would be ignored. The lack of responsibility shown by many local authorities in the adoption and enforcement of bye-laws was also evident in the laxity regarding means of escape in case of fire. Local authorities already had such a statutory responsibility for factories and workshops, but only four per cent acted in a responsible manner by adopting bye-laws for this purpose (for bye-law content, see *Appendix 13*).[40] This again showed clearly the lack of concern on important matters of health and safety. The Commission was suggesting that consolidation would enable a fresh start to be made and the simplification of administration and up-to-date bye-laws would overcome the difficulties and frustrations. This approach needed legislation and this the government avoided, choosing instead to continue with prompting and advising local authorities of their role and responsibilities.

Ministry of Health Circulars

The government's lack of commitment to restructuring the building control system on the lines recommended by the Departmental Committee was the main reason why local authorities continued with the haphazard approach to their responsibilities. This was not helpful to the building industry. Similarly, the government's approach to increasing the stock of houses met problems, and a rapid increase in the price of houses occurred. Prices soared, rising to £1,000 from an average pre-war price of £250, an inflated price due to excess demand, limited materials and lack of skilled labour. These prices very soon stretched beyond the reach of even the middle classes, and when demand slackened prices dropped very quickly – by almost 30 per cent in six months. Between 1920 and 1922 prices halved, brought about by an increase in the supply of materials, cheaper transport costs, lower interest rates and building costs as builders with a steady supply of work were willing to accept a lower level of profits.[41]

The prices in some areas would probably have dropped even further if many of the older bye-laws had been removed or updated. The high prices had led to a greater demand for new houses built for, and managed by, local authorities. The government, who were financing this form of housing,[42] had taken a similar line to that expressed by the supporters of the Housing of the Working Classes Bills by ensuring exemption from bye-law control for local authority and Housing Society developments. This attitude not only suggested the lack of importance given by the Conservative government to the health and safety building bye-laws, but also provided an easy way out of the dilemma it faced. Consolidation and improvement of the Public Health Acts was a possibility and a way in which the problems could have been minimized. The government's role, in association with councils, of providing houses had given them the attitude of a developer to avoid bye-laws and obtain exemption. Consequently, it continued with its policy of relaxation and encouraged the updating of building bye-laws. This approach was another advance in the powers of central authority in that it could switch from one political incentive to another without the need for the law to be changed. There was of course no guarantee that local authorities would respond; after all, they jealously guarded their powers of discretion displayed by their slowness in adopting or updating their bye-laws.

Circular of 1st September 1922

The circulars of 1906 and 1912 only drew a limited response and this led to another circular being issued on the 1st September 1922 informing local authorities of the urgent need for revising building bye-laws and referring to the current urban, intermediate, and rural models.[43] It was emphasized that there was no justification in retaining bye-laws that might hinder private development and which were not required for safety or sanitation. Whilst the Departmental Committee in 1918 had advised updating bye-laws every ten years, the Ministry of Health considered that more frequent revision was necessary. Authorities were reminded that they could provide temporary relief by relaxing bye-laws in respect of dwellings only by using the provisions of Section 25 of the Housing and Town Planning Act of 1919. This circular did not draw an immediate response, given the slow process of updating bye-laws as stated in Dolton's evidence on the Departmental Committee.[44] Although questions in the House of Commons prompting the Minister to take action had no immediate effect (see p.103), some progress was being made so that by the end of 1928 some 1,270 local authorities had brought their bye-laws up-to-date.[45] The tendency was for local authorities to adopt the rural and intermediate models which indicated a movement towards less control and greater freedom for developers.

Circular 56 of June 1926

Despite this slow progress of revision, by 1933 there were 60 rural authorities which still did not have a single bye-law. This did not affect government policy, as not having bye-laws curbed complaints from developers and avoided the need for an update. It did of course highlight the variety of bye-law control, or lack of it, that was being exercised nationally. In addition to the frustration of complying, the variety of bye-laws was having a significant effect on the cost of construction. Circular 56 of June 1926 again emphasized the updating of bye-laws stating that it was of the utmost importance for the revival of trade and general well-being that proper methods of building should not be forbidden by local bye-laws. It pointed out that in other manufacturing countries, such as the USA, Germany, Czechoslovakia and Poland, the policy had been to remove restrictions on building and this had benefits in reducing costs and other important undefined areas. It was stated that bye-laws before 1913 had impeded invention, mass production, standardization and industrial recovery, though this was not borne out by the Housing (Building Construction) Committee report of 1918. This report gave clear descriptions of various parts of the construction process where standardization and mass production methods could be introduced, with bye-laws helping the process. However, different bye-laws restricted the development of standardization, as it was pointless to manufacture components or materials which were acceptable in one area and not in another and this could occur between adjoining authorities. The Ministry in 1926 had sought some degree of uniformity, and had advised on the necessity of local authorities adopting current bye-laws.[46] But it was not just bye-laws that were creating the problems, there were also those authorities who were enforcing their own Improvement Acts which had a building control content. Whilst the government had some control on bye-law matters, they had little effective control over the administration of Improvement Acts, and the approach towards relaxation and exemption continued. The Ministry of Health (Temporary Relaxation of Bye-laws) Regulations of 1922 allowed interested parties to appeal to the Minister of Health against local authorities who had refused to relax their bye-laws.[47] This encouragement towards relaxation is further illustrated by Circular C.80 of January 1928 where the Minister thought it undesirable to adopt building bye-laws governing the strength of timber unless authorities had the staff to enforce them. This meant at least one full-time building inspector. The Minister was concerned that this would mean regular site visits and taking measurements, and for this reason, there have never been any such bye-laws in the model series after 1918.

This statement would seem to suggest that the government did not wish to have any requirement in the bye-laws that would demand regular inspection of building works and in many cases the appointment of full-time surveyors. Local authorities were expected to administer them as a form of gentlemanly code of conduct! The circular added that apart from large towns employing inspection staff, other authorities should refrain from enforcing their bye-laws in the interests of economy of administration as well as liberty in building.

These suggestions would only add to the indifference of enforcement and were likely to draw even stronger complaints. No great benefit would derive from the exercise, as it is not possible to expect a local authority exercising a lawful discretion to adopt and enforce building bye-laws to do so without making any form of check on the construction of buildings. The submission of plans and their checking is only an aid to the builder; he is able to vary the construction on site and it is really in effective site control that the benefits of building control can be achieved. This was being virtually disregarded by the Ministry of Health.

This circular clearly advised the non-adoption and enforcement of bye-laws controlling the strength of timber, a requirement designed to avoid excessive deflection or even structural collapse. If bye-laws were over-demanding in respect of timber sizes, the Minister should have informed local authorities of more economic timber sizes which would be strong enough to sustain their design loadings, rather than advising authorities not to enforce the law. Furthermore, it was clear that local authorities were not encouraged to engage full-time enforcement staff and this itself would have an effect on the equality of enforcement. These were matters that gave rise to discontent and aggravation where builders were subjected to such bye-laws in one area and not another. This was a problem recognized later by the Ministry who, in a memorandum attached to the Model Bye-laws, Rural Series, of 1932, referred to the problem experienced by builders and architects working in different areas with varying requirements based on the same bye-law. It was suggested that assistance could be obtained from the British Standards Institution on points of issue causing difficulty in interpretation or enforcement.

Effects of the circulars

The series of circulars centred on three main aspects of building control. Firstly, the need to provide a common base; a uniformity of requirement and application. Secondly, the recognition of British Standards and codes of practice and the work of the British Standards Institution, and thirdly, the role of the local authority surveyor. The Departmental Committee highlighted four different modes of control and advised against relaxation as an acceptable option. The government disregarded the advice and continued with the policy of relaxation of bye-law requirements on local authority housing, bringing about modifications within the building control system by means of advice through circulars.

Not only were matters relating to building construction raised, but even economies of local authorities themselves. The printing of large numbers of building bye-laws booklets for sale to the public was not recommended, as many were likely to be wasted when the authority updated its bye-laws.[48] Whilst costs were involved, it was more likely that there would be a delay in the introduction of updated bye-laws until the stock of bye-law booklets had been sold. Some authorities had reintroduced fees for building bye-law control, presumably to aid their income, reintroducing old Improvement Act practices, but they were promptly advised against this practice which was not only illegal but regarded as highly objectionable by the builders.[49] Builders did not seem to object to paying fees under the London system but took every opportunity to ensure that the practice did not spread beyond London. Costs were all important, but whilst the government ensured that the cost of public house building and other schemes approved by the LGB would not be impeded by bye-laws, the same did not apply to private sector building. Total relaxation was not encouraged and those who sought to achieve this were told that it was not necessary in areas where building bye-laws had been brought up-to-date.[50] The recommendations of the Departmental Committee on Building Bye-laws, on improving the bye-law system, were gradually becoming self-evident to the Ministry. The need for updating was recognized, as even bye-laws over five years old were considered out-of-date.[51] The problems of interpretation and enforcement required an independent arbitrator, and the Departmental Committee proposed an appeal system. Although this was not law, the Minister advised local authorities that he would give an opinion on such matters if both sides agreed to refer to his arbitration.[52] Similarly, the Departmental Committee advised that the reasons for refusing plans should be stated, and whilst this recommendation had not been brought in as law, the Minister chose to recommend that local authorities adopt such practice.[53]

The administrative procedures of building bye-law control varied considerably, and these circulars were an intrusion into local issues, advising on points of law which should be adhered to and practices that should be carried out, even where there were no legal requirements, or the legal requirement was considered by the Minister to be out-of-date. Such was the situation regarding habitation certificates which were issued on the satisfactory completion of construction of houses. This was a procedure which some authorities retained under old bye-laws, but as the new model bye-laws did not contain this provision, it was requested that the practice stop.[54] Many local authorities adopted the practice of retaining deposited plans, but the Minister advised that they were not empowered to do this unless they had adopted Section 16 of the Public Health Act 1907 which permitted them to do so.[55]

Despite trying to improve the system, especially on matters of practice and procedure, control by circular was clearly not desirable. It was subject to political and economic trends which were erratic and could cause as much confusion as it sought to overcome. Circulars were looked upon as an intrusion into local self-government and consequently it was not surprising to find that they were often ignored. The solution to the erratic control by circular was to introduce legislation based on the recommendations of the Departmental Committee. This the government failed to do and consequently the problems remained.

Chapter 7
The Professional Approach

The construction specification in the Housing (Building Construction) Committee report was an example of how professional assistance could produce a document that was understandable, informative, practical and related to sound economic building. The involvement by the DSIR showed the immense value that could be obtained from research into building materials and technology, and this professional approach to research developed further when the DSIR recommended the establishment of a Building Research Board (BRB) in January 1919.[1] The tasks of the Board would be:

1. to increase scientific knowledge of most materials used in buildings;
2. to assist in the development of new materials;
3. to assist in the process of manufacture;
4. to investigate methods of construction, giving assistance to government departments on questions raised by them;
5. to conduct research on fire prevention and fire resistant construction; and
6. to instigate research on the construction of roads, drains and sewers.

Establishment of the Building Research Board

The government did not foresee any responsibility for research falling on the building industry itself or on the associated professions, as it was to be regarded as a matter of public interest. The proposal to establish the BRB was strongly supported by RIBA and the Society of Architects. Accordingly, the Board was set up in February 1920, having acquired premises in Acton in London together with temporary accommodation at the Brixton School of Building. It later moved to permanent accommodation at Garston, near Watford, where a large country mansion had been acquired and where the Board has remained to this day, although it is now know as the Building Research Establishment (BRE). In its first published report, the Board set out amongst its duties:

a. research into the behaviour of building materials; and
b. the application of existing knowledge to resolve immediate problems.

Thus began a practical scientific approach, which in later years would encompass other fields including the formulation of building bye-laws.

The use of steel

One of the early problems the Board was involved in was the use of steel for construction purposes. Steel had made considerable advances in its use as structural frameworks or component elements of buildings since earlier times when cast iron had been used. The ability of steel members to span large openings and to support greater floor and roof areas gave architects greater freedom in design, eagerly demanded and accepted by Victorian entrepreneurs.

Building bye-laws had not fully taken account of the use of steel as a load-bearing structural element, despite its increased use. Bye-laws remained firmly entrenched in the use of masonry to carry the main loads of the building, although regulations were introduced in London in 1909 to control the construction of steel frame building at the same time as regulations were also introduced to control reinforced concrete.[2] The situation arose where masonry regulations were applied alongside the steel regulations, and consequently masonry walls were required to be of full load-bearing thickness despite their load-bearing steel framework. This produced expensive and unnecessary construction. Building bye-laws permitted external walls to be of a framework that could include the use of steel, provided it was of sufficient size and strength and properly framed together. It was not uncommon for local authorities to permit different working stresses for the steel, which in turn affected the size and consequently the cost. Not unnaturally, builders objected.[3]

The development of steel-framed buildings

Steel-framed buildings were increasing in popularity following the development of large skyscraper buildings in America. From 1866, steel joists were rolled whole, although beams continued to be made from steel plate riveted together. When Dorman Long began rolling steel joists in 1885, the use of cast and wrought iron soon became uneconomical.

The economic use of steel depends upon its quality and its working stress. Structures have two main problems, buckling and bending, and theories in calculating these two properties in steel were established in 1759 and 1826,[4] to be refined later. These theories were continually developed, enabling a more confident use of steel in buildings. To arrive at a reasonable working stress, a factor of safety against failure was assessed and this was generally taken as a quarter of the average ultimate strength of the material. On this basis, London City Council determined that the working stress of steel was seven and a half tonnes per square inch. A higher factor of safety was introduced for columns to allow for imperfections in the material that introduced some bending in addition to compression.[5]

Dead loads were calculated on the weight of materials while live loads were a matter of guesswork. To arrive at a reasonable working live load for domestic or small office premises, a factor of safety had to be allowed for. As we have seen, steel stresses were a quarter of the ultimate stress and when this principle was applied to an ultimate load of a tightly packed crowd of people, say about 160 pounds per square foot, then the working live load would be 40 pounds per square foot. This calculation would be made in respect of industrial and commercial loading to produce live loading for various types of building.

When these principles were applied to multi-storey buildings, it tended to produce an over design which added to construction costs. It was most unlikely that every floor of a multi-storey building would be loaded to the maximum working live load and therefore some reduction could be made. The Americans were in advance of the British when it came to constructing multi-storey buildings, and the building regulations of Chicago and New York had taken account of this problem. A five per cent reduction was allowed in live loads to each floor below the topmost floor. Thus the top floor was 100 per cent, 95 per cent for the floor below, 90 per cent for the floor below that, and so on. However, no floor load could be reduced to below 50 per cent. This principle was adopted in the London Building Acts of 1909, but it did not appear in the model building bye-laws until after 1936, which only emphasized the need for the legislative changes the Departmental Committee had recommended in 1918.

Despite the bye-law requirement, it is also necessary for any architect or engineer to ensure that a building remains sound. Any collapse would ruin the designer's reputation and retard the further development and use of steel or indeed reinforced concrete. Consequently, many buildings were over-designed, invariably resulting in costly construction. To introduce new materials into low cost housing, a reduction of cost had to be achieved. This required a reappraisal of stresses, strain and the theory of structures to produce smaller and more economical sections using higher quality steels that had improved working stresses. Bye-laws were not made to accommodate new materials or methods but merely to restrict or prohibit the use of existing products that were known from experience to perform badly.

The Building Research Department

Research encouraged the development of building technology. There was a growing need to move from the more traditional empirical approach to a scientific approach which accepted investigation, analysis and experimentation as a sound basis for accepting constructional changes, and until this step had been made, progress in bye-law development and acceptance was some way off.

This approach began when the problems surrounding the evaluation of methods and regulations for the design of steel structures were referred to the Building Research Department (BRD) by the Minister of Health.[6] London County Council had been criticized for being backward in not updating their bye-laws, although this was partly due to the lack of resources the London County Council had available for the investigation of this particular problem. Hence the value of the BRD, who were in an independent position to produce a professional report in which political issues were hard to place. Consequently, the reports of the BRD helped produce some degree of uniformity in London Building Act requirements and building bye-laws. An update of the 1915 London County Council regulations on reinforced concrete was sought for the same reasons, and the Minister was also challenged on the need for local authorities to update their bye-laws on these matters.

Some improvement had been made in this area, but it was noticeable that technological advances in structural steel and reinforced concrete were outstripping the government's ability to keep its statutory requirements abreast of these changes. A further example was the advances in the manufacture of cement and the Ministry was questioned on this matter, as it was alleged that London County Council were using obstructive tactics and it was thought that such regulations were no longer necessary.

British Standards for steel and concrete

The continuing problem of local authority discretion was again surfacing but in this case it provided the Minister with the excuse that he was not able to control the way local authorities administered their responsibilities. This was by no means a satisfactory answer, but it did again emphasize the problems of discretionary control. Meanwhile the BRD was working on a code of practice for the use of structural steel in buildings and their recommendations were incorporated into British Standard 449. This was the first national code for structural steel work and as a result of this work the London County Council asked the BRD to prepare a similar code for reinforced concrete. These codes of practice not only provided uniformity, but also an understanding of building problems and their solutions. As we have seen, these codes were used as a footnote to bye-laws and were a guide to meeting the requirements of the bye-laws. These footnotes helped to produce a more uniform interpretation and application that could be acceptable to all local authorities. Eventually they were written into the bye-laws and became known as 'deemed to satisfy' specifications. The use of British Standards in this way, and the availability of the BSI to give advice to local authorities on interpretation and enforcement, were valuable contributions which emphasized the importance of the professional approach as a necessary ingredient in the statutory control of building. The basis for uniformity of understanding and application was at last established. Further work added greatly to understanding the application of building technology to meet design criteria, easing the problems of making and enforcing building bye-laws. However, research takes time and time is also needed to assess the overall performance of new materials and methods.

The work of the Building Research Station (BRS, previously the BRD) was proving an asset in the solution of building problems but it was not specifically structured to provide a solution to the problems surrounding building bye-laws, although their involvement with bye-laws has evolved through the practice of research.[7] This involvement was based on concern; concern about having spent considerable time and effort solving a building problem only to find the results of that research thwarted by an outdated bye-law modelled in specific terms. This had to be avoided if research was to become creditable and readily acceptable. The Board firmly expressed the view that bye-laws should specify the performance to be obtained, leaving open the method of attaining the required standard. These views were made known to the London County Council in 1931 at a time when a revision of their regulations was contemplated and again in the Board's Annual Report of 1936.[8] The issue of circulars and the addition of footnotes to bye-laws was one way in which the Ministry of Health indicated that to some extent they shared those views.

Ministry of Health circulars

The further problem that the MOH circulars tried to control was the way in which bye-laws were enforced, despite the views previously expressed by the Minister of Health. This depended not only on the attitudes of the elected representatives to these responsibilities, but also on the structure of the local authority staff, and in particular the professional and technical skill of the persons responsible for the administration and enforcement of the bye-laws. Unlike the London Building Acts and the Improvement Acts of Liverpool and Bristol, there was no statutory requirement to appoint surveyors, thus allowing the appointment of persons without regard to the nature of the officer or his qualifications. This gave local authorities wide scope and whilst many appointed knowledgeable surveyors, we have already seen that many did not. The criticisms that were directed at those surveyors were rarely directed towards the district surveyors appointed under the London Building Acts. District surveyors were unique amongst surveyors in England and Wales who administered building law. They were paid by fee income and they also enjoyed private practice which provided further income. District surveyors who did not have a private income found that fee income was inadequate, and rather than accept a salary as proposed by the London County Council, in 1906 their association unsuccessfully sought removal of the restrictions on private practice which had been creeping in since 1901. The situation remained unsatisfactory until the district surveyors became salaried officials in 1940.

Salaries

The salaries of officials outside London varied considerably. Whilst the senior officials such as town clerks and borough surveyors enjoyed a salary commensurate with their qualifications and experience, this did not apply amongst the junior staff. In 1899 some sanitary inspectors in the London area were being paid less than £2.00 per week, a sum which was considered a reasonable wage.[9]

The appointment of surveyors

The Local Government Board did not seek to influence local authorities in their appointment of surveyors. These posts usually covered many tasks in addition to building bye-law administration, including such matters as sewage disposal, drainage, street works and municipal building maintenance. The larger borough and urban authorities tended to appoint engineers who would have the additional responsibility of enforcing building bye-laws, but this was not apparent in the smaller authorities because there were less extensive municipal works. Often these works were designed and carried out by private consultants and contractors appointed by the authority. The growth of municipal works being undertaken by the authorities led to the formation of the Institution of Municipal Engineers (I.Mun.E.) in 1873. This Institution first conducted examinations in 1886, which included the subject of building construction and law and bye-laws.[10] However, many of the local government officers qualified by such examinations did not carry out the inspection of plans and building works but appointed junior staff for this purpose. There were no criteria or examination structure for such officers, but when the 1936 Act proposed a more uniform system of building bye-laws throughout England and Wales, with an improved administrative system, the Institution introduced an examination for Building Inspectors in 1937.[11] This examination was not the first of its kind. RIBA, founded in 1834, became involved in examining the competency of suitably experienced candidates for the office of building surveyor to local authorities as required by the Metropolitan Building Act of 1855. The first meeting to consider what conditions should apply was held on the 22nd December 1855. The first candidates were awarded Certificates of Competency on the 29th January 1856.[12] This examination was primarily related to the administration of the London Building Acts, and later developed into the District Surveyors Examination.

RIBA maintained the examinations for candidates for the office of Building Surveyors to local authorities, but neither this examination nor that of the Institute of Municipal Engineers of 1937 was a statutory pre-requisite to appointment with local authorities. Consequently, the standard of surveyors varied considerably throughout England and Wales, and no doubt contributed to the widely differing standard of interpretation and enforcement. Other professional bodies also catered for the professional needs of building surveyors. The Institution of Surveyors, formed in 1868, and now known as The Royal Institution of Chartered Surveyors (RICS), introduced examinations in 1881 which became compulsory as a professional qualification for all candidates in 1891.[13] The examination had three divisions, one of which was building surveying. These examinations have been maintained and improved, but the specific subject of Building Regulations has only been included in the examination syllabus since 1972. However, the subject matter relating to building control was at a standard that would permit a successful candidate to understand and apply the specific requirements of the building bye-laws. The Incorporated Association of Architects and Surveyors (IAAS), formed in 1925, was eventually to provide a separate examination and division for municipal building surveyors whose main responsibility was the administration of building bye-laws and associated law, but this was not effective until 1952.

The Departmental Committee in 1918 did not recommend that local authority surveyors needed to be statutorily appointed and qualified in a similar manner to the district surveyors of London. Such a recommendation was outside the scope of their brief. Nevertheless, the point could have been made as the London system was recognized not to cause so many problems amongst builders. The independence of local authorities was also another matter that had to be considered. Governments were reluctant to require building bye-laws to be administered in defined ways and it has been said that local authorities are responsible bodies who best know how to conduct their own affairs. This maintained the discretionary independence over the adoption and enforcement of bye-laws.

Publications

An aid to the better understanding of building bye-laws was the publication of books explaining bye-law requirements, such as *Knight's Annotated Model Byelaws*. The first edition of this book appeared in 1883 and gave a background to the making of the bye-laws, notes on their requirements and comment on ministry circulars and legal judgements. Publications such as this made a substantial contribution to the application of building bye-laws and were valuable to the builder, architect and enforcing surveyor in trying to achieve some degree of uniformity. Helpful as these publications may have been, it still remained essential for the surveyor to have a good understanding of building technology so as to enforce building bye-laws correctly. The professional bodies recognized this within the examinations and requirements of entry to membership. Neither the Public Health Acts nor the Local Government Acts required authorities to appoint certain officers, although the posts of clerk, treasurer, and surveyor were quite common. It was not until the Local Government Act of 1933 that local authorities were required to appoint certain officers, one being a surveyor.[14] Only rural district councils had the discretion not to appoint such an officer. This in many respects was reasonable, as small rural authorities did not require a full-time officer. In such circumstances, the duties of building bye-laws administration were often undertaken by the sanitary inspector. Whilst the Act specified the post, it did not specify any qualifications for the appointment, and an opportunity was lost to improve the building control system. As Thomas Cubitt, in evidence to the Poor Law Commission in 1842, had said, 'Anything in the nature of a building Act that is not equally and skilfully administered will aggravate the evils intended to be remedied' (see p.24). He had been proved right, yet the quality of enforcement, although criticized as poor, was still not remedied despite the interest of professional bodies in raising their standards.

As we have seen, the increasing complexity of building construction necessitated the establishment of the Building Research Station to investigate the technology of building materials to provide a greater understanding and a solution to many of its problems. The work of the BRS, and their assistance in the development of British Standards and building bye-laws meant that the complexities of such technology found their way into the codes and bye-laws. If the technical and professional qualifications of the officers enforcing the bye-laws were not of an acceptable standard then this matter could not be resolved where local authorities maintained their independence as to the selection of staff they wished to appoint and the government would not aggravate the situation by insisting on such standards. However, until uniformly high standards were introduced, the differences of interpretation, administration and enforcement remained, often to the annoyance of industry and the professions. This necessitated the willingness of local authorities to undertake their responsibilities by adopting the latest bye-laws and taking the trouble to ensure that their enforcement was properly carried out. The recommendations of the Departmental Committee were still sitting on the shelf and needed to be taken down, dusted off, and brought into effect. The Housing (Building Construction) Committee had clearly shown the need to construct houses to a high standard. This was by no means unrealistic or utopian, as a lot of consideration had been given to the problems facing the building industry, its economics, and the benefits of standardization. [15] 'Up- to-date' bye-laws were a vehicle by which this could be done, but, as Dewsnup points out, no great improvement will be achieved unless bye-laws and regulations are enforced.[16] This important aspect of building control was constantly put aside by both local authorities and by the MOH, who tried to achieve their aims through circulars instead of updating the legislation. It is quite clear that this approach had limited success, and while the continuing prodding of local authorities encouraged many to respond, an equal number did not, often increasing the problems rather than diminishing them. In those areas the benefits of up-to-date bye-laws on new development did not accrue nor did they stimulate the technological advances the building industry wished to apply. Circulars that at one moment criticized local authorities for acting in an *ultra vires* manner and then sought their assistance to do just that, demonstrate the indifference of local authorities to political pressures that varied quite frequently. The Departmental Committee had at least made an attempt to find a solution, yet its recommendations had been ignored. The RSC in 1871 had stated, 'Whatever concerns the whole nation must be dealt with nationally, whatever concerns only a district must be dealt with by the district'.[17] The problems unearthed and the solution put forward by committees, commissions, and the interference imposed by circulars, clearly indicate that even local administration was becoming a national issue and ultimately could only be solved by national governmental action. Since 1918, legislation had been consolidated in respect of education, town planning and poor law; the laws related to highways, housing and public health needed similar attention.

Consolidation of the law

In 1930, the government appointed a Departmental Committee for the consolidation of the law relating to local government and public health whose terms of reference were 'with a view to the consolidation of the enactments applying to England and Wales (exclusive of London) and dealing with (a) Local Authorities and Local Government, and (b) matters relating to the public health to consider under what heads those enactments should be grouped in consolidating legislation and what enactments of the existing Law are desirable for facilitating consolidation and securing simplicity, uniformity and conciseness'.[18]

Certainly the demands of the building industry were simplicity, uniformity and conciseness, and the Departmental Committee on Building Byelaws had made constructive proposals on that basis in 1918. After 12 years, the responsibility to review and introduce those recommendations fell on the new committee, and there was no guarantee that the recommendations made in 1918 would be accepted and implemented by the government in the 1930s. The committee produced its first interim report in March 1933, together with the draft of a Local Government Bill which would deal with the first part of the terms of reference, namely consolidation of local authority legislation.

Minor amendments were made to the draft bill in consultation with local authorities and various government departments, and it was eventually passed by both Houses, receiving royal assent on the 17th November 1933. The Local Government Act 1933[19] reduced the number of local authorities by permitting agreed boundary changes. Large, and enlarged, boroughs could obtain 'county' status and this enabled those authorities to undertake county council responsibilities, yet at the same time retain the responsibility to enforce building bye-laws. These enlarged authorities could now afford to increase or improve resources allocated for enforcing these, provided they had the political will to do so.

The appointment of officers

The Act recognized the need for the appointment of certain officers to conduct the administration of the council's responsibilities. These officers were county clerk, treasurer, medical officer of health, and surveyors, while boroughs and districts had to appoint in addition sanitary inspectors. There were no set standards of qualification for any of these officers, or defined areas of responsibility, but it was normally found that the tasks of the post determined the necessary professional expertise and qualification of the particular officer. Consequently, it is not surprising to find that the work of a clerk required the appointment of a solicitor, that of a medical officer of health, a doctor, while the surveyor needed to be a civil or municipal engineer, and the work of the treasurer required the expertise of an accountant. This was not always the case in smaller authorities. Boroughs, urban and rural districts alike often combined the post of surveyor and sanitary inspector, or clerk and treasurer, and it was not unusual to find responsibilities relating to housing, town planning, drainage, sewage disposal, water supply and building bye-laws enforcement being carried out by unqualified assistants or encompassed within the control of a person qualified in other matters.

Whilst the statutory requirement to appoint certain officers was helpful, it did not extend far enough into specific responsibilities such as building control. Neither was there a requirement for such persons to be qualified by examination as we find in the London system. The consolidation process did not permit account to be taken of the London system and a further opportunity was lost in seeking uniformity that could be helpful on a national scale. This situation continued to permit local authorities the discretion of staff selection and where vested interests dominated, the quality and quantity of building bye-law surveyors varied enormously.

Second interim report of the Local Government and Public Health Consolidation Committee

The Local Government and Public Health Consolidation Committee presented their second interim report in January 1936. This report contained that part of the terms of reference dealing with the consolidation of the public health law. The Committee began work on this task in November 1933 and held 59 meetings. Sixteen Public Health Acts had been introduced between 1875 and 1932, but only the 1875, 1890 and 1907 Acts related to building bye-law control. Even these three Acts required simplification to avoid duplication and to be consolidated into a single enforceable Act. This was not an easy task. The 1875 Act itself was a consolidation of a larger number of Acts, each drafted by different Parliamentary draftsmen using their own drafting language, yet in the end these different Acts had to be united into one comprehensive Act. Many of the previous Acts were adoptive, and the Committee considered that although the principle of adoption was reasonable, it had in the past been abused. It was now necessary to review the principle and how, if at all, it should be retained in the new Bill.[20]

The basic system of building control based on the adoption and enforcement of building bye-laws was not to be changed. This proposal was originated by the Departmental Committee on Building Byelaws, who considered that the system of control was not in dispute, only the mode of control. Despite the problems caused by the discretionary power to adopt bye-laws, the Bill proposed to retain this power with a proviso that would enable the Minister to make bye-laws in areas where it was considered desirable either by public demand or ministerial enquiry.[21] This power of intervention, however, did not extend to the day-to-day administration or to the quality or extent of enforcement, although this was always a possibility through departmental circulars.

The Consolidating Committee was aware of the considerable controversy and litigation over building bye-laws and that the subject had been extensively investigated by the Departmental Committee on Building Bye-laws. This was an opportune (and long-awaited) time to incorporate recommendations of that committee into any consolidation proposals. Since 1918, many more authorities had adopted building bye-laws, due partly to urbanization creeping into rural areas following the improved road and rail communications which encouraged such development. In these rural areas, lower land costs enabled cheaper houses to be built, which was attractive to buyers. There had been continual, if infrequent, reminders by the Ministry of Health to adopt or revise bye-laws. The Committee was in agreement with the three different models, urban, rural and intermediate, as many areas of sparse population did not require complex bye-laws.[22]

Whilst it was politically expedient to agree with the retention of three different models of bye-laws on the assumption that they did not cause problems especially to speculators, this situation was building up problems for the future. Bye-laws could have been framed to include all types of development and due regard given to isolated properties. What may be considered to be rural development at one time could easily be urbanized by infill development and isolation distances reduced, whereby spread of fire through extensive use of combustible material was significantly increased. Similar situations applied with drainage and sewage disposal.

The draft bill imposed an obligation on authorities to make bye-laws but did not bind them to do any more than this, even when required by the Minister.[23] This freely allowed local authorities to make bye-laws, and yet not effectively administer or enforce them in any manner that would restrict jerry building, in much the same way that the provisions of the Public Health Act had been adopted and not acted upon. Although this criticism had abated due to the removal of many rigid and stringent bye-laws, nevertheless the law allowed indifference to persist. The opportunity should have been taken to place a greater emphasis on the duty of a local authority; if the government considered building bye-laws had beneficial social effects in terms of public health and safety, there should have been no discretion and more positive direction given to administration and enforcement.

The government was to maintain its control of local government through the imposition of ministerial control and penalties. One important change was the power for the minister to make bye-laws in any local authority's area where that authority had failed to do so.

Revision of bye-laws

The Consolidation Committee considered that existing bye-laws should be revised after a period of three years, after which they should be reviewed every ten years as recommended by the Departmental Committee. This was inserted into the Bill with the proviso that the Minister could extend the period if necessary.[24] This, in effect, meant that existing bye-laws would no longer be effective after 31st July 1939. The Committee recommended that any extension should only be for periods of six months up to a maximum of 18 months, allowing ample time to enable local authorities to renew their bye-laws, failing which the Minister would make them. The bill retained the provisions of the 1907 Act in that approved plans would be of no effect where building works had not commenced after three years, thereby placing the onus on the developer to resubmit plans and construct in accordance with the current building bye-laws. The approval of plans could only be withdrawn by notice. Not to withdraw approval would be reasonable if the local authority had not altered its bye-laws in the past three years but alternatively, the authority would be lacking in its responsibilities if it failed to withdraw approvals where the bye-laws had been updated.

Noise control

The original intention was that the builder would derive financial benefit from complying with updated bye-laws. This was true in many instances where revised bye-laws, for example, permitted thinner walls. However, it had the opposite effect where bye-laws had been extended and placed controls on parts of the structure that had not previously been controlled. This was particularly apparent where the content of building bye-laws had to take account of local variations due to local Acts. This had extended the bye-law making powers of Section 157 of the 1875 Act and Section 23 of the 1890 Act. These Acts had qualified the making of bye-laws as to their purpose 'for securing stability and prevention of fire and for the purpose of health' and 'to secure a free circulation of air'. The Committee considered that by excluding these qualifications it would be possible to make bye-laws covering most, if not all, of the matters Parliament had given in local legislation.[25] In addition, it would make it possible to make bye-laws to deal with materials used in buildings to control transmission of noise. This was a matter of concern to the Building Research Station which had started conducting tests in 1929 to measure sound transmission between flats in a building.

The construction of buildings containing flats represented a growing trend in low cost housing, especially in areas with high land prices. The density of units was much greater, permitting a lower cost. The construction, using traditional materials, meant that timber floors separated the flats which allowed sound to pass through all too easily. Noise generated from another source intruding into the home can affect a person's health, and this was beginning to be recognized as a health problem. Much of the problem could be prevented by constructing separating walls and floors using dense material such as brickwork and reinforced concrete, but until the building bye-laws had been amended to permit the use of these materials and this mode of construction the problem was likely to get worse. Accordingly, the Committee recommended the all-embracing wording of 'the construction of buildings, and materials used in the construction of buildings'. This amendment would enable a more flexible approach to the making of bye-laws, which was a distinct advantage in terms of technological requirement, but had the disadvantage to the speculative builder that bye-law making powers could be extended without the need to extend the legal base. There were sections of the Public Health Acts that applied controls on drains, sewers and sanitary conveniences, and the Committee considered that these were allied matters and in effect part of a building, so that to divorce these requirements from bye-law making powers would be wrong in that it would destroy effective administration (see *Appendix 14*). However, it was considered bye-law making powers relating to streets and to unfit houses would be adequately covered by highway and housing Acts. This, in effect, enabled public health law to be streamlined and not to affect requirements on matters not associated with the construction and sanitation of buildings.

Complaints

The administration of bye-laws had always brought about complaints, sometimes of the bye-law itself, but more frequently of the way it was (or was not) administered. The Departmental Committee in 1918 had recommended that it was essential that where plans had been refused, the local authority must state the bye-law that had been contravened. This enabled aggrieved parties to challenge the local authority to justify their reasons in a Magistrates Court. In addition to the right to refer disputes to the courts, parties could jointly submit their case to the Local Government Board for determination. This was the softer, less expensive option. These provisions had been recognized by the Consolidation Committee, and incorporated in the new Bill, a voluntary practice agreed by the Minister in 1932 (see p.111). In conclusion, the Consolidation Committee emphasized that they were conscious that their task was not to produce an ideal law of public health but a working consolidation of existing law. Parliamentary time did not allow further consideration and therefore the report had been produced at the risk of errors and omissions. The Committee's report was presented on 10th January 1936, with a draft Public Health Bill which the Minister of Health announced publication of on the 27th February.

The recommendations put forward by the Committee represent another incremental advance in the development of the bye-law system. The Committee was restrained as to what action it could propose. It was not able to produce a radical solution that either threw off the chains of central government or discarded local authority control in favour of an alternative system. The Committee was not allowed to consider the London Building Act system and its consolidation with the rest of England and Wales.

The London system and the new model code

With the development of the bye-law system, the London system, despite its longer history, was becoming an anomaly in building control terms. Its inflexible Acts, together with the wide discretionary powers of the district surveyors, were often held as a shining example of how building control should be administered. Certainly it did not accumulate objections in the manner that the local authority bye-law system did. Much of the strength of the London system lay with the powers of interpretation, application and administration held by the district surveyors who were able to resolve constructional problems on site, as opposed to the local authority system of criticizing deposited plans and frequently avoiding or being asked to avoid, site control.

The Departmental Committee had thrown out control by an Act because of its inflexibility to respond quickly enough to technological change, consequently favouring the bye-law system which appeared to be more flexible. However, the experience gained from the way local authorities undertook their role showed that the system was frequently far from flexible. Yet the mode of administration did have distinct advantages, offering a solution to the problem of control being exercised by central authority through a delegated system of district surveyors. This could have broken the polarities of interest between the central and local approach. Total centralization was not welcomed and this action would no doubt have been fought against by the various associations of local authorities, but the recommendations did not go far enough in placing a duty on enforcement which was more in keeping with the views of the Departmental Committee in 1918. Instead, the Committee recommended greater control by giving the Minister power to require local authorities to make bye-laws, but failed to find a solution to force them to respond by enforcing bye-laws they had made. Consequently, the weaknesses remained which would permit the continuance of indifferent interpretation, application and enforcement.

The recommendation that all existing bye-laws would have to be replaced by new bye-laws was a distinct advantage. For once, all authorities would be adopting a new model code and apart from a few variations that no doubt would be sought by some councils, the new code would at least allow some positive progress towards uniformity. When presented to the House of Lords, the Bill was referred to a joint committee of both Houses.[26] The exemption clauses were viewed with concern, but the Board of Education had no intention of relaxing the exemption rights which they had obtained in 1909 and this subject was not pursued when assurances were given that the Board would maintain bye-law standards.[27] This was a step in the right direction in that due recognition was given to maintaining basic standards of health and safety without the interference of local authorities.

Increase in the use of British Standards

To assist in achieving bye-law standards, greater use of British Standards was called for, especially where bye-laws were not clear or were inappropriate.[28] It would have been advantageous to develop British Standards and Codes of Practice so that these documents could have been accepted as the legal standard. However, codes and standards go far beyond that needed for health and safety reasons, and to adopt the whole document would have extended building control beyond the criteria of health and safety. Whilst it was possible for certain sections of codes to be specially quoted in a bye-law, it was better to leave bye-laws, codes and standards as separate documents. Furthermore, it was too big a step to be taken at this time. It seemed better to allow local authorities and developers to agree the areas of compatibility between bye-laws and codes and these areas could grow closer together when bye-laws were updated every ten years. This period of time, as we have already noted, was too long, allowing inefficient local authorities not to bother with their own periodic updating. The period should have been reduced to five years. The proposal to review building law so as to consolidate it into a single separate Act was beyond the scope of the Bill. However, in itself it was a consolidation of the public health aspects of building law since 1875, going some way to meet that proposal and could be considered as an expression of government agreement with that idea.[29]

The bill was not perfect, but it did make compulsory what was previously adoptive and as public health law developed, similar amendments in the same direction should follow. (For a summary of the growth of building bye-laws from 1858–1936, see *Appendix 19.*) In completing its passage through Parliament, it was expressed that the bill would be of great benefit to administrators, owners and builders alike. The bill was not put forward as an ideal code, but as a foundation on which future amendments could be solidly built.[30] On the 31st July 1936, the bill became law, and its success can be measured by the total lack of amendments necessary to the building control measures in the next 25 years.[31]

CHAPTER 8
Towards a Building Act

The provision within the Public Health Act 1936, which in effect nullified all old bye-laws by July 1939, was the legislation that necessitated local authorities to adopt new and modern bye-laws based on the 1937 model (see *Appendix 15*). This positive step forward ensured a better alignment and uniformity of bye-laws across the two countries. The discretion to adopt or not adopt remained with local authorities but the Minister now had powers to require local authorities to adopt, or indeed make, such bye-laws where they had so far failed to do so. In 1936, however, dark clouds were again looming over Europe. The fear of war was occupying most minds, but despite this, most authorities had new bye-laws in place by 1939.

Rebuilding after World War II

The majority of new building between 1936 and 1939 was of a military nature, and was of buildings that were exempt from compliance with building bye-laws because of their Crown status. During the whole period of the war building materials were in short supply, as priority was given to work classified as essential to the war effort.

Considerable numbers of buildings were destroyed or extensively damaged during the war especially during the Blitz of 1940 and 1941. Between September 1940 and May 1941, in London alone, some 1,150,000 houses were damaged. In Hull, only six per cent of the housing stock escaped damage. One in four houses was bombed out of use in Plymouth, and in Coventry, one air raid alone in November 1940 destroyed 2294 houses whilst a further 50,000 were damaged.[1] Over the whole country, out of a housing stock of 13,000,000 houses, 20,000 had been destroyed and 3,750,000 damaged.[2] A survey of the damaged buildings revealed many inherent defects, which gave rise to the opinion that buildings constructed between the wars were substandard and that a new code of building bye-laws should be introduced.

> 'I have heard people talk about buildings built between the wars. A state of affairs that should never have existed has now been disclosed. In a certain town recently, when I had some men clearing up after bomb damage, I found that not a single roof tile had been nailed, and dampness three feet high in the walls due to lack of a damp-proof course. I visited a house with a friend and was able to shake hands

through the fireplaces as there were no backs. Jerry builder, who is he? He is someone who comes into the industry to speculate and knows nothing about the business. There should be a standard code from one end of the country to the other and it should be enforced. Building inspections are not carried out by Local Authorities. A good builder has nothing to fear because it will stop the man who wishes to exploit it. Thorough building inspection and an up-to-date code will stop bad building.'[3]

Comments such as this reflected badly on the performance of many local authorities who were trying their best to apply their building bye-laws in a reasonable way, but as has been noted, professionalism was lacking in the delivery of this public service.

National versus local bye-laws

The need for national, as opposed to local, bye-laws was raised once again when the government debated the need for new housing after the war. This was an opportunity to avoid shoddy building. Some of the housing needs, it was felt, could be satisfied by constructing prefabricated buildings, which necessitated national bye-laws as localized and old forms of bye-laws hampered new methods of building.[4] As it was alleged that differing interpretations of bye-laws by local authorities could add as much as £600 to a house, possibilities of uniformed interpretation were also being explored at this time.[5] One problem that led to lack of uniformity arose from rural and urban model bye-laws. It was considered that a general code for timber use, one that took account of the quality and strength of timber, not merely quoting sizes, was needed. This also applied to brickwork as both the quality and strength of bricks had improved and specific bye-laws took no account of this.[6]

Some assistance had been given to designers, constructors and building inspectors with the excellent technical appendices in the *Housing Manual 1949*. Much research had been carried out since the publication of the 1944 *Housing Manual*, which included post-war building studies, the work of the British Standards Institute and the Building Research Station. The technical appendices are interesting in that they set out a form of functional standards, followed by details very similar to the form building regulations would take some 36 years later.[7]

Prefabricated buildings

As already mentioned, the construction of prefabricated buildings was seen as a major solution to satisfying the demand for new housing after the war, and was a new method of construction that did not comply with building bye-laws. When challenged on this matter, the Minister of Health indicated that it was a subject under discussion, but that the bye-laws would not stop the construction of factory-built houses as it was considered that the 'deemed to satisfy' clauses would enable this form of construction to comply.[8]

Thousands of single-storey prefabricated houses were constructed and erected in many towns after the war to replace destroyed and badly damaged housing. The construction programme had to be rapid and economic. The buildings, often better than those they replaced, were well liked by their occupants and contained modern facilities, provided privacy, spatial layout of development and remained in use for many years (see *Plates 9a and b*). Whilst a lot of these buildings have been replaced, there are many which remain occupied today, such as those in the Kingswood area of Bristol and some of the smaller towns around Bristol. The fact that these buildings provided very useful units of accommodation for so long and at low cost was an indicator as to how out-of-date the building bye-law system was, as the buildings certainly met the functional criteria at that time and continued to do so. The real value of these properties would not emerge for some years, and in the meanwhile the bye-law system with all of its problems would continue.

The differing models of bye-law and local variations did little to establish a common pattern of housing. Differences offered opportunities which could not only be exploited by jerry-builders, but which also confused the established house builder. As a measure to minimize this problem, an approach was made by the government to the National House Builders Registration Council (NHBRC) for the registration and certification of new houses, constructed to an approved standard. This would, for the purposes of Section 5 of the Building Societies Act of 1939, make the houses more easily mortgageable.[9]

The Building Byelaws of 1939 were intended to be replaced by 1949. This did not happen, as by that time a new set of model bye-laws were under review. To assist in the development of new bye-laws the Minister formed an advisory panel comprised of members from 15 relevant institutions.[10] In 1952, modified in 1953, a new set of model bye-laws emerged (see *Appendix 16*). This was one model for all areas, thus avoiding the problems caused by the previous rural and urban models.[11] The 1953 model was very similar to the 1935 urban model, but added 'deemed to satisfy' provisions such as the acceptance of design and work in accordance with British Standards.

The Public Health Act 1961

Despite these advances, uniformity was not achieved. Seventy per cent of local authorities adopted the model whilst the remaining 30 per cent had bye-laws roughly in conformity with the model. For example, three out of 126

Lancashire authorities required that the ground floor room height was more than seven feet six inches. These authorities had agreed that a smoke-laden atmosphere, low levels of sunshine and high density development necessitated this room height. Whilst the Minister had tried to achieve uniformity, he accepted the long tradition of occasional non-conformity.[12] However, these variations, even though they were minor, added to the cost of construction. The method of expressing requirements was considered in the report of the Committee on Building Legislation in Scotland in 1957. The report favoured the functional requirement, in that requirements of a specific nature, based on construction and materials, restricted the progress of technological development (see *Plate 10*). This approach had been advocated before and had also been supported by the Building Research Board in 1936.[13]

The need for uniformity remained a justifiable aim and this was incorporated into the Public Health Bill of 1961. Apart from giving new powers to local authorities, the bill proposed the replacement of local bye-laws with national regulations. It was agreed that the bye-law machinery was time-wasting and led to inefficiency,[14] and there would be greater control and authority with the new regulations. There was little opposition to these proposals, although they reflected badly on local government's ability to manage its own affairs.

Means of escape in case of fire

The search for uniformity was not restricted to building regulations, as moving in parallel was another important issue in the design and construction of a building – the provision of a satisfactory means of escape in case of fire. Whilst this is an essential facility for users of any building in all matters of emergency, at this time the debate centred on factories. In 1937 the Factories Act enabled local authorities, under section 34, to issue certificates in respect of means of escape in case of fire in factories to which the Act applied. At that time, local authorities were fire authorities, and it was relatively easy for the staff responsible for building and for fire to work together to implement these requirements. However, whilst this happened in some authorities, it was not widespread throughout England and Wales. The duty was not new; it had been imposed by the Factories Act of 1901 which required all factories employing 40 or more persons to have a certificate from the District Council regarding adequate means of escape in case of fire.

Model bye-laws to this effect were issued by the Local Government Board in 1906 but by the end of 1919, these bye-laws had been adopted by only 52 councils,[15] being less than four per cent of the whole number of local authorities in England and Wales.

The situation was not improved by the Act of 1937 and was not helped when the responsibilities for fire brigades were passed from district councils to county councils. During the debate on the Factories Bill 1959, it was considered that these responsibilities were a heavy task for local authorities, many of whom did not have the knowledgeable staff to do this work, and some employed fire brigades to carry out these duties (illegally of course); this practice had been going on since 1948.[16] The problem of conflict of interests was raised in that it was foreseen that district councils applying building bye-laws would conflict with fire authorities requiring structural building work to provide a means of escape in case of fire.[17] This was a frequent occurrence, especially when the first building regulations appeared in 1965, and the situation was eventually resolved with formal consultation procedures imposed by the Fire Precautions Act 1971.[18] Nevertheless, the responsibility for the certification of factories passed from district councils to fire authorities on the 29th July 1959[19] and was retained within section 40 of the Factories Act 1961.[20]

The importance of means of escape in case of fire re-emerged with the introduction of the Fire Precautions Bill in June 1970.[21] Requirements for means of escape were fragmented amongst a number of Acts, mainly the Factories Act, Offices, Shops and Railway Premises Act 1963, and the Public Health Act 1936. The measures in the Bill were based on the Holroyd published in 1970,[22] which recommended formal consultation between building and fire authorities. These consultations would avoid the need for fire brigades to employ their own professionally qualified civilian staff for fire prevention duties. The principles established were that authorities responsible for building regulations would control the construction of buildings, and fire authorities would control the building in use. As such, the building authority would be the arbiters as to compliance with the building regulations. The Bill also provided for the Secretary of State to make building regulations for means of escape in case of fire, to be administered by the building authority. This recommendation was accepted and became section 11 of the Act. The first of these regulations appeared in 1973 as the first amendment of the Building Regulations 1972[23] came into effect 31st August 1973. Since that date, authorities responsible for building and fire have developed a close working relationship which has helped to smooth out any possible areas of conflict between their respective responsibilities.

The Building Regulations Advisory Committee

With the introduction of the Public Health Act 1961 it was now clear that the regulation of building was a central government responsibility administered through local authorities.[24]

The Act provided the Minister with powers to form an advisory committee to be known as the Building Regulations Advisory Committee (BRAC) and R.M. Wayne-Edwards was appointed chairman in April 1962. The committee was made up of 10 members, one of whom was a local authority building inspector, Mr Harry Fellows, whilst another was a surveyor and public health inspector, Mr P. Gilby.[25] A lot of hard work was involved in structuring a new system and regulations, and other interested bodies, both professional and commercial, were consulted. During this time, the Minister was questioned several times regarding the delay. A survey had shown that 91 per cent of all new housing was faulty to some extent and that new regulations would help to address the problem.[26] Faced with the challenge of producing workable relevant regulations within the administration set out in the 1961 Act, BRAC took their time in producing the new regulations in the summer of 1965 (see *Appendix 17*), which would take effect from April 1st, 1966.

Local authorities had little time to become acquainted with the format and content of the regulations, although many of the requirements were based on, and were similar to, the previous bye-laws. The regulations remained of a specific nature, but there was a greater element of flexibility, such as greater acceptability of British Standards and codes of practice, greater use of calculated assessment of risk, especially in matters of fire safety, and the introduction of formal relaxation of the specific requirements (or indeed dispensation) providing a suitable case could be made.

Published guidance

Both the BRE and the FRE contributed to the formation of the new regulations and many requirements were based on their research work. Reference to their published documents could be used to support or refuse applications for relaxation. As we have seen, relaxation was not a new concept, having been raised by the Departmental Committee in 1918 and incorporated into the Public Health Act 1936. However, it had never been developed for use in the manner that the 1936 Act had sanctioned. Disputes over interpretation or application of a requirement could be resolved by reference to the courts or by a formal application to the Minister for determination. Technical handbooks such as the one prepared by the Incorporated Association of Architects and Surveyors (IAAS) began to appear.[27] These guidebooks were extremely beneficial to both designers and enforcers, being well-illustrated and supported by explanatory text.

Despite these excellent attempts to give helpful guidance it was soon alleged that the regulations were too complex and that a simplified code should be introduced for small buildings. Local authorities appeared to be enforcing 'deemed to satisfy' provisions as the actual regulations, as some of their staff lacked the knowledge and skills to understand and accept other methods of meeting the mandatory requirements.

Health & Safety at Work Etc. Act 1974

The new administration system did not appear to be any speedier than that which had existed under the bye-laws. More research was called for, as it was contended that modern methods of construction would otherwise be unduly hindered.[28] Objections continued to be raised on almost every occasion that amendments were introduced; so much so that the Minister prepared another review. In addition, it was considered that there was a need for higher standards of insulation,[29] flexibility of application for buildings designated as being of architectural and historical importance[30] and even suggestions that all qualified building inspectors be employed by central government because of the indifference within local government.[31]

The Minister accepted the need for change and consulted a wide range of interested organizations.[32] A consultative document was prepared in which a Building Act was proposed by consolidation of existing legislation and the incorporation of wider powers. Unnecessary local Acts would be repealed, improvements for resolving disputes would be made, and there would be greater flexibility in the procedure for approving plans and the procedures to bring them into line with modern building practices. The provision for charging fees would assist in offsetting the cost of administration. It was suggested that the scale of fees would follow that already existing in London, linking building regulations with other similar statutory controls so as to avoid conflict and anomalies and the removal of many categories of exemptions. It was also proposed that some regulations should impose a continuing requirement, for example requiring that a means of escape in case of fire remain effective.

Whilst it was accepted that building inspectors needed to be qualified and experienced, this would not be specified in law as it was the government's policy to impose as few constraints as possible on the managerial arrangements of local authorities. Nevertheless, the consultative document recognized the need to provide training schemes for building control surveyors. As Scotland and London had separate systems it was proposed that the Bill should include provisions for bringing the systems of London and England and Wales together, and new provisions in the Bill would follow Scotland closely, bringing about a more uniform arrangement throughout Great Britain. Of the professional bodies who made their views known, The Institution of Municipal Engineers, who examine the majority of building inspectors, made it plain that it did not want to see its hold on the responsibility it had in the training and qualification of building inspectors loosened in any way. And while it endorsed the need for modernization and rationalization, as most did, it felt that the resultant statutory instrument would be cumbersome and prejudice the flexibility sought.[33]

Many of the proposals were contentious, but there was agreement on the majority of them. In the end, however, there was insufficient Parliamentary time to create a Building Act and the proposals were appended to the Health and Safety Bill to become the 'Etc.' part of the Health and Safety Etc. Act 1974.[34]

The effect of building failures on building control

During the period from the late 1960s to the 1980s, serious building failures came to light mainly as a result of tragic accidents of disastrous proportions which highlighted the difficulty of existing building controls and the need to strengthen both the requirements and the enforcement.

Notable failures

Ronan Point

Ronan Point was a 22-storey block of flats in Canning Town, London, UK, built of reinforced concrete structural components using the Larson Nielson system of construction. On May 16th 1968, an explosion occurred on the eighteenth floor, blowing out an external load-bearing flank wall of the living room and bedroom of Flat No. 90. The flank walls and floors immediately above collapsed, and the additional weight caused progressive collapse below. Four people died as a result of this accident, while many were injured and suffered shock. The resultant enquiry revealed that building regulations did not cover the possibility of progressive collapse, and whilst the approach to control, with functional requirements and complying with 'deemed to satisfy' provisions was right, nevertheless it was incumbent on the government to keep regulations up-to-date. As a result of this accident, regulations were amended so as to prevent a similar occurrence.[35]

Birkenhead Sports Hall

The collapse of a sports hall in Birkenhead in July 1976 revealed that pre-fabricated timber roof trusses had not been adequately braced, leading to progressive roof loads being transferred to a masonry gable end wall and causing its collapse.[36] Investigations by the BRE led to the publication of advisory documents on compliance with the structural requirements of the regulations.

Summerland Leisure Centre, Isle of Man

In August 1973, the Summerland Leisure Centre at Douglas, Isle of Man, suffered extensive damage due to a fire in which there was a tragic loss of life. The Commission of Enquiry revealed that relaxation of bye-laws had been granted whereby the standard of structural fire resistance had been reduced and approval given for the use of combustible inner screens. The rapid spread of fire was assisted by the poor surface resistance of the materials and lack of fire stopping in cavities. The building was subject to the Isle of Man building bye-laws, but there were sufficient lessons to be learnt resulting in amendments to the regulations in England and Wales.

Woolworths, Manchester

Ten people died as a result of a fire at a Woolworths store in Manchester in 1979.[37] The Home Office enquiry into the accident considered that the tragedy could have been avoided if Manchester City Council had applied the building bye-laws more vigorously by requiring compartment walls or sprinkler systems when the building was extensively altered some 12 years previously.

Concrete problems

Collapse of pre-fabricated reinforced concrete beams where calcium chloride has been used as a curing agent caused much concern, and this led to a regulatory amendment.[38] Spalling concrete from load-bearing elements of system-built houses erected between 1947 and the mid-1950s revealed that the concrete was losing its protection to the reinforcement, resulting in thousands of the properties being extensively rebuilt in later years.

Cavity wall insulation

Area formaldehyde foam was used to fill the cavities of masonry walls so as to increase the thermal insulation properties of the building. However, this foam had the tendency to shrink, allowing cracks to occur through which water penetrated to the inner leaf, causing dampness. Hundreds of buildings had to be partly demolished and rebuilt. The demolition often revealed wall ties with mortar bridging the cavity and assisting rain penetration. The foam also gave off a gas which would find its way into the building, producing unpleasant effects to the eyes, throats and respiratory system with an associated risk of lung cancer.[39] In America the product was banned, although this ban was lifted a year later.[40] Nevertheless, tighter controls were introduced by amended regulations.[41]

These examples are a few highlighted cases, but the presence of building defects and the risk of disasters will still remain as buildings are constructed, modified and used in a manner reflecting the residential and commercial pressures of the time. Well-targeted building research will assist in identifying potential problems which could enable regulations to be effectively amended so as to reduce the possibility of further tragic accidents. Building defects not only have the potential to affect the safety and health of persons using the building, but they are often expensive to correct.

Compensation claims

Local authorities were not exempt from claims for compensation. In Bognor Regis, Mrs Sadie Dutton, a houseowner, had contended that Bognor Regis Council was negligent through the agency of their building inspector who had inspected the building works and approved them when he knew, or might have known, that the foundations were inadequate. The court found that the council, through their building inspector, owed a duty of care to Mrs Dutton and was negligent, and consequently liable to costs.[42]

The findings of this case were strengthened by the case of Anns vs. London Borough of Merton, which had been referred to the House of Lords. The case revolved around a block of flats with latent defects in the foundations that the council had failed to inspect, or having done so, failed to notice the inadequacy of the foundations. The House of Lords determined that the case of Dutton vs. Bognor Regis District Council had been rightly decided and accordingly dismissed the appeal. The further case of Haig vs. London Borough of Hillingdon determined that the council was negligent and liable in damages for inadequacy of inspection in that their inspector had failed to inspect a new steel beam which was critical to the load-bearing capacity of the structure and consequently failed. These cases started alarm bells ringing in local authorities, and their procedures both in plan-checking and site inspection were reviewed. Many authorities adopted policies after advice from professional bodies and legal sources.[43]

Reviews

It was contended that the local authority building control system had received its greatest shake up yet,[44] and now recognized the importance of good quality building inspection and control. Local authorities not only revised their procedures but also their staff both in terms of qualification and experience. Training would be needed and proper inspection records were required to be kept along with a review of insurance cover.[45]

These matters were seemingly long overdue and the majority of councils took their responsibilities seriously with the result that they increased their effectiveness by raising their professionalism. Professional bodies had been arguing this approach for some considerable time, but local authorities, in attempts to keep administration costs as minimal as possible, were not able and often did not want to attract professionally qualified surveyors into the building control service.

Despite the reviews undertaken, the situation did not significantly change in the following ten years, as in 1989 a report showed that difficulties remained in recruiting qualified professionals. It was revealed that the gap in salary levels between public and private sectors was 20 per cent and widening, and it was taking some eight months to fill a local authority post. This did little to maintain staff resources and morale, and fears were expressed that important projects would not be inspected. The local authority trade union, NALGO, organized strikes to emphasize the need for improved salaries, but this had the effect of reducing even further the number of building inspections.

In 1989 the pressure of facing claims for negligence was reduced. In the case of Murphy vs. Brentwood District Council, judgement was given against the council who had approved foundations of a house which later failed. The council had used the services of a civil engineering consultancy to scrutinize the plans of the design and it was held that the council was responsible for the advice given. The case was upheld on appeal, whereafter it went to the House of Lords. They ruled in favour of Brentwood Council, thereby overturning the judgement given in Anns vs. London Borough of Merton. The ruling determined that the duty of a local authority in their administration and enforcement of building regulations did not extend beyond actual injury to a person or impairment to their health or to the defective property itself. Economic loss could no longer be the basis of a claim. The burden of having to contend with claims of negligence had been considerably reduced, but it was not a reason to refrain from seeking improvements to the system of building control.

The improvements made by many local authorities in the mid- to late 1970s did not prevent further calls for changes in the system. Building control legislation remained fragmented. Regulations, although moving towards functional requirements, were, in the main, specific and seen as restrictive. The system of relaxation was cumbersome, bureaucratic, and did not produce the flexibility and speed of response needed. Disasters, defects and negligence only highlighted the deficiencies and made a further review inevitable.

The then Prime Minister, Margaret Thatcher, and her Conservative government were to leave few stones unturned in their review of the way the state conducted its business. Both central and local government functions were under review and building control was no exception. Michael Heseltine, then

Secretary of State for the Environment, stated that he would be conducting a fundamental review of the system without reducing standards of health and safety. In a speech at the NHBC annual dinner in December 1979, he highlighted aspects of this review and suggested it would appear appropriate that certain elements of the control system could be carried out by persons other than local authorities. Over 400 responses to his speech were received and would be taken into account when formulating and publishing a consultative document. The extensive and detailed proposals were contained in a Command Paper in February 1981.[46] The principles of the review were clearly set out: *maximum self-regulation*; *total self-financing*; *minimum government interference*; and *simplicity of operation*.

It was considered that these aims could be achieved by wider exemptions, new arrangements for appeals and determinations, revised building regulations based on functional achievements rather than specific requirements, and supported by a range of approved documents, simplified administration giving a choice whether or not to deposit plans. The technical standards of Inner London, England and Wales were to be aligned as far as possible, and certification by Approved Inspectors who would be qualified, experienced professionals would be introduced.

The principle of change had been firmly set out. The radical nature of the proposals generated considerable conflict and consultation. It was not surprising to find that the NHBC supported the proposals[47] whilst the local government organization vigorously opposed.[48] The Incorporated Association of Architects and Surveyors (IAAS) and the Institute of Building Control (IBC), both heavily influenced by members who worked in local authority building control opposed,[49] whilst RIBA welcomed the proposals with open arms.[50] These differences indicated the individual and often personal interests that would arise during the consultation period. The *Builder* magazine invited comment on the proposals and had so many responses that extra pages were allocated to readers' reactions.

Fees

The first step necessitated introducing an element of commercialism and this had been achieved by charging fees for the services provided. Fees were not new; they had been part of the London system for over a hundred years and were the subject of consultation in 1972, accepted and incorporated into the Health and Safety at Work Etc. Act 1974. (The provisions to charge fees were introduced and became operative on April 1st 1980.[51])

One single Act

The second step was the consolidation of building control legislation into a single Act, a Building Act. For over 140 years, such an Act had been advocated and now the moment had arrived with the introduction of the Housing and Building Control Bill.[52] In the debates that followed, there was much support to introduce consolidated legislation, incorporating the London Building Act and simplifying administrative proposals, but the most controversial was the new form of certification by Approved Inspectors. Those in favour spoke of the need to have choice; the avoidance of one local authority approving a house design and the same then being refused by another local authority as is the case in the present system of control that is democratically accountable.[53]

The views expressed by the professions, industry and local government varied. As can be expected, local authority organizations and those heavily influenced by them objected on many of the issues. London did not like losing its Building Acts, or indeed its district surveyors system, a highly professional and respected system that had no equal in the United Kingdom.[54] The IAAS agreed on the need for improvement, the introduction of fees and wider exemptions but expressed concern on self-regulation, differing bodies enforcing regulations and proposed an even bigger bureaucratic control with regional authorities co-ordinated by a National Building Council.[55] Other professional bodies had differing ideas, the results of which could more easily be ignored. Even the building press leader columns changed over time, from 'a step in the right direction',[56] to 'a half-baked idea the Government should drop',[57] and 'Uniformity on regulations must be achieved'.[58]

From the summation of the press reports it appeared that certification was not widely accepted by the professions. Concern remained over the role and influence of insurance companies who provided the cover under which Approved Inspectors would operate, the feeling being that ultimately building control might be entirely insurance-based. The building control system in France had similarities to that being proposed and that system appeared to function quite adequately. However, the arguments put forward were insufficient to persuade the Government to change their strongly held views. Change was not only desirable but also essential. The system had to be more flexible to meet the stated criteria, and there was, after all, a role for the National House Building Council, especially in the vast house building market.

The Bill did not complete its passage through Parliament, but was resubmitted the same year. The proposals were in two parts. Part I would enable provisions for local authorities to dispose of their housing stock and Part II the certification of compliance with building regulations by approved inspectors and public bodies.

The debate continued with the independence of the approved inspector being queried, and the possibility of qualified local authority staff moving to the private sector, diminishing resources with these authorities. On the other hand, private certification was considered a huge advance, and there was a need to modernize the system. It was alleged there could be few better examples of something that could be better or more responsibly done by the private sector.[59] Despite the resistance expressed outside the House, where such views were seemingly more press-worthy than those of support, they had not changed the principle of the Bill, although it had been conceded that the role of the Approved Inspector would be independent of the design and construction process, other than minor work, and that adequate insurance would be necessary in order to practise. The weight of political argument against the Bill was not strong enough to prevent the Government obtaining the majority needed in the debates. The Bill became an Act in June 1984, and before the ink was dry the provisions had been included into a consolidating bill presented in the House of Lords. The bill consolidated building control provisions of 42 Acts and four statutory instruments into one Building Act. The political battles to prevent change had been fought and lost, and when the consolidation bill was presented to the House it was passed without debate,[60] completing its Parliamentary passage on 31st October 1984.[61]

One hundred and forty-three years had passed since Slaney and Normanby put forward their proposals for a national Building Act. During that time there had been occasions for the call to be repeated, and Parliament had been close to securing such an Act but opposing pressures had always been strong enough to prevent it happening. The combined forces of industry and the political weight of the Conservative government produced the most radical shake-up of the building control system since the demise of local Improvement Acts and the establishment of the system of building bye-laws.

The task was now to introduce the changes that the Act sought to achieve.

Chapter 9
A New Beginning

In July 1985 the government set out its proposals for modernizing the building control system very clearly in the Command Paper 'Lifting the Burden'.[1] These proposals included the simplification of procedures, the option of private certification, and the removal of unnecessary regulations. Whilst these proposals were aimed at the systems of England and Wales, it was stated that there would be also be a complete recasting of the Building Standards (Scotland) Regulations. In these there would be an element of self-certification, type approval of repetitive designs, and the greater exemption of agricultural, industrial buildings and minor house extensions. The reference to Scotland is important in that the quest for uniformity within Great Britain, harmonization with Scotland was equally desirable. The first stage of implementation would be the introduction of new building regulations.

The 1984 Building Act

New building regulations took effect just over a year after the assent of the 1984 Building Act. These new regulations (see *Appendix 18*), introduced in July 1985,[2] were a radical departure from the 1976 regulations which had been amended four times since their introduction, the last being in 1985 to bring about controls to ensure adequate access and facilities for disabled persons.[3] The aims of the 1976 regulations were achieved mainly through 310 pages of specific requirements and 'deemed to satisfy' clauses backed by 12 detailed schedules. The 1985 regulations were 24 pages comprising 20 regulations and three schedules. The reduction was brought about by introducing functional requirements, other than for 'Means of Escape in Case of Fire', which stated the aim of the regulation, not the means of achieving the requirement. For example, Building Regulation 4 Schedule 1 F1 states that 'there shall be means of ventilation so that an adequate supply of air may be provided for people in the building'. This one statement replaced five specific requirements and is deemed to satisfy provisions. Furthermore, it reduced the necessity of seeking formal relaxation of the specific requirements if those requirements appeared to be not relevant to the case in question. At first this seemed very simple, but the problem lay in what would be defined as 'adequate' to satisfy the aim of the regulation.

Approved documents

The regulations were backed by 12 booklets of guidance for architects, surveyors and builders, known as Approved Documents, together with a manual explaining the procedures involved in the administration of the regulations by local authorities and the newly-designated Approved Inspectors. Some 334 pages of detailed information were contained in the approved documents and had to be consulted to establish the standard necessary for acceptance. Most of this guidance followed the specific requirements of the 1976 Regulations.

Other than in London, there has never been a requirement for local authorities to appoint professionally qualified staff for the enforcement of building regulations. Therefore, with the indifference shown by local authorities to this responsibility, the explanatory guidance would be seen as helpful. Guidance was needed if only to avoid local authorities enforcing the approved documents as if they were a specific requirement, as the flexibility sought by both designer and constructor would be lost in their enforcement process. Not surprisingly, the approved documents became covert regulations.

London

The unification of the London system with that of the rest of England and Wales, the intent of which was made clear in 1972 (see p.134), came about on the 6th January 1985 with the introduction of the Building (Inner London) Regulations 1985. These regulations brought into effect the majority of the 1985 Building Regulations with certain limited exceptions. The constructional bye-laws made under the London Building Act no longer applied. The provisions for Approved Inspectors to operate in London also applied on that date. In order for a smooth transition from one system to another, it was proposed that the Greater London Council District Surveyors Service would remain responsible for the administration until 1st April 1986 when it would pass to the London Boroughs and the Corporation of the City of London.[4] So ended a service of high professional standard that had served the people of London for 319 years. It was an enormous task for the new system to continue this effectiveness but it would rest squarely on the shoulders of those now responsible.

Approved Inspectors

Local authorities were no longer the sole arbiters as to the interpretation of the regulations. Interpretation could also be undertaken by Approved Inspectors, and consequently departures from the approved documents could occur whereby differing constructional solutions could be accepted as meeting the requirement of the regulation. Approved Inspectors had to conduct their responsibility through the Approved Inspector Regulations 1985[5] (see *Appendix 18*). Those regulations required the Approved Inspector to notify the local authority prior to commencement of work that they would be responsible for building regulation administration and provide information to enable the local authority to register that interest. Similarly, on completion the Approved Inspector would inform the local authority of satisfactory completion. Enforcement would revert to the local authority should an Approved Inspector not be able to certify compliance with the regulations. The Building Act provided severe penalties to deter reckless and misleading certification.[6]

Role of the Secretary of State

It was the Secretary of State's responsibility to grant approved status to suitably qualified and experienced individuals or organizations. The Secretary of State could also approve a corporate or incorporated body to grant approved status. Whilst in the formative years the Secretary of State took on the responsibility, it was later devolved to the Construction Industry Council to approve both individuals and companies.[7] 'Has the Secretary of State approved any Inspectors for private certification?' asked John Heddle, MP for Mid-Staffordshire in the House of Commons on the 11th November 1985.[8] It was of course little surprise when John Patten (then Minister of State for the Environment, Housing, Urban Affairs and Construction) replied that as from that date the National House Building Council had been made an Approved Inspector, and was able to certify the construction of dwellings up to four storeys. The insurance scheme operated by the NHBC was considered satisfactory for this purpose.

The National House Building Council (NHBC)

For the first time, local authorities had a competitor able to provide a building regulation approval and certification service. The prime purpose of the regulations remained for the benefit of health, safety, welfare and convenience of those using the buildings, but to many a local government officer it was a basis for employment which was strongly supported by NALGO, as was apparent in the consultation phase of the Building Act. The fact that competition existed prompted a response from local authorities. Prior to the Act, local authorities, through their Chief Building Control Officers, had voluntarily formed into county groups, providing a basis on which to exchange views and to try and establish common working practices. Through these groups came many ideas and initiatives which helped to ease any frustrations experienced by builders.

Competition between the NHBC and local authorities

The NHBC had one distinct advantage in that their inspectors were able to inspect not only for purposes of their warranty, which was necessary for mortgage purposes, but also for compliance with the building regulations. This meant there was one less inspector on the site, thus avoiding differences that had previously occurred on matters of interpretation of materials and requirements. To counteract this, the local authorities sought to attain a similar warranty, and by prompting the Municipal Mutual Insurance Company, who provided insurance facilities for the majority of local authorities, a warranty scheme was devised and introduced in January 1989. This was called Foundation 15, with the number fifteen representing the years' cover of the warranty, and exceeding the NHBC warranty by five years.[9] This was later added to by the introduction of Conversion 10 for refurbishment work.[10] Municipal Mutual were now embarked on obtaining a viable share of the previous monopoly service once provided by the NHBC.

Local authorities continued to look for further initiatives to promote their service in the face of competition. It was obvious that they would not be able to maintain a monopoly, but there was no reason why they should not aim to be the major service provider. In doing so, they had to work together, as diversity was, and remains, one of the weaknesses of this area. Because of the operational independence of each local authority, there was no likelihood of total equality of administration and enforcement, but there was every chance that both the general public and the construction industry would benefit from initiatives that were aimed to improve the service.

The appointment of Rhys Jones Consultants to establish a marketing strategy for local authorities under the auspices of the National Promotion of Local Authority Building Control achieved much in uniting the approach by authorities to their responsibilities.[11] This, together with the appointment in 1987 of Denis Stokes as the National Director of the Local Authority Building Control Steering Group, indicated how authorities were promoting a local service in a national environment, yet at the same time recognizing and accepting differences at local level. These initiatives brought about the wider acceptance of house type approvals, whereby a house type of a developer approved by one local authority would be accepted without question by all other local authorities. This balanced neatly with the national approach of the NHBC, and was so successful that the scheme was extended to include commercial buildings. In 1990, the NHBC had acquired approximately 20 per cent of the building regulation administration of the new house building market and were expanding their interests.

Denis Stokes, a quantity surveyor, former housebuilders' manager and local authority councillor, was well aware of the mountains of red tape, bureaucracy and committee meetings that have to be gone through before the simplest of decisions can be agreed. He urged the introduction of business plans to develop better delivery of services, if local authorities wanted to fend off competition.[12] Many authorities were well aware that more effective management and better staff training were needed.[13]

Cheltenham District Council was one such authority that had developed a management strategy to effectively deliver a service within a competitive environment.[14] They were not the only authority to do so, but amongst these positive initiatives there were a number of uncompetitive practices developing within local authorities.[15] These included the imposition of conditions in local authority building contracts that contractors had to use the local authority building control service. This also occurred with the provision of council land for development, the withholding or delaying of planning permission, exercising public health functions so as to obstruct builders, not accepting notices given to them by Approved Inspectors, promotion of the Municipal House Warranty, and indifference to that available from the NHBC, and the giving of factual and impartial advice. This approach hampered the efforts of those serious in establishing local authorities as a deliverer of a first class service able to retain the major share of what was now seen to be a competitive market.

Fees

First introduced in 1980, fees provided the financial background within which a competitive service could operate, but the service provided by the local authorities remained subsidized by public taxation while this was not the case in the private sector. It was quite important that the question of cost was equated to actual administration of the system. Local government once again found itself losing out in the recruitment and retention of qualified staff. It could take up to eight months to complete the appointment of qualified staff, and the salary differences between public and private sector was 20 per cent and widening.[16] Staff shortages, especially in the London area, raised the fear that shoddy work would go undetected through lack of inspections. In 1989 a series of two-day strikes in support of a pay claim had the effect of reducing even further the number of building inspections carried out.[17]

A survey carried out in 1988 had established the current level of fee income in comparison to expenditure.[18] It had always been the intention of the government to raise building control fees to a level where the service was self-financing, and the survey established that 90 per cent of local authorities recovered their costs on current building control expenditure. Fees recovered in respect of commercial work subsidized the costs of the service in other sectors, especially home extensions. The survey averted the danger of a considerable increase, and consequently fees were only to increase by seven per cent.[19]

By 1990 the changes brought about by the Building Act 1984 and the new Building Regulation of 1985 had settled down and become accepted. Differing systems of control, and minor variations of interpretation, applications and administration were not seen to be the problems originally envisaged. Graham Fuller, Head of the Building Regulations Division of the Department of the Environment, told delegates attending the third annual conference of the Institute of Building Control that disputes between developers and local authorities referred to the Department on the interpretation of requirements had dropped from 1000 to 300 per annum. [20] Competition was bringing about the changes it was intended to. The reduction in bureaucracy, changing attitudes of local authority officials, the flexibility of interpretation of regulations, the choice of service delivery and of provider, increase in fees, were all steps towards meeting the criteria on which the Act was based – maximum self-regulation, minimum government interference, simplicity of operation and total self-financing.

As the twentieth century draws to a close, further steps in the meeting of those criteria have been made. These include amendments to the approved documents to keep public health and safety requirements in line with current expectations, widening the scope and number of Approved Inspectors, continuing improvements in local authority service, the requirement for local authorities to introduce self-financing fees, and the role of the Construction Industry Council in the granting of Approved Inspector status.

Conclusion

Over 150 years have passed since the first demand for building regulation in England (outside the metropolitan area of London) and Wales. The introduction of building control and its development has been a slow process of public administration. We have noted how public interest was established, demands made and legislation introduced firstly by local government, and secondly by central government. The problems relating to the type of controls introduced, whether by rigid Acts, specific but changeable bye-laws or functional regulations have been considered, as have the difficulties associated with enforcement. These three elements, *legislation*, *regulation* and *enforcement*, are the basis of any system of building control and they have social and technological implications.[21]

The aim of the building bye-law system, introduced by central government, was to produce the 'sanitary house', a building with sanitary facilities, drainage, ventilation, open space, daylight, sunlight, and walls that gave stability, durability and insulation. These buildings were capable of remaining structural units able to accommodate further improvement thus extending their useful life and allowing money to be invested elsewhere in the local economy. The first important issue is the development of a good working bye-law that achieves its aim, yet permits a tolerance of freedom or flexibility without such a substantial increase in cost as to financially prohibit achieving its aim.

Controlled building brought about an improvement in housing,[22] and the development of the 'sanitary house' by means of building bye-laws contributed to the gradual but significant improvement in the housing and health of working classes.[23] By the turn of the nineteenth century, the housing problem was contained and the motivation to build below standard had been substantially removed.[24] The aim of an improvement in the standard of health was partly achieved by building better houses, as could be seen in the falling urban death rates,[25] but the problem of improving the slum houses erected prior to bye-law control remained.[26] Despite opposition to building bye-laws, they generally achieved their aim, not always eradicating bad building, but certainly reducing the scope for it,[27] and where bye-laws were correctly enforced they ensured that houses were adequately built and healthy to live in.

One aspect that clearly emerges is the need for housing that offers an acceptable degree of protection in respect of health and safety ensuring that the cost of the building does not exceed an acceptable amount when related to construction, rent and profit.[28] This fine balance is frequently thrown out by national economic trends such as the booms and depressions to which the building industry is so vulnerable. Where money has been freely available many excellent building have been constructed, but where this is not available, buildings can become a hazard to the health and safety of their occupants. The area of low cost housing is where this trend is most common.

The extensive expansion of industrial and commercial activity during the Victorian era meant that the same criteria had to be given to the construction of buildings for those purposes and the bye-laws structured to take account of this form of development. Tremendous inroads had to be made to change the type and construction of buildings from local traditional types to the planned approach. This required consideration being given to town layout, infrastructure as well as the buildings themselves, and all within an economic plan. Consequently, many prejudices were uncovered which resulted in obstructions to the development of common and acceptable building standards. Building controls have to be finely tuned, able to respond to both changes in technology and the needs of society. To meet this need, legislation has to be national and mandatory, thus enforcing the enforcing authority to respond by implementing the law. Local discretion, especially of a political nature, is undesirable, as the main issues have been resolved by Parliament.

However, local discretion is not so objectionable when considering the acceptance or otherwise of plans or construction work in meeting the byelaws or regulation requirement. These requirements should be flexible, capable of being changed quickly when needed and adaptable to the widest range of technical solutions. Functional performance-based requirements are the better type to use; specific requirements should be avoided and only used if it is absolutely necessary to ban a hazardous material. All required standards should be capable of being met within known and recognized building methods which take account of traditional as well as scientifically assessed methods. If requirements are clear, easily understood and capable of application, the enforcement is that much easier. There is less likelihood of misinterpretation leading to disputes between designer, construction and builder. To ensure that the flexibility of the system is used to the best advantage of all concerned it is essential that the regulations are administered and enforced by those of a professional standard equal to that of the designer or manager of the construction. It is only through efficient and effective administration that the public benefits of controlled building really emerge (see *Plate 11*). When the factors are out of balance, frustration, argument, indifference and unnecessary expense creep in to generate another incremental adjustment in an attempt to maintain stability. It is alleged that an industry free of constraints would be able to meet the demand for houses,[29] and this also applies to all buildings. Meeting demand is one aspect but producing a building that is less prejudicial to health and safety is another. The consequence of such an approach results in statutory intervention to restore the balance, a balance that on reflection is worth the costs involved.

Many examples have been given in previous chapters where this balance has been tilted by the action or inaction of local authorities. Much of the blame and criticism of inept administration, so forcefully expressed in evidence to inquiries referred to in this book, must be placed squarely on their shoulders. The mere fact that by 1936, 60 local authorities had not adopted a single building bye-law, while many of those that did neither had the desire, or the means, to enforce them, justifies that criticism.

Within the framework of the law these actions were permitted as an exercise of discretionary powers. The government, quite rightly, checked the abuse of these powers, as credibility had to be established within the system of building control. This they did by introducing the Public Health Act 1936, which, although a major piece of legislation, was just another incremental step in maintaining the balance.

Further incremental steps were taken with the Public Health Act 1961 and the Health and Safety at Work Etc Act 1974, both of which increased the powers and involvement of central government, paving the way for an easier acceptance of the more radical measures contained in the Housing and Building Control Act 1984. Consolidation of legislation within the framework of the Building Act 1984, the flexibility of requirement, the recognition of the independent professionalism of Approved Inspectors and the retention of enforcement of local authorities provided a fresh impetus to the maintenance of a building control system adapted to meet the needs of both users and beneficiaries. There are many changes yet to come, and this has to be expected if the legal and technical base of the control system is to keep pace with the changing needs of society. Nevertheless, the system of building control in England and Wales has, since 1840, been generally successful and has stood the test of time.

Appendix 1

The City of Bristol Building Act 1788 – Geo 3 c.66

This appendix does not contain the complete text but provides a résumé of the requirements.

Section	Requirement
1.	Regulations for building external walls. This required that all new walls should be built perpendicular. This would avoid the construction of external walls where the upper storeys oversailed the lower storeys, thus reducing the distance between buildings across narrow streets at upper floor levels.
2.	No bow window to be built or extended beyond the line of the street, except for projections for decoration. This did not apply to the replacement of bow windows.
3.	Regulating the building of party walls. The regulation required that walls built of stone should be 2 feet thick in stone and 18 inches thick in brickwork to the ground floor, 21 inches thick stone and 14 inches brickwork at the first floor, and requiring a 12-inch projection above rake of roof and gutter.
4.	Regulating the building of chimneys. This required 9 inches of non-combustible material between chimneys built back-to-back and 4½ inches of non-combustible material at the back of other chimneys.
5.	Directions concerning jambs and chimneys; a requirement of the size and the extent of chimney press.
6.	A requirement controlling the construction of recesses and chases in party walls.
7.	Regulations of party walls between intermixed properties.
8.	Owners may be compelled to join in building party walls.
9.	Builders to be paid part of the expense according to the verdict. The verdict being related to the appointed surveyors in compelling owners to construct party walls.
10.	Court may fine the sheriff making default, and also any witness making default in any hearings brought before the court.
11.	Old party walls and party arches when decayed shall be rebuilt.
12.	Owners of houses to give three months' notice in writing before pulling down old party walls.
13.	Owners of houses having partitions of wood may give three months' notice to owners of adjoining houses of their design to pull down the frame.
14.	Buildings not having distinct side walls in the manner of building party walls described.

15.	How owners who have built said partitions or party walls are to be reimbursed part of their expense and in what proportions.
16.	Penalty upon master builders etc., acting contrary to the directions of the Act.
17.	Further penalty for allowing the irregularities to continue.
18.	Penalty on the workmen or servants.
19.	The mayor, alderman and common council to appoint surveyor being a discreet person skilled in the art of building as the council may think fit. This appointment was a yearly appointment renewable every year. The surveyors were required to take an oath, this oath being:
	(I), one of the surveyors appointed in pursuance of an Act of Parliament passed in the 28th year of the reign of King George III for regulating buildings and party walls within the City of Bristol and the liberties thereof do swear that upon receiving notice of a building or wall to be built or other builders work done in the district under my inspection, not being by illness or otherwise lawfully prevented, I will diligently and faithfully survey the same, and to the utmost of my abilities endeavour to cause the rules, directions and restrictions in the said Act prescribed, to be strictly observed and that without favour, or affection, prejudice or malice. So help me God.
20.	Surveyors may be displaced.
21.	Rate or classes of building. This section classified four rates as follow:
	i) every house or building not exceeding 9 squares and 30 feet high (a square is 100 square feet);
	ii) every house or building between 5 and 9 squares and 22–30 feet high;
	iii) every house or building between 3 and 5 squares and 13–22 feet high;
	iv) every house or building not exceeding 2 squares and 13 feet high.
22.	Owners to apply to magistrates in case they shall think themselves aggrieved by the surveyor's measurements.
23.	Detached offices deemed of the same rates as any other building.
24.	That master workmen shall give notice of building works to surveyor and fees to surveyors.
25.	Penalty on persons who shall begin any building without giving notice to the surveyor, or neglecting to give notice to the surveyors, or refusing admission to inspect and irregular buildings to be pulled down.
26.	If workmen do not observe the rules of the Act, surveyor to give notices to the justices.
27.	Surveyor to survey and make affidavit of houses being built in conformity with the Act.
28.	Funnels for conveying smoke not to be put on the outside of houses.
29.	Penalty for surveyor neglecting his duty. Maximum £10 fine.
30.	Power to hear and determine offences. This section provided that at least two Justices of the Peace was the minimum to determine offences.
31.	Penalty of witnesses refusing or neglecting to attend mayor or justices.

32. Directing the manner of serving notices.
33. Ascertaining and recovering costs.
34. Application of penalties.
35. Inhabitants may be witnesses.
36. The form of conviction.
37. Persons agreed may appeal to quarter sessions.
38. Limitation of actions.
39. Public Acts.

Appendix 2
The Bristol Building Act 1840 – 3 Vict c.77

This appendix does not contain the complete text but provides a résumé of the requirements.

An Act for regulating buildings and party walls within the City and County of Bristol and for widening and improving of streets within the same.

Section	Requirement
1.	Previous Act repealed.
2.	Contracts etc. to continue, notwithstanding Act repealed.
3.	Monies due under former Act may be recovered under this Act.
4.	Officers under former Act to account (re books, documents, papers and other effects).
5.	Present officers to continue in office until removed.
6.	Act to be put in execution by Mayor, Alderman and Burgesses or by the Council.
7.	An Improvement Committee may be appointed (17 or more persons).
8.	Construction of terms.
9.	Proceedings to be minuted.
10.	Officers to be appointed (as the Council may think proper), and fix salaries, wages and allowances.
11.	Such person not to be clerk or treasurer.
12.	Penalty for officers taking any fee or reward except as prescribed by the Act.
13.	Officers to account.
14.	Buildings within city to be divided into classes as per second schedule.
15.	Rules as to rates of buildings to be affixed as additions to any existing building.
16.	Surveyors to be appointed and districts assigned to them (as the Council thinks proper). Surveyor to make declaration.
17.	Fees to be paid to surveyor (by builder, tradesman, owner or any person causing building or alteration work).

Fees

	New Building	Alterations
First Class	£3.03s	£1.11s.6d
Second Class	£2.10s	£1.05s
Third Class	£2.02s	£1.11s
Fourth Class	£1.10s	£0.15s
Fifth Class	£1.20s	£0.10s

APPENDIX

	Non-payment of fees to be reported by surveyors and summons may be issued by any two Justices of the Peace, penalty may be imposed for non-payment of fees.
18.	Notice to be given to surveyor of the intention to build, alter or work on any party or partition wall.
19.	Penalty for not giving notice of intention to build or repair.
20.	External walls to be carried up perpendicular or as the surveyor may determine. Appeal to the Justices may be made against the determination of the surveyor.
21.	Compensation to be made for building thrown back.
22.	No projection to be erected except in certain cases.
23.	External walls to be constructed of bricks or stone (except lintels, joist ends, internal plates, all of which to be at least $4¼$ inches from the face of the wall).
24.	Party and separate side walls to be constructed of certain materials (fire resisting, $4½$ inches either side of wall).
25.	No cutting to be made in the rough party walls except for communication or for tying in adjoining building or erecting steps etc.
26.	If party wall is defective one owner may give notice to the other requiring the arbitration of two surveyors, and in case of default, may appoint a surveyor.
27.	Mode of building party walls and separate walls.
28.	How owners, who have built partitions or party walls, are to be reimbursed part of their expense and in what proportion. Rates for building party walls.
29.	When building erected over a public way or divided into separate tenements, party arches or party walls to be erected.
30.	Owner of party wall may raise the same under certain restrictions. Adjoining chimneys and flues to be raised.
31.	Backs of chimneys to be pargetted with mortar and openings and hearth stones to be clear of timber.
32.	If building now standing it shall hereafter be built under regulation of this Act.
33.	Gutter may be made to carry off water discharged on the proposed site of a building.
34.	Houses to be roofed but not with boards or thatched (slates, tiles, copper, lead or other incombustible material).
35.	Funnel for conveying smoke not to be erected next to any road or nearer to any timber than 14 inches.
36.	Names of streets and numbers of houses to be put up.
37.	Penalty for erecting buildings contrary to the directions of the Act. Further penalties for suffering irregularities to continue (sum not exceeding £20).
38.	Penalty on surveyor for neglect of duty (£20 maximum).

Sections 39–75 relate to street widening, improving, compensation, and purchase of houses and lands.

76.	Nuisances by persons in public streets.
77.	Prohibition of other nuisances.

Sections 78–97 relate to monies, mayoral duties and administration.

The second schedule of the Act defined the class of buildings as follows:

First Class: Chapel or place of worship, brewery, distillery, manufacturing of whatever height or extent of frontage, or every dwelling or other building exceeding 44 feet high or 27 foot frontage.

Second Class: Every dwelling or building including walls, fences, etc., not exceeding 44 feet high or 27 foot frontage.

Third Class: As Second Class, not exceeding 36 feet high, and not exceeding 21 foot frontage.

Fourth Class: As above not exceeding 32 feet high and 15 foot frontage.

Fifth Class: Not exceeding 15 feet high and any frontage.

The schedule gave thickness of external walls and party walls and backs of flues, chimney backs in party walls and external walls. For example, in a third class building, external and party walls were required to be 1½ bricks thick in the cellar and first floor, and 1 brick thick for the rest, whilst if constructed of stone, the thickness would be 1 foot 10 inches and 1 foot 6 inches respectively. The backs of flues etc. were required to be 1 brick thick. The schedule described the footings required to the base of the wall on First and Second Class buildings, and a 5 inch projection on the remaining classes, apart from internal walls where the projection could be 4½ inches.

Appendix 3
The Liverpool Improvement/Building Act 1825 – 6 Geo 4 c. 75

This appendix does not contain the complete text but provides a résumé of the requirements.

Section	Requirement
1.	Future buildings erected or altered according to regulations.
2.	Every building contrary to be declared a common nuisance.
3.	Buildings deemed nuisances to be taken down by order of Justices and material sold to defray expenses.
4.	Court of Quarter Session to appoint surveyors skilled in the art of buildings (these surveyors would not be surveyors of the Corporation of Liverpool). Surveyors appointed to take an Oath of True and Impartial Execution of Office. The Oath to read: (I) being one of the surveyors of buildings appointed in pursuance of an Act of Parliament passed in the sixth year of the reign of King George IV entitled an Act for the Better Regulation of Buildings in the Town of Liverpool, do swear I shall diligently, impartially and faithfully execute the said Office of Surveyor of Buildings and to the utmost of my abilities cause the provisions and regulations in the said Act to be strictly observed and without favour, affection, prejudice and malice to any person or persons. So help me God.
5.	Notice of building to be given to surveyor of district.
6.	No notice if only door or window opening.
7.	In case surveyor of district cannot attend, the surveyor of another district may do so.
8.	Salary of surveyors, to be paid by Mayor and bailiffs and burgesses of Town of Liverpool such sum as the Justice of the Peace of the Quarter Sessions may think so.
9.	Penalty on persons neglecting to give notice of building or alterations or refusing inspection to be £20.
10.	Surveyor to give information on buildings or acts constructed contrary to the Act. A Notice may be issued as a result of two Justices declaring a common nuisance.
11.	Persons inadvertently making default in conforming with Regulations, no action taken where surveyor had not given notice to the Justices within 10 days of default, provided that default does not affect the safety of the building.
12.	Penalties on workmen.
13.	Buildings or alterations to be surveyed within 14 days of completion. Surveyor to make oath of satisfactory completion to the Mayor or Justice of the Peace.

14. Surveyors neglecting to do their duty could be fined a sum of £20 following which they would be incapable of being re-appointed a surveyor.
15. No timber to support chimney breast.
16. No projection into street except shop windows of certain dimensions.
17. Openings in external walls to be supported according to direction of surveyors.
18. Water from buildings to be conveyed to drains. No smoke to be discharged from fronts of buildings.
19. How pipes for conveying water shall be laid.
20. Cellar openings to be covered.
21. Thickness of side walls in case parties cannot agree to erect party walls.
22. Party walls becoming decayed.
23. Expenses of party walls.
24. Certain buildings exempted from the operation of the Act (warehouses and other buildings over 18 foot from the street and churches of the Church of England).

Appendix 4
Bill for Regulating Buildings in Large Towns – 3rd May 1841

This appendix does not contain the complete text but provides a résumé of the requirements.

Section	Requirement
1.	Bill for the council of every borough which is within the Acts passed for the regulation of Municipal Corporations in England and Wales, Scotland and Ireland, shall within six months of passing the Bill appoint surveyor or surveyors of buildings to be responsible for a district in the borough and who may have assistant surveyors.
2.	Surveyors to make a declaration: 'That I will diligently, faithfully and impartially perform the duties of my office to the utmost skill and endeavour to cause the said Act for the regulation of building in the borough to be strictly enforced without fear, favour or malice towards any person whomsoever'.
3.	Council to provide an office for the surveyor. The cost to be paid by surveyors out of the fees provided.
4.	Commissioners shall be authorized to act for the borough in Oxford.
5.	Commissioners to be authorized to act for the borough in the hamlets of Duddleston and Nechells in the Parish of Aston near Birmingham.
6.	Surveyors to be entitled to fees as set out in schedule.
7.	Three days before any party wall, outside wall or chimney back of any building is pulled down, built or rebuilt, notice to be given to the surveyor by the builder.
8.	Surveyors to act where notice has not been given. Any irregularities to be notified to the Justice of the Peace, or in Scotland the Sheriff, who shall cause irregularities to be amended.
9.	Where the surveyor of a district cannot attend a building site, a surveyor of another district may do so.
10.	Surveyor to give notice of any defect to owner/occupier, master builder, workman or any other person employed. Any defects nor corrected within 48 hours, notification be given to Justice of Peace, or Sheriff, who shall cause an inquiry into that contravention and if confirmed cause the removal or amendment of the contravention.
11.	Buildings and alterations being inspected within one month of completion and a declaration be given stating that the building is in conformity with the Act.
12.	Penalty on builder for neglecting to give notice.
13.	Penalty on workmen offending.

14.	Penalty on refusing surveyor permission to inspect.
15.	Houses not to be built below the level of the ground without areas, such areas being open and not less than 3 feet wide from the floor of such room to the top of the area adjoining the front or back of the property.
16.	Occupation of cellars in houses may be used as a storehouse or warehouse, not to be used for habitation if cellar does not have a window, chimney and open space.
17.	Occupation of cellars already built/penalties in respect of contravening Sections 16 and 17.
18.	House not to be built back-to-back. Not applicable to corner houses, nor to any buildings in a street which was laid prior to the passing of the Act. Rear space between back-to-back of any other house but not applicable to any back addition or outbuilding belonging to either house, the height of the extension being limited to half height of the wall and not to extend more than two thirds along the back.
19.	Regulation of street widths, 30 foot between houses, 20 foot in the case of alleys and foot passages where there is no carriageway.
20.	Houses not to be built in close alleys except mews and stables.
21.	Floor levels to be at least six inches above the level of footway or road adjoining such houses.
22.	Regulating height of rooms in small houses. Eight foot and not less than 7 foot in the other storey.
23.	Only one storey may be constructed in the roof of a building.
24.	Yards and necessary houses to be provided to small houses. Privy to be properly fenced from public view. Yard to be enclosed. Maximum area covered by outbuildings one sixth of the yard area.
25.	All buildings erected contrary to the Act to be abated. A report submitted to the Justice of the Peace or Sheriff who may authorize the alteration or removal of the offending building.
26.	Neglect or evasion of Act.
27.	Future buildings in towns not within local Building Acts to be according to this Act. Provisions for securing against fire.
28.	Buildings to be distinguished as in Schedule A.
29.	Rules to the rates of additions to existing buildings.
30.	Regulations as to rates as buildings, heights of walls.
31.	Regulations as to outer walls. To be built of stone or brick being bonded with a good mortar of one-to-three cement sand mix.
32.	Openings in outer walls of shops or warehouses to be supported according to direction of surveyors. Brick or stone arches, iron cradling, lintels or bressummers over 10 feet span be provided with posts.
33.	Mode of building party walls and separate side and end walls. Party wall brick or stone. Any timbers in the wall to be nine inches away from other timbers.

APPENDIX

34. Party walls to be carried through and above roof as to form a parapet not less than 12 inches high measured perpendicular from the gutter and right angles from the roof.
35. Thickness at back of flues and chimney openings. No flue nearer than 9 inches to face of a party wall or 4½ inches to any other flue or chimney opening. Thickness of back of chimney one and a half brick (13½ inches) in cellars or 8½ inches in any other case.
36. Timber not to be within nine inches of any chimney opening or flue.
37. Construction of chimney openings. Arch of brick or stone or bar of iron over every chimney opening.
38. Ovens and furnaces to have protecting walls. Refers to bakers, smiths or other tradesmens' furnace: wall thicknesses a minimum of 9 inches.
39. Heights of chimney shafts. Not to exceed 6 foot above roof or 22 inches wide unless built back-to-back. May be in excess of this height if secured with straps approved by surveyor.
40. Chimneys to be pargetted.
41. The position of flues to be painted on the outer face of buildings adjoining vacant land. The flues to be so painted on buildings adjoining vacant land – painted mark 3 inches wide on party wall (this was to identify the position of flues in order that any timbers in the adjoining property would not be placed in close proximity to that flue).
42. Houses to be roofed with incombustible material (this did not apply to any woodwork in dormer windows).
43. Roof water not to be allowed to drip into street.
44. Projections from the face of the building (this was not applicable to copings and cornices).
45. Regulations as to raising buildings.
46. Adjoining chimneys and flues to be raised. Buildings raised at greater height than adjoining chimneys of smaller buildings to be raised at the expense of the builder or the extended building. Chimney to be as high as extended building.
47. Regulating the mode of cutting into existing party walls.
48. Openings through party walls. (Secured with iron doors.)
49. Notice of cutting through party wall. (Three clear days' notice to the surveyor.)
50. Penalty for improper cutting into party walls.
51. Penalty for fraud in erecting party walls.
52. A notice to be given of intention to build old party walls, arches and partitions.
53. Surveyors to be appointed to view party walls, arches and partitions.
54. Form of notice re party wall and appointment.
55. If walls are certified ruinous by the surveyor, copy of notice to be delivered to owner within three days.
56. Owners thinking themselves aggrieved may appeal to General Quarter Sessions.
57. Powers of penalties intending to repair or rebuild in default of appeal.

58.	Payment of surveyors of party walls if not condemned.
59.	How owners are to be reimbursed of their expense of building party or partition walls.
60.	How expenses of party walls shall be formed between land owners and tenants.
61.	Persons requiring a wall or a higher rate of building shall build a separate side or end wall.
62.	Regulations as to buildings over passages.
63.	Such buildings as shall be prescribed as nuisances shall be pulled down.
64.	Expenses borne by owner.
65.	Persons taking down and repairing buildings shall set up sufficient fence with platform for foot passengers and to be lit at night. Penalty for neglect.
66.	If chimneys are ruinous, notice may be given by surveyor for repair.
67.	Occupier may deduct the expenses from the rent.
68.	Regulations relating to fire in sheds.
69.	Existing contracts not to be vitiated.
70.	Respecting contracts for leases.
71.	Recovery of penalties.
72.	Persons aggrieved may appeal to Quarter Sessions.
73.	Distress not unlawful for want of form.
74.	Plaintiff not to recover after tender of amends.
75.	Decision of sheriff to be final.
76.	Interpretation.
77.	The Act may be amended.

Appendix 5
Building Regulation Bill No. 2 – Bill No. 371 27th May 1842

This appendix does not contain the complete text but provides a résumé of the requirements.

Section	Requirement
1.	Councils to appoint surveyors.
2.	Declarations by surveyors.
3.	Surveyor's office to be provided.
4.	Fees.
5.	Oxford Commissioners.
6.	Surveyors under Local Acts to be surveyors under this Act.
7.	Buildings and additions to be surveyed.
8.	Penalty.
9.	Penalty for refusing inspection.
10.	Houses below ground.
11.	Occupation of cellars.
12.	Occupation of cellars in buildings already built.
13.	Penalty.
14.	Width of streets.
15.	Level of ground floors.
16.	Height of rooms.
17.	Only one storey in a roof.
18.	Yards to be provided.
19.	All buildings erected contrary to the Act to be altered.
20.	Neglect or evasion of Act.
21.	Height of walls.
22.	Buildings presented as nuisances may be taken down.
23.	Expenses borne by owner.
24.	Persons taking down a building shall construct a fence and platform for foot passengers which shall be lit at night.
25.	Ruinous chimneys.
26.	Occupier may deduct expenses from rent.
27.	Existing contracts not vitiated.
28.	Respecting contracts for leases.
29.	Receiving of penalties.
30.	Persons aggrieved may appeal to Quarter Sessions.
31.	Distress not unlawful for want of form.
32.	Plaintiff not to recover after Tender of Amends.

33. Decision of sheriff final.
34. Interpretation.
35. May be amended.

Schedule granting London and Bristol exemption from the Act.

Appendix 6
The Liverpool Building Act 1842 (5 Vict c.44)

This appendix does not contain the complete text but provides a résumé of the requirements.

Section	Requirement
1.	Repeal of former Act.
2.	Council to appoint a Committee known as a Health Committee.
3.	Surveyors appointed to assist Committee.
4.	This section contained rules for regulating widths of streets.
5.	Houses not to be built in close courts.
6.	Level of ground floors (6 inches above footway adjoining).
7.	Regulating size of rooms.
8.	Only one storey in roof.
9.	Regulating windows (every room provided with at least one window 5 feet by 3 feet wide and 3 square foot in attic rooms).
10.	Cellars in courts not to be occupied as dwellings.
11.	Cellars not to be let as dwellings unless a room height of 7 foot.
12.	Penalties.
13.	Owners of house to provide privy and ashpit for same.
14.	Privies to be provided.
15.	Owners of houses to keep privies and ashpits in repair.
16.	Owners of courts and passages to keep them flagged and in repair.
17.	Private drains, privies, cesspools etc. to be cleaned by occupants.
18.	Provisos.
19.	Nothing to authorize the Council to act in any public or private sewer without consent of proper authorities.
20.	In case any house is filthy and unwholesome in condition magistrates may order same to be cleansed.
21.	In case of tenants opposing execution of Act.
22.	Nuisance bye-laws.
23.	Nuisance bye-laws.
24.	Nuisance bye-laws.
25.	Nuisance bye-laws.
26.	Graves (two feet six inches of soil on top).
27.	Fine on Secton for second offence.
28.	The vaults.
29.	Power to appoint surveyors.
30.	Surveyor to make declaration.
31.	Council to provide officer for surveyors.

32.	Notice of building or repair of building to be given to surveyor.
33.	No notice required for construction of door or window.
34.	Surveyors to act although notice has not been given.
35.	If surveyor of the district cannot act, another may act for him.
36.	Surveyor to give information on buildings or alterations constructed in contravention of the Act.
37.	Buildings or alterations to be surveyed within one month after finished. Declaration to be made of conformity to the Act.
38.	Penalty on builder neglecting to give notice.
39.	Penalty on workmen offending.
40.	Penalty on persons refusing inspection.
41.	All buildings erected contrary to this Act to be altered and to comply.
42.	Fines for neglect or evasion of the Act.
43.	As to persons inadvertently making default of conforming to regulations.
44.	Future buildings to be erected according to this Act.
45.	Buildings distinguished as in Schedule A.
46.	Rules as to the rates of building to be affixed to any existing building.
47.	Regulations as to the rates of buildings, heights of walls etc.
48.	Definition of an outer wall
49.	Regulations as to outer walls (non-combustible materials bedded in mortar of one-to-three cement or lime sand, timbers 4½ inches from face of wall).
50.	Openings in outer walls of shops or warehouses to be supported according to directions of surveyors (arches, lintels, bressummers).
51.	Mode of building party wall and separated side walls (non-combustible materials).
52.	Rules as to thickness of party walls.
53.	Parapets may be formed.
54.	Party walls in Third Class buildings erected prior to 1834 exempt from this Act.
55.	Regulations as to fireplaces and flues (flues 4½ inches from face of wall, timber not nearer than 9 inches to a flue).
56.	Construction of chimney openings.
57.	Ovens and furnaces to have projecting walls.
58.	Height of chimney shafts.
59.	Chimneys and flues to be pargetted.
60.	Flues to be painted externally on the wall which abuts adjoining vacant land.
61.	Sizes of joists, purlins, rafters as per Schedule B.
62.	Of what material houses shall be roofed (slate, tile, glass, copper, lead, zinc or artificial stone or stucco).
63.	Water from buildings to be conveyed to drains.
64.	How pipes shall be laid.
65.	No smoke or steam to be discharged from front of building.
66.	Cellar openings to be secured.
67.	Projections in front of buildings.

APPENDIX

68.	Regulations as to raising buildings.
69.	Adjoining chimney and flues to be raised.
70.	Regulations for and mode of cutting into party walls.
71.	Openings through party walls (how to be made).
72–82.	Sections relating to party walls.
83.	Persons requiring a wall for higher rate of building to build separate end and side walls
84.	Regulations as to buildings over passages.
85.	Corporation empowered to fence off or take down such buildings as may be presented as a nuisance.
86–89.	Hoardings and fences to buildings.
90.	Ruinous chimneys.
91.	Owner may deduct the expense from his rent if there is no agreement.
92.	Fires in sheds.
93–131.	Relate to streets and administration.

An example of the timber sizes quoted in Schedule B:

Floor joists; span 7 foot – 10 foot, 6 inches depth, 2 inches width or equal area, span 10 foot – 12 foot, 6 inches by 2½ inches, span 12 foot – 14 foot, 7 inches by 2½. Rafters 6 foot clear span, 3 inches by 2 inches, 7½ foot clear span, 3 inches by 2½ inches, 9 foot clear span, 4 inches by 2½ inches.

Appendix 7
Structure of Building Bye-laws Made Under Section 34 of the Local Government Act 1858

This appendix does not contain the complete text but provides a résumé of the requirements.

These bye-laws were generally in accordance with the following format:

Section	Requirement
1.	With respect to the structure of walls of new buildings for securing stability in the prevention of fires.

    a) walls of new buildings to be constructed of the thickness specified in the schedule attached and foundations to rest on solid ground or concrete;

    b) external or party walls of new buildings which adjoin any other buildings to be carried up to form a parapet of not less than six inches. Thickness of party walls and backs of chimneys;

    c) incombustible materials to be used in construction of roofs, chimneys, fire-places, etc.

    d) chimneys, fireplaces etc.

2. With respect to sufficiency of space about new buildings to secure free circulation of air and with respect of ventilation of such buildings.

    a) open space to be provided in the rear or at the side of building;

    b) open space not to be built upon afterwards;

    c) windows;

    d) ventilation of rooms;

    e) ventilation (relating to public buildings).

3. With respect to drainage etc.

    a) to provide drains;

    b) construction of drains;

    c) drains, etc. to be trapped and ventilated;

    d) subsoil drains to be provided where necessary;

    e) construction of water closets and privies;

    f) no cess pool to be constructed unless where unavoidable and including mode of construction of cess pools;

    g) ashpits;

    h) buildings unfit for human habitation.

4. As to the giving of notices, etc.

    a) notices to be given of intention to erect new buildings and plans and sections to be deposited;

    b) borough surveyor to inspect works and persons performing works to give notice to the borough surveyor before commencement and completion of same;

c) works not executed in conformity with bye-laws to be pulled down and laid open on receipt of notice from surveyor;

d) notice to be given to surveyor within a month after completion of any works to inspect same;

e) town council may pull down any works not executed in accordance with bye-laws;

f) penalty;

g) offences by workmen.

Appendix 8

Sections 124 to 142 Relating to Building Control Matters St Helens Improvement Act 1869 (32 & 33 Vict.) c. 20

This appendix does not contain the complete text but provides a résumé of the requirements.

Section	Requirement
124.	Rules as to erection etc. of dwelling houses.
125.	Backyards to new buildings.
126.	Buildings and dwelling houses not to be converted so as to provide dwellings in contravention of bye-laws as to dwellings erected after commencement of the Act.
127.	Size of areas of courts, alleys etc.
128.	Level of ground floor.
129.	Only one storey to be in the roof.
130.	Size of rooms.
131.	Elevations of buildings in front land to be subject to approval of corporation.
132.	Penalty on letting buildings contravening Act etc. which no other penalty specifically provided.
133.	Waterspouts to be affixed to houses and buildings.
134.	Regulations as to external walls.
135.	Corporation may regulate height of chimneys.
136.	Prohibition of thatch.
137.	Restrictions as to pipes and funnels for conveying smoke etc.
138.	Respecting existing contracts for building.
139.	Alteration of contracts for building.
140.	Measurement of front elevation.
141.	The corporation may make bye-laws with respect to all or any of the following matters: • With respect to the width, level and construction of new streets and courts, and the provisions for the sewerage thereof; • With respect to the structure of the foundations and walls of new buildings with a view to the prevention of fires; • With respect to the structure of new buildings of public entertainment, for securing efficient means of egress therefrom in case of fire or accident; • With respect to the sufficiency of the space about buildings to secure a free circulation of air; • With respect to windows and the ventilation of buildings; • With respect to the drainage of buildings, and in water closets, privies, cess pools and ashpits in connection with buildings and to their situation;

Provided always that no bye-laws for any of the purposes aforesaid shall affect any building, not being a new building within the meaning of this Act.

The corporation may also make bye-laws with respect to all or any of the following matters:
- With respect to the thickness, material and construction of walls near ovens and furnaces, and of walls of ovens and furnaces not used for manufacturing;
- With respect to the closing of buildings or parts of buildings unfit for human habitation, and to prohibiting the use thereof for human habitation.

And the corporation may provide for the observance of any bye-laws made under this Section by enacting therein such provisions as they think necessary:
- as to the giving of notices;
- as to the deposit of plans and sections by persons intending to lay out new streets or to construct or alter buildings;
- as to inspection by the corporation; and
- as to the power of the corporation to remove, alter or pull down any work begun or done in contravention of the Act or of such bye-laws;

Provided always, that no such bye-laws shall apply to the construction of the new roads authorized to be made by the London and North-Western Railway Company under the powers of 'The London and North-Western Railway Additional Powers Act 1866', or to any building erected or to be erected on any lands belonging to any railway company for the purposes of their undertaking.

142. If the corporation for the space of one month after any plan or section is submitted to them for their approval neglect to notify their determination with reference thereto in writing to the person submitting the same, the Corporation shall be deemed to have approved of such plan or section.

Appendix 9
Model Building Bye-laws 1st Series (Local Government Board 7th Annual Report, 1877/78, Appendix A, p. 86)

This appendix does not contain the complete text but provides a résumé of the requirements.

The subject contents of the Model Bye-laws 1877 were as follows:

Section	Requirement
1.	Interpretation.
2.	Exempted buildings.
3-8.	Related to streets.
9.	Buildings not to be erected on filled sites impregnated with faecal matter.
10.	Over sites – 6 inches of concrete.
11.	Walls of bricks, stone or other incombustible material – bonded with cement joints.
12.	Cross wall as external walls.
13.	Walls not to project overall unless arch feature.
14.	Walls bonded angle.
15.	Walls to rest on proper footings.
16.	Walls to rest on solid ground on concrete or solid sub-structure.
17.	DPCs of slate, lead, ash fault or other durable material impervious to water.
18.	Heights of storeys and walls and length of walls.
19.	Thicknesses of walls of domestic buildings.
20.	Wall thickness of public or warehouse buildings.
21.	Cross wall thicknesses.
22.	Walls of stone.
23.	Opening size in walls.
24.	Wood frames in warehouse class.
25.	Building with 15 feet of other buildings.
26.	Party walls.
27.	Parapets.
28.	No openings in party walls.
29.	No recesses in party walls.
30.	Chases.
31.	No wood in party walls.
32.	Bressummers or joists in party walls.
33.	Girders.
34.	Bressummers.
35.	Openings in walls.
36-52.	Chimneys and flues.

APPENDIX

53.	Front open space.
54.	Rear open space.
55.	Sufficient number of windows.
56.	Under floor ventilation.
57.	One window per habitable room.
58.	Rooms without fireplaces to have air brick.
59.	Public buildings to be provided with adequate ventilation.
60–66.	Drainage.
67–89.	Privies, ashpits, WCs, cess pools.
90.	Closing of buildings or part unfit for human habitation.
91.	Details to be submitted.
92.	Building plans.
93.	Notices to surveyors.
94.	Notices of contravention by surveyor.
95.	Access to site for surveyor.
96.	Completion notice re streets.
97.	Completion notice re buildings.
98.	Penalties.
99.	Persons receiving contravention notice may on a duly appointed day show the local authority why the work did not contravene or need to be pulled down. If the local authority is not satisfied, they are empowered to remove, alter or pull down the work.

Appendix 10

Model Building Bye-laws 1899
Additional bye-laws that could be made by local authorities who had adopted the provisions of the Public Health (Amendment) Act 1890

This appendix does not contain the complete text but provides a résumé of the requirements.

Section	Requirements
1.	Interpretation.
2.	Exemption.
3.	Secondary means of access (for removal of refuse – Section 23 PHAA of 1890).
4.	Sized and spans of timbers used in roofs of ordinary construction.
5.	Timbers of certain roofs not within preceding bye-laws (extra strength).
6.	Roof battens.
7.	Laying and fixing of slates or tiles.
8.	Sizes of timbers to be used in the construction of floors or ordinary construction.
9.	Timber sizes used in floors not within the preceding bye-laws.
10.	Floors of public buildings and warehouse (7 inches deep × 2½ inches wide timber would be permissible to span between 10–12 feet).
11.	Bridging or strutting of joists.
12.	Thickness of floorboards 7/8 inches thick or ¾ inches in sleeping rooms.
13.	Hearths.
14.	Staircase (required to have a minimum of 8 inches tread and a maximum of 9 inches rise) be provided with a handrail, the thickness of the strings to be 1¼ inches, thickness of tread 1 inch thickness, of riser ¾ inches.
15.	Staircases of public buildings and warehouses.
16.	Heights of rooms 8 foot 6 inches – rooms with a roof to have a room height of 9 feet of an area equal to 2/3 of the floor area measured at a height of five feet.
17.	Paving of yards and open spaces in connection with dwelling houses.
18.	Open spaces – 150 square foot to be paved.
19.	WCs provided with flushing cisterns and water supply.
20.	Deposit of plans for streets.
21.	For preventing buildings which have been erected in accordance with bye-laws from being altered in such a way as not to comply with those bye-laws.
22.	Notice of intention to alter buildings including the deposit of plans and sections.
23.	Notice of commencement of work.

APPENDIX

24. Notice to amend work (by surveyor). Notice of completion of amendments.
25. Inspection of work in progress.
26. Inspection on completion of work.
27. Penalties of £5 and 40s a day for continuing offences.
28. Power to pull down work.

Appendix 11
Model Building Bye-laws – Rural Series

This appendix does not contain the complete text, but provides a résumé of the requirements.

These byelaws were limited to the following items: Interpretation – exempted buildings – structure of walls and foundations of new buildings for the purposes of health – over sites to be covered in concrete – DPCs to be provided in walls – parapets to be coped – space to be provided about buildings – drainage – WCs – earth closets– privies – ash pits – cess pools – water supply to cisterns WCs – notices, plans and inspection of building works – alterations and additions – penalties – repeal.

There was a reprint in 1928 whereby information contained in memoranda were included in the bye-laws and there was an alteration to the form of bye-law on intercepting traps. Shorter and clearer clauses were introduced with some explanatory footnotes. These amendments took into consideration suggestions from local authorities and professional bodies.

Appendix 12
Model Building Bye-laws Series 4 Urban – 1912

This appendix does not contain the complete text but provides a résumé of the requirements.

Section	Requirement
1.	Interpretation.
2.	Exempted buildings. Added to the list of exempted buildings were buildings used for the treatment of tuberculosis, and partial exemption was granted for domestic outbuildings.
6–12.	Relate to street bye-laws.
13.	New buildings or foundations of any building not permitted on a site which has been filled with material impregnated with faecal matter, animal and vegetable matter.
14.	On damp sites the whole ground surface within the external walls of the building to be properly asphalted, or covered with a layer of concrete at least 6 inches thick or 4 inches thick if properly grouted.
15.	Sites which had been excavated. The ground floor to be elevated as to prevent dampness.
16.	Low-lying sites. Building sites to be built up to a level related to the Ordnance Survey datum level.
17.	External and party walls, including hollow external walls.
18.	Walls to be true and plumb.
19.	Return walls and piers to be bonded.
20.	Foundations of walls and piers.
21.	Construction of footings.
22.	DPCs to walls (6 inches above ground level).
23.	Rules of measurement for walls and storeys.
24.	Thickness of walls – domestic (minimum 8½ inches thick).
25.	Thickness of walls – public and warehouse class building.
26.	Thickness of cross walls 2/3 of that required by previous bye-laws (minimum 8 ½ inches thick).
27.	Walls of materials other than bricks (stonework to be at least 1/3 thicker than brick walls).
28.	Openings in external walls.
29.	Party walls to extend up to roof – slates etc. to be solidly bedded in mortar or cement on top of the wall.
30.	Parapets to external walls of certain buildings.
31.	Parapets to be coped.

32.	No openings in party walls.
33.	Recesses in external and party walls.
34.	Chases in walls (maximum 4 inches deep, maximum 14 inches wide in 8½ inch wall – 13½ inches from other chases and 13½ inches from return walls).
35.	Timber in party walls.
36.	Templates under bressummers.
37.	Materials for chimneys.
38.	Construction of chimneys.
39.	Chimney flues to be pargetted inside.
40.	Outside of flues to be rendered (where less than 8½ inches thick).
41.	Brickwork about certain flues to be extra thick.
42.	The support of chimney breast above opening.
43.	Jambs of chimney openings (8½ inches wide).
44.	Thickness of brickwork about chimney flues (minimum 4 inches thick).
45.	Thickness of chimney backs (4½ inches and 8½ inches thick).
46.	Thickness of brickwork in certain flues (not less than 45 degrees 8½ inches thick).
47.	Minimum height of chimneys above roof (3 feet).
48.	Maximum height of chimneys (6 times width).
49.	Metal joist holders not nearer to flues than 2 inches.
50.	Timber not to be nearer to flues than 9 inches.
51.	Face of certain brickwork about chimneys to be rendered (2 inches from any timber).
52.	Openings in chimneys.
53.	Roof covering (allows use of combustible material if building is twice its height away from boundary).
54.	Open space in front of new buildings (minimum 24 feet).
55.	Open space at rear of new buildings (minimum area of 150 square feet at a depth of 15 feet where the height of the building is less than 25 feet – 20 feet where the building height is less than 35 feet and 25 feet where the building height is less than 50 feet).
56.	Windows to be provided.
57.	Ventilation of space beneath lowest floor.
58.	Window to habitable rooms to be of a size equal to 1/10th of the floor area, half of which shall be capable of being opened.
59.	Ventilation of rooms without fireplaces (provision of air bricks to give ventilation area of 100 square inches).
60.	Drainage of sub-soil.
61.	Drainage materials.
62.	Drains to be trapped from the sewer.
63.	Ventilation of drains.
64.	No drainage inlet within buildings.

APPENDIX

65.	WCs.
66.	Earth closets.
67.	Ashpits.
68.	Movable ashpits.
69 and 70.	Cess pools.
71.	Existing buildings – ashpits, WCs, privies and cess pools.
84.	Water supply for WC cistern.
85.	Notice and plan of new streets.
86.	Notice and plan etc. of intended new building.
87.	Notices etc. (24 hours' notice in writing at commencement, covering up sewer, drain, foundations and DPC – provisions to serve notice to open up – notice to be given of completion of alterations or amendments – surveyor to have access to building – notice of completion).
88.	Surveyors' assistants to have access to building works.
89.	Alterations and extensions to buildings.
90.	Penalties.
91.	Work done in contravention of bye-laws may be removed, altered, or pulled down.
92.	Repeal of previous bye-laws.

Appendix 13

Model Bye-laws – Issued from the Ministry of Health – XVIII –Means of Escape from Fire in Certain Factories and Workshops – 1935

This appendix does not contain the complete text, but provides a résumé of the requirements.

The Factory and Workshop Act of 1901 (Section 15) empowered town councils, urban district councils and rural district councils to make bye-laws providing for means of escape from fire in factories and workshops. Section 14 of that Act dealt with factories and workshops in which more than 40 persons were employed, and therefore the model bye-laws were confined to factories and workshops in which not more than 40 persons were employed. The Act also required that the means of escape from fire provided in compliance with the bye-laws were to be maintained in good condition and free from obstruction.

Bye-laws

Section	Requirement
1.	Interpretation.
2.	Bye-laws not to apply to any factory or workshop in which more than 40 persons were employed.
3.	Rules relating to the construction of a new building or alteration in form of structure of an existing building. a) an adequate staircase or flight of stairs; b) staircase to be constructed of incombustible fire resisting material; c) where more than 10 persons were employed or readily inflammable materials or explosives are stored or used, an external staircase be provided, or similar external means of escape or access to the roof and to the roof of the adjoining building; d) rooms in which persons are habitually employed which are above the ground storey or on the ground storey and where there is not direct and unimpeded access to open space on the outside of the building, those rooms shall have at least one window or other means of exit from the building; e) windows or other means of exits shall be distinctively marked; f) window or door or other means of access to any external staircase or flight of stairs shall be distinctively marked;
4.	Persons not to begin to use building as a factory or workshop until it has been adapted to comply with the rules.
5.	Owner of a building which is used as a factory or workshop at the date of the confirmation of the bye-laws shall execute all works as necessary to make the factory or workshop comply.
6.	Penalties.
7.	Repeal of previous bye-laws.

APPENDIX 14

The Public Health Act 1936 (16 Geo. 6 & 1 Edw. 8 c.49). Sections of the Act, in addition to Section 64, which enabled local authorities to refuse, or conditionally approve deposited plans.

This appendix does not contain the complete text, but provides a résumé of the requirements.

1. Section 25. Plans that indicated a building or extension would be built over a public sewer. Approval could be given and the local authority could impose conditions. This power was a consolidation of the powers of Section 26, Public Health Act 1875 which was applicable to urban areas and had been extended to other areas in 1931.
2. Section 43. Plans that do not show satisfactory sanitary closet accommodation consisting of one or more water or earth closets as the local authority may require unless they are satisfied that they may properly dispense with this requirement. This Section replaces Section 35 of the Act which was later amended by the 1907 Act.
3. Section 53. Plans of a building which show that a building will be constructed using materials which are short lived or unsuitable for permanent construction. This Section is new in form and substance but based on Section 27 of the Public Health Act 1907 and similar provisions in local Acts. This Section provided local authorities with control over temporary type buildings by either refusing the plans or using discretion to approve fixing conditions in a time limit as to the use of the building may be put.
4. Section 54. Refusal of plans showing a building to be erected on land which had been filled with faecal or animal or offensive material unless the local authority is satisfied that the material in question has been rendered innocuous. This Section replaced Section 25 of the Public Health Act 1890 which gave independent control not related to the deposited plans. This provision could be adopted by rural authorities. In addition, the Ministry Model Bye-laws of the 1935 addition contained a similar provision which could be adopted in areas where Section 25 of the 1890 Act was not enforced.
5. Section 55. Plans of a house or extension to a house that did not show satisfactory means for the removal of refuse and faecal matter would be refused. This Section did not apply to houses that had been approved by the Minister in respect of housing operations to which Section 99 of the Housing Act 1925 applied, being local authority housing or Housing Association or Trust

Development. This was another example of a provision exempting local authority housing from building control. Some local authorities had made bye-laws in respect of refuse removal under the Public Health Act 1890 but these were now repealed.

6. Section 59. Plans which did not show that buildings or extensions to buildings would have satisfactory entrances and exits, passageways and gangways could be refused. This Section applied to buildings used for public purposes, such as theatres or halls of public resort, restaurants, shops, stores or warehouses, to which members of the public were admitted and where more than 20 persons were employed, and clubs required to be registered under the Licensing (Consolidation) Act 1910, schools not exempt from the building bye-laws, and churches, chapels or other places of public worship. The provisions of this Section could be applied to existing buildings. This Section replaced Section 36 of the Public Health (Amendment) Act of 1890, where the provisions of this Act could be applied independently but did not relate to the deposit of plans. Furthermore, the provision did not apply to rural districts although those districts could adopt the section. It could also have been put in force in a rural authority by order of the Ministry of Health. To some extent, this provision did also accommodate some of the views expressed by the Royal Commission of Fire Brigades and Fire Prevention.

7. Section 137. Where plans did not show that a house would be provided with a supply of wholesome water sufficient for domestic purposes they could be refused. This Section was a new provision based upon Section 6 of the Public Health (Water) Act of 1878, but unlike that Section, this provision extended to urban and rural areas.

Appendix 15
Model Building Bye-laws, Ministry of Health, July 1937

This consisted of 55 pages of 129 bye-laws and two schedules.

Part 1: Introduction
1.	Interpretation
2.	Application
3.	Total exemptions
4–7.	Partial exemptions

Part 2: Buildings
8.	Bricks and Blocks
9.	Cement
10.	Sand
11.	Water
12.	Mortar
13.	Aggregate
14.	Damp-proof course
15.	Structural steel
16.	Timber
17.	Other materials
18.	Application of materials
19.	Sites
20.	Prevention of damp
21.	Elevation of sites
22.	Foundations (Buildings)
23.	Foundations (Walls)
24.	Foundations (Piers)
25.	Structural walls
26.	Domestic exemptions
27–31.	Walls
32.	Buildings (n.e. 3 storey)
33.	Warehouses
34.	Hollow walls
35.	Timber in hollow walls
36.	Damp-proof courses
37.	Walls of housing
38.	Rules for walls

39–44.	Thickness of walls, reinforced walls – piers, recesses, bays, cross walls
45.	Walls built of stone
46–48.	Chases and openings in masonry walls
49.	Bressummers
50.	Over hanging
51.	Bonding
52.	Coping
53.	Party walls
54–77.	Chimneys and flues
78.	Height of chimneys
79.	Short-lived materials
80.	Front open space
93.	Rear open space
94.	Access width
95.	Buildings abutting two streets
96.	Measurement lower storey
97.	Unobstructed space
98.	Stables
99.	Alterations to buildings
100.	Ventilation
101.	Courts
102.	Ventilation of lower floor
103.	Larders
104.	Ventilation of rooms exc. flues
105.	Ventilation of staircases
106.	Height of rooms
107–109.	Drainage
110.	WCs
111.	Urinals
112.	Earth closets
113–114.	Ashpits
115.	Cesspools
116.	Tanks for trade effluent
117.	Wells
118.	Water tanks and cisterns
119–121.	Other fittings
122.	Giving of notices, etc.
123.	Notice/plan for drainage
124.	Plans in duplicate
125.	Notices to surveyor
126.	Signature and giving notice
127.	Penalties

APPENDIX

128.   Prescribed period
129.   Repeal of bye-laws

Schedule 1: Loading
Schedule 2: Permissible stresses

Appendix 16
Model Building Bye-laws 1952 & 1953

Model Bye-laws 1952 Ministry of Housing and Local Government
Bye-laws prepared with the assistance of the Building Bye-laws Advisory Committee. Representing the RICS, Mr G. Biscoe; representing RIBA, Mr C.S. White; representing the IAAS, Mr S.D. Studd; and representing the I.Mun.E, Mr J. Chadwick.
This consisted of 36 pages of 116 bye-laws, and 5 schedules.

Part 1: Introduction
1.	Interpretation
2–6.	Application of bye-laws, plans, notices etc.
7–12.	Exemptions

Part 2: Buildings
13–14.	Materials
15–18.	Sites
19–21.	Foundations
22–27.	Load-bearing requirements
28–31.	Walls, resistance to weather and damp
32–33.	Fire resistance
34–38.	Fire resistance of small houses
39–42.	Buildings other than small houses
43–45.	Separating and fire division walls
46.	Fire resistance of floors, columns, etc.
47–50.	Fire resistance of walls
51–52.	Roofs
53–68.	Chimneys, flues, and hearths
66–73.	Factory chimney shafts
74–78.	Space about buildings
79–82.	Ventilation
83.	Dimensions of rooms
84.	Thermal insulation of houses
85–99.	Drainage
100.	Earth closets
101–103.	Sanitary conveniences
104–105.	Ashpits
106–107.	Cesspools
108.	Wells

109.	Water tanks and cisterns
110–113.	Fireplaces, stoves and other fittings
114–116.	Miscellaneous
Schedule 1:	Giving of plans and notices
Schedule 2:	Calculation of loading
Schedule 3:	Rules for walls
Schedule 4:	Notional periods of fire resistance
Schedule 5:	Spans for timber sizes

Model Bye-laws 1953. Ministry of Housing and Local Government, July 1953

Substantially a reprint of the 1952 edition. This consisted of 80 pages of 111 bye-laws, and 4 schedules.

Amendments resulted in the removal of clauses that had not been adopted by local authorities and placing them in an appendix together with one or more other clauses which local authorities had used beneficially.

The reprinted model allowed for fire resistance to walls being based on British Standard fire tests in place of the standard published in 1932 and to substitute the new timber economy memorandum for the fifth schedule which had been based on an earlier memorandum. A few alterations in the drafting were made, and the fourth schedule, relating to fire resistance of floors, was extended.

Clauses moved to appendices covered elevation of sites, factory chimney shafts, ashpits, habitable rooms over garages and stairs for flats.

Appendix 17
The Building Regulations 1965, 1972, 1976

The Building Regulations 1965

Statutory Instrument 1965 No. 1373
This was made 6th July 1965 and came into operation 1st February 1966. It was made up of 15 parts with 11 schedules.
Part A: General – 14 regulations dealing with application and administration
Part B: Materials – 5 regulations regarding the suitability of materials
Part C: Preparation of site and resistance to moisture – 10 regulations
Part D: Structural Stability – 17 regulations
Part E: Structural Fire Precautions – 16 regulations
Part F: Thermal Insulation – 7 regulations. Applicable to dwellings only
Part G: Sound Insulation – 4 regulations. Applicable to dwellings only
Part H: Stairways and Balustrades – 6 regulations
Part J: Refuse Disposal – 4 regulations. Applicable to dwellings only
Part K: Open Space, Ventilation and Height of rooms – 8 regulations. Dwellings only
Part L: Chimneys, flue pipes, hearths and fireplace recesses – 21 regulations
Part M: Heat producing appliances and incinerators – 10 regulations
Part N: Drainage, private sewers and cesspools – 17 regulations
Part P: Sanitary conveniences – 4 regulations
Part Q: Ashpits, wells, tanks and cisterns – 3 regulations
11 schedules relating to partially-exempted buildings, giving of notices and depositing plans, relaxation and dispensation and standard of compliance.
These regulations were amended on seven occasions:
1st 10/01/1966 SI 1965 No. 2148
2nd 01/11/1966 SI 1966 No. 1144
3rd 15/12/1967 SI 1967 No. 1645
4th 01/07/1969 SI 1969 No. 639
5th 01/04/1970 SI 1970 No. 109
6th 01/11/1971 SI 1970 No. 1335
7th 01/11/1970 SI 1971 No. 1600

The Building Regulations 1972

Statutory Instrument 1972 No. 317
This was made 29th February 1972, and came into operation 1st June 1972. It was comprised of 15 parts and 12 schedules

Parts A–Q: as the 1965 Regulations. Part A increased to 16 regulations, Part D increased to 21 regulations, Part L increased to 22 regulations, and 1 additional schedule.
These regulations were amended on three occasions:
1st 31/08/1973 SI 1973 No. 1276
2nd 31/01/1975 SI 1974 No. 1944
3rd 01/12/1975 SI 1975 No. 1370

The Building Regulations 1976

Statutory Instrument 1976 No. 1676
This was made 7th October 1976, and came into operation 31st January 1977.
It was comprised of 14 parts and 12 schedules.
Parts A–P followed the 1965 and 1972 regulations. Part A increased to 16 regulations. Part B reduced to 4 regulations, Part D increased to 20 regulations, Part E increased to 23 regulations, Part F reduced to 4 regulations, Part G increased to 6 regulations, Part H increased to 7 regulations, Part M increased to 11 regulations, and Part Q relating to ashpits, wells, tanks and cisterns was deleted.
These regulations were amended on four occasions:
1st 01/06/1979 SI 1978 No. 723. Introduced new Part FF: Conservation of Fuel and Power in Buildings other than Dwellings plus a new schedule 11A.
2nd 01/12/1981 and 01/04/1982 SI 1981 No. 1388. Introduced new Part Q: Control of space and water heating systems, new Part R: Thermal insulation of pipes, ducts and storage vessels, and added 2 further regulations to Part F.
3rd 31/03/1983 SI 1983 No. 195 Introduced new Part S: Toxic substances (control of urea-formaldehyde foam in cavity walls).
4th 01/08/1985 SI 1985 No. 488 Introduced new Part T: Facilities for disabled persons.

Appendix 18
The Building Regulations 1985; The Building (Approved Inspectors etc.) Regulations 1985

The Building Regulations 1985

Statutory Instrument 1985 No. 1065
This was made 11th July 1985 and came into operation 11th November 1985. It comprised 20 regulations and 4 schedules. Nineteen regulations referred to application and administration by a local authority. Regulation 4 required that all building work to which the regulations applied had to comply with the requirements of the 1st and 2nd schedules.

Schedule 1 comprised of 9 parts:
Part A: Structure A1 Loading; A2 Ground Movement; A3 Disproportionate Collapse
Part B: Fire B1 Means of Escape; B2–4 Internal and external fire spread
Part C: Site preparation and resistance to moisture; C1–4
Part D: Toxic Substances D1 – Cavity insulation
Part E: Resistance to the Passage of Sound E1–3 Airborne and impact sound
Part F: Ventilation F1 Ventilation; F2 Condensation
Part G: Hygiene G1 Food storage; G2 Bathrooms; G3 Hot water; G4 Sanitary Conveniences
Part H: Drainage and Waste Disposal H1–3 Drainage; H4 Solid Waste Storage
Part J: Heat producing appliances J1 Air supply; J2 Discharge; J3 Protection of Building
Part K: Stairways, Ramps and Guards K1 Stairways/Ramps; K2 Protection; K3 Barriers
Part L: Conservation of Fuel and Power L1–3 and L5 Insulation; L4 Heating Controls

Schedule 2
Facilities for disabled people

The Building (Approved Inspectors etc.) Regulations 1985

Statutory Instrument 1985 No. 1066
This was made 11th July 1985 and came into operation 1st September and 11th November 1985. It was comprised of 10 parts and 8 schedules.
Part 1: General
Part 2: Grant and withdrawal of approval
Part 3: Supervision of work by Approved Inspectors
Part 4: Plans Certificates
Part 5: Final Certificates
Part 6: Cessation of Effect of Initial Notice

Part 7: Public Bodies
Part 8: Certificates Relating to Deposited Plans
Part 9: Registers
Part 10: Effect of Contravening Building Regulations

The Building Regulations 1985 were amended on two occasions (1987 and 1989), prior to being replaced by The Building Regulations 1991; The Building (Disabled People) Regulations 1987 SI 1987 No. 1445; The Building Regulations (Amendment) Regulations 1989 SI 1989 No. 1119; The Building Regulations 1991 SI 1991 No. 2768.

Appendix 19
Legislative Growth of Building Bye-law Powers

This appendix does not contain the complete text, but provides a résumé of the requirements.

Local Government Act 1858, Section 34

i) Structure of walls of new buildings for securing stability and prevention of fire.
ii) Space about buildings so as to secure a free circulation of air and with respect to ventilation of buildings.
iii) Drainage of buildings, WCs, privies, ashpits and cess pools.
iv) Giving of notices, deposit of plans, inspection of work.

Public Health Act 1874

Extended to walls, roofs, foundations and waterspouts for purposes of health.

Public Health Act 1875

As above, but extended to cover chimneys.

Public Health (Amendment) Act 1890

Extended to cover floors, hearths, staircases and height of rooms, water supply to WCs.

Public Health Act 1936

i) construction of buildings including materials.
ii) space – lighting and ventilation.
iii) height of buildings, chimneys.
iv) sanitary conveniences and drainage of buildings.
v) wells etc.
vi) sewers.

vii) stoves etc.
viii) existing buildings.
ix) change of use.

Public Health Act 1961

Section 4: Power to make building regulations.
Section 5: Application to building regulations of statutory provisions concerning building bye-laws.
Section 6: Relaxation of building regulations.
Section 7: Appeals.
Section 8: Advertisement of relaxation proposal.
Section 9: Consultation with Building Regulation Advisory Committee.

Fire Precautions Act 1971

Section 11: Power to make building regulations as to the provision of means of escape in case of fire.

Health and Safety at Work etc. Act 1974

Section 62: Further matters for which building regulations may provide.
Section 65: Continuing requirements.
Section 66: Type relaxation.
Section 67: Power of Secretary of State to approve types of building.
Section 68: Power to require tests.
Section 79: Power to make building regulations for Inner London.

Building Act 1984

Section 1: Power to make building regulations.
Sections 2–135: Consolidation of provisions contained in the above Acts.

Notes to the text

Introduction pp xiv–xvi
1. Knowles, C.C. and Pitt, R.H. (1972). *The History of Building Regulations in London 1189–1972.* London: Architectural Press.
2. The Building Act 1984, c.55.
3. Harper, R.A. 'Evolution of the English Building Regulations'. (Unpublished PhD thesis, University of Sheffield, 1978, number 4316.)
4. Harper, R.A. (1985). *Victorian Building Regulations, Summary Tables of the Principal English Building Acts and Model Bye-laws 1840–1914.* London: Maxwell Publishing Ltd.
5. Gaskell, S. Martin (1983). *Building Control – National legislation and the introduction of local bye-laws in Victorian England.* London: Bedford Press.

Chapter 1: The Building Regulation Bill 1841–1842: Antecedents and Failure pp 1–19
1. For example, Entwhistle refers to the Babylonian Code of Hammurabi (2200 BC) in which the death penalty was imposed on any builder who constructed a building which collapsed and caused the death of an occupant. Entwhistle, F.D. (1974). *Building Regulation, Practice and Procedure*, p.3. London.
2. Knowles, C.C. and Pitt, P.H. (1972). *The History of Building Regulations in London 1189–1972*, p.6. London: Architectural Press.
3. The London Building Act 1667, 9 Car. II c.3.
4. Knowles and Pitt *op. cit.* (note 2), p.44.
5. Cave, L.F. (1981). *The Small English House*, p.143. London: Robert Hale.
6. The London Building Act 1772, 12 Geo. III c.73.
7. The London Building Act 1774, Geo. III c.78.
8. An Act for the Better and More Easy Rebuilding the Town of Northampton 1675, 27 Chas. II.
   Act for the Rebuilding of the Town of Warwick 1694, 6 and 7 Will. III c.1.
   An Act for the Better and Easy Rebuilding of the Town of Wareham 1763, 3 Geo. III.
   An Act for the Better and Easy Rebuilding of the Town of Chudleigh 1808, 48 Geo. III c.89.
   An Act for the Better and More Easy Rebuilding of the Town of Blandford 1731, 5 Geo.
   An Act for the Better and More Easy Rebuilding of the Town of Tiverton 1731, 5 Geo.
9. Calais Paving Act 1548, 2 & 3 Edw. VI c. 38.
10. An Act for Regulating Buildings and Party Walls Within the City of Bristol 1778, 28 Geo. III c.66.
11. Chambers, J. (1985). *The English House*, p.176. London: Guild Publishing.
12. An Act for Regulating Building and Party Walls within the City and County of Bristol

and Widening and Improvement of Streets within the Same 1840, 3 Vict. c. 77.
13. The fees prescribed by the Act were:

	Building			Alterations		
1st class	£3	3s	0d	£1	11s	6d
2nd class	£2	10s	0d	£1	5s	0d
3rd class	£2	2s	0d	£1	1s	0d
4th class	£1	10s	0d		15s	0d
5th class	£1	1s	0d		10s	0d

14. The sectional headings of this Act are given in *Appendix 2*. The Act also required street names and numbers to be displayed, a feature of other town improvement Acts later in the century.
15. James Newlands, 1813–1871. Civil engineer appointed under the Liverpool Sanitary Act of 1846. Became Associate of the Institution of Civil Engineers in 1848 and a member in 1857.
16. Newlands, J. (1858). *Liverpool Past and Present*, p.11. A paper presented to the Health Section of the National Association for the Promotion of Social Science in October 1858.
17. An Act for the Better Regulation of Buildings in the Town of Liverpool 1825, 6 Geo. IV c.25.
18. Gaskell, S. Martin (1983). *Building Control – National legislation and the introduction of local bye Laws in Victorian England*. London: Bedford Press.
19. Pelling, M. (1978). *Cholera, Fever and English Medicine 1825–1865*, p.32. Oxford.
20. Checkland, S.G. (1964). *The Rise of Industrial Society in England 1815–1895*, p.27. London.
21. Buer, M.C. (1926). *Health, Wealth and Population in the Early Days of the Industrial Revolution*, p.31. London.
22. Southwood-Smith, Thomas, MD. 1788–1861. Presented reports to the Poor Law Commissioners on preventable sickness among the poor (1835–39). Founder member of Health of Towns Association (1840), and of the Metropolitan Association (1842). Gave evidence to Health of Towns Commission in 1844, member of Board of Health (1848), becoming a permanent member in 1850 on leaving private practice. Wrote recognized works on quarantine (1845), cholera (1850), yellow fever (1852), and sanitary improvements (1854).
23. Report as to the removal of some causes of disease by sanitary regulations. *Poor Law Commissioners 4th Annual Report*, 1838, Appendix A, No. 1. House of Commons Papers P.P. Vol. 28, pp 62–96.
24. Pelling, M. *op cit.* (note 19), p.252.
25. Gauldie, E. (1974). *Cruel Habitations*, p.103. London.
26. Slaney, Robert John, 1792–1862. MP for Shrewsbury in 1826. Often raised the issue of poor law reform and moved the appointment of a committee for enquiring into the condition of the labouring classes. Chairman of the Committee on the Health of the Poor Classes in Large Towns in 1849 and was an active commissioner on the Health of

Towns Commission from 1843–1846.
27. House of Commons Papers, Vol. 2, 1840, p.384.
28. Cubitt, Thomas, 1788–1855. Master carpenter who also undertook house building. Member of the Institution of Civil Engineers. Gave evidence on a number of House of Commons committees and took a leading part in the preparation of the Metropolitan Building Act of 1844. Concerned about the sewage of the metropolis, and also with smoke nuisance from large chimneys.
29. House of Commons Papers, Vol. XI 1840, p.383.
30. Ibid.
31. Macdonagh, O. (1977). *Early Victorian Government*, p.20. London.
32. Phipps, Constantine Henry, 1st Marquis of Normanby, 1797–1863. Entered Parliament as MP for Scarborough in 1819. Supported Lord John Russell's proposals for parliamentary reform. Re-entered Parliament in 1822 as MP for Higham Ferrers. Became Lord Lieutenant of Ireland in 1835 and Secretary of War and the Colonies in 1839.
Normanby was summoned by the Queen to form a Government in 1839 but was unable to do so and returned to the Colonial Office. Later transferred to the Home Office until 1841, from which he introduced the Building Regulation Bill.
33. *Hansard*, 3rd ser., vol. 41, 1293. Report of the Third Reading of the Bill, 30th April, 1841.
34. Gauldie, *op cit.* (note 25), p.104.
35. The headings of the 77 clauses are set out in *Appendix 4*.
36. Municipal Corporation Act 1835, 5 & 6 Will. IV c.76.
37. *Hansard*, 3rd ser., vol. 58, 1300.
38. *Hansard*, 3rd ser., vol. 60, 94.
39. *Hansard*, 3rd ser., vol. 61, 316.
40. Building Regulation Bill 1842, No. 33, Vol. 1, p.257.
41. Building Regulation Bill No. 2 1842, No. 52, Vol. 1, p.319. Hansard, 3rd ser, vol. 63, 884.
42. The fees proposed by the Bill were:

First Rate	£3.10s	Fourth Rate	£2.00s
Second Rate	£3.00s	Fifth Rate	£1.00s
Third Rate	£2.10s	Sixth Rate	£1.00s

43. This committee was empowered to report the minutes of the evidence taken before them to the House. Fifteen persons gave evidence, including Richard Kelsey, surveyor to the Commissioners of Sewers for the City of London and previously a district surveyor in the City of London; Joseph Franklin, surveyor to Liverpool Corporation; William Scott, Master of Works, Dundee; and Ebenezer Robbins and John Kempson, both surveyors from Birmingham.
44. *Hansard*, 3rd ser., vol. 64, 635.
45. Building Regulation Bill 1842, No. 371, Vol. 1, p.367.
46. The sectional headings of the bills are given in *Appendix 6*.
47. Gauldie, E. *op. cit.* (note 25), pp.117–118.
48. Macdonagh, O. *op. cit.* (note 31), pp.18–19.
49. Gauldie, E. *op cit.* (note 25), p.115.

50. Gaskell, *op cit.* (note 18), p.13.
51. Burnett, John (1978). *A Social History of Housing 1815–1970*, p.24. Cambridge: Cambridge University Press.
52. *Hansard*, 3rd ser. Vol. 65, 356.
53. Gauldie, *op cit.* (note 25), p.104.

Chapter 2: Local Improvement Acts and the Health of Towns pp 20–34

1. Report on the Sanitary Conditions of the Labouring Population of Great Britain 1842 by the Poor Law Commissioners. Edwin Chadwick, Secretary to the Poor Law Commissioners and Barrister at Law – 14th July 1842.
2. See Chapter 1 this book, p.12.
3. *op. cit.* (note 1), p.16.
4. Ibid.
5. Loudon, John Claudius, 1783–1843. Landscape gardener and horticultural writer. Author of essay on 'Observations on Laying Out Public Squares', published *Encyclopaedia of Gardening* in 1822 and *Encyclopaedia of Cottage, Farm and Villa Architecture* in 1832.
6. Vetch, James, 1789–1869. Captain, Royal Engineers. Joined Royal Engineers in 1805 undertaking military engineering work. Resident engineer for Birmingham and Gloucester Railway from 1836–1840, designed sewage system for Leeds in 1842 and engaged on drainage works for Windsor in 1843. Appointed Consulting Engineer to the Admiralty in 1846, retiring in 1863. Author of *Structural Arrangement Most Favourable to the Towns* (1842), and also several works on engineering relating to railways, harbours and sewage.
7. *op. cit.* (note 1), p.328.
8. Ibid., p.282.
9. Ibid., p.282.
10. Ibid., p.282.
11. Ibid., p.329.
12. Dyos, H.J. (1908). The Speculative Builders and Developers in Victorian London, *Victorian Studies*, XI, supplement p.650.
13. Muthesius, S. (1982). *The English Terraced House*. London: Book Club Associates. Page 34 refers to a cartoon in *Punch*, dated 11th October 1890.
14. *op. cit.* (note 1), p.328.
15. Ibid., p.329.
16. Ibid., p.330.
17. Ibid., p.333
18. Ibid., p.287
19. *Hansard*, 3rd ser, vol. 73, 393.
20. Macdonagh, O. (1977). *Early Victorian Government*, p.9. London.
21. The Liverpool Building Act 1842, 5 Vict. c.44, Sections 49–61. Mortar used in the construction of walls was required to be one part of cement or lime to three of sand. Structural timber: a 6" × 2" floor joist had a maximum acceptable span of 10 feet, a 6"

× 2½", 12 feet, and a 7" × 2½", 14 feet, whilst rafter sizes of 3" × 2" were restricted to a 6'0" span – other sizes of structural timber were similarly controlled.
22. The Bristol Building Act 1847, 10&11 Vict., c. 129, 2nd July 1847.
23. Newcastle Improvement Act 1837, 7 Will. IV and 1 Vict. c.172.
24. Leeds Improvement Act 1842, 5–6 Vict., Cap., 104.
25. Hole, J. (1866). *The Homes of the Working Classes*, p.35. London: Longman Green & Co.
26. Ibid., p.129.
27. Gauldie, E. (1974). *Cruel Habitations – A History of Working Class Housing 1780–1918*, p.104. London.
28. Gauldie, E. *op cit.*, p.127.
29. Ibid., p.128.
30. Ibid., p.125.
31. Town Improvement Clauses Act 1847, 10&11 Vict. c.34.
32. *Hansard*, 3rd ser., vol. 74, 541. Lord Normanby in question to the Duke of Buccleuch.
33. Health of Towns Commission Enquiry into the State of Large Towns and Populous Districts, 1845. Second Report. House of Commons Papers, 1845, Vol. 18, p.1.
34. House of Commons Papers, 1845, vol.18, p.1.
35. Ibid., p.57.
36. Gaskell, S. Martin (1983). *Building Control – National legislation on introduction of local byelaws in Victorian England*, p.15. London: Bedford Press.
37. House of Commons Papers, 1845, vol. 18, p.59.
38. House of Commons Papers, 2nd Report of the Health of Towns Commission, 1845, p.19–20.
39. Gauldie, E. *op. cit.* (note 27), p.104.
40. *Hansard*, 3rd ser., vol. 82, 1076.
41. *Hansard*, 3rd ser., vol. 91, 617.
42. Public Health Act 1848, 11&12 Vict. c. 63.

Chapter 3: The Local Government Act 1858 and Building Bye-laws pp 35–44

1. Cooper, Anthony Ashley. Seventh Earl of Shaftesbury 1801–1885. Entered Parliament in 1826 as Lord Ashley MP for Woodstock and in 1831 to 1846 for the county of Dorset. In 1834 became a lord in the admiralty. Interested in the Lunacy Acts, reform of law for workers in mines and factories, children working in mines and the treatment of chimney sweep apprentices. In 1847 as MP for Bath he visited the slums of London which intensified his interests in the improvement of the dwellings of the people. Chairman of the Central Board of Health and chairman of the Sanitary Commission for Crimea.
2. Finer, S.E. (1952). *The Life and Times of Sir Edwin Chadwick*, p. 350. London.
3. Ibid., p. 431.
4. Lewis, R.A. 1952. *Sir Edwin Chadwick and the Public Health Movement*, p.302. London.
5. Ibid., p.302.
6. Finer, *op. cit.* (note 2), p.432.
7. Toulmin-Smith, Joshua, 1816–1869. Publicist and constitutional lawyer. Called to the

Bar in 1849. Called attention to health matters during the 1847 outbreak of cholera, particularly in his home area of Highgate. His practice then concentrated on local responsibilities. When proposals were made to raise sanitary conditions and municipal life in London he spoke and wrote on the subject and objected to the Public Health Act of 1848.
8. Toulmin-Smith, J. (1851). *Local Self-government and Centralisation*, p.207–208. London.
9. Ibid., p.12.
10. Ibid., p.3.
11. Richardson, B.L. (1887). *Health of Nations: A review of the works of Chadwick*, p.178–191. London.
12. Wright, L. (1960). *Clean and Decent*, p.204. London.
13. Calder, J. (1977). *The Victorian Home*, p.87. London: Book Club Associates.
14. NobleTwelvetrees, W. (Ed.)(1923). *Rivingtons Notes on Building Construction – Part III Materials*, 7th edn, p.337. (Revised 1910.) London: Longman Green & Co.
15. Hellyer, S. S. (1884). *The Plumber and Sanitary Houses*, 3rd edn., p.9. London.
16. Local Government Act 1858, 21&22 Vict. c. 98.
17. Public Health Act 1858, 21&22 Vict. c. 97.
18. *Laissez-faire*. A French phrase used to characterize a particular type of policy which left social and economic matters to the free operation of private enterprise. In this case, the freedom to adopt and enforce building bye-laws was left to the discretion of local authorities.
19. Perkin, H. (1969). *The Origins of Modern English Society 1780–1850*, p.33. London.
20. Simon, Sir John 1816–1904. Officer of Health to City of London 1848–1855. Medical Officer to Privy Council 1878–1879. President of Royal Society 1877–1880.
21. Toulmin-Smith, J., *op cit.* (note 8), p.230.
22. Gaskell, S. Martin (1983). *Building Control – National legislation and the introduction of local byelaws in Victorian England*, p.24. London: Bedford Press.

Chapter 4: The Growth of the Building Bye-law System pp 45–68
1. Burnett, S. (1978). *Social History of Housing*, pp 21. Cambridge: Cambridge University Press.
2. Ibid., p.16.
3. Wright, L. (1960). *Clean and Decent*, 2nd edn, p.106. London.
4. Borough of Barnstaple Building Byelaws, 1875, bye-law 20.
5. Hellyer, S.S. (1877). *Water, Air and Light*, p.192. London.
6. Borough of Brighton Building Byelaws, 1866, bye-law 69.
7. Gaskell, S. Martin (1983). *Building Control – National legislation and introduction of local byelaws in Victorian England*, p.26. London: Bedford Press.
8. Stockton Improvement Act 1869, 32&33 Vict. c.73. An Act for extending the boundaries of Stockton – consolidating and amendment Acts in force in relation to the management of and improvement of streets, to sewage of buildings, to police and other workings of local government.

9. St Helens Improvement Act 1869, 32&33 Vict. c.20. An Act to repeal the St Helens Improvement Act of 1855 and to constitute the Corporation for improving and governing the Borough.
10. Annual Report of the Local Government Board 1873, St Helens, as one of the 73 local authorities who during 1873 adopted building bye-laws under the provisions of the Local Government Act 1858.
11. Gaskell, *op cit*, (note 7), p.38.
12. Hole, J. (1866). *The Homes of the Working Classes*, pp 8–9. London: Longman Green & Co.
13. Pridgin-Teale, Thomas, MA, Hon DSc, FRS, 1831–1923. Senior Surgeon Leeds Public Dispensary. Developed interests in public health and preventing sickness. Published works: *Dangers to Health; Economy in Coal Fires – Principles of Fireplace Construction; Dust and Fresh Air, How to Keep One Out and the Other In*. Member of the General Medical Council 1876–1907.
14. Pridgin-Teale, T. (1878). *Danger to Health: A pictorial guide to domestic sanitary defects*. Commentary to plate 50. London: J&J Churchill.
15. Public Health Act 1890, 53&54 Vict. c.59.
16. *Journal of the Royal Agricultural Society of England*, 52, 1892. A paper presented to the Journal by Dr T. Pridgin-Teale following a meeting held on October 29th, 1892. The paper was produced at the request of Earl Cathcart, Chairman of the Journal Committee.
17. Ibid., p.26.
18. Simon, J. (1893). *English Sanitary Institutions*, p.470. London.
19. Cave, L.F. (1981). *The Smaller English House*, p.227. London: Robert Hale.
20. Housing (Building Construction) Committee, Cd 9191, 1918, p.4.
21. Gauldie, E. (1974). *Cruel Habitations – A history of working class housing 1780–1918*, p.195. London.
22. Tarn. J. (1971). *Working Class Housing in the 19th Century*, p.43. London.
23. Public Health Act 1866, 29&30 Vict. c. 40.
24. Dutton v. Bognor Regis District Council 172 (QB373) and Anns v. Merton London Borough Council [1977] 2WLR 1024. These two law cases held that local authorities were under a duty to give proper consideration to carrying out their building control duties. In doing so they must discharge that duty with reasonable care and the standard of care had to be related to the duties to be performed, namely to ensure compliance with regulations (bye-laws). As a result of these two cases, many local authorities have been sued for damages in respect of negligently carrying out their building control duties.
25. Lambert, R. (1963). *Sir John Simon and English Social Administration*, p.391. London.
26. Stewart, A.P. and Jenkins, E. (1867). *Medical and Legal Aspects of Sanitary Reform*, p.97. London. Reference to a recommendation (No. 4) of a memorial to the President of the Privy Council, the Duke of Marlborough, by the National Association for the Promotion of Social Science.

NOTES

27. 2nd Report of the Royal Sanitary Commission 1871, C 281, Vol. 35, Vol. 1 (the report), p.1.
28. Adderly, Sir Charles Bowyer. 1st Baron Norton 1814–1905. Sought to develop his property along enlightened principles. He helped to plan the street layouts to avoid slums and could be said to be the father of town planning. MP for North Staffordshire in 1841, retiring in 1872. Advocate of local self-government. Responsible for first Local Government Act, inventing the term 'local government'. Chairman of Sanitary Commission in 1871 and President of Board of Health 1874.
29. *op cit.* (note 27).
30. Ibid. Nuisances Removal and Disease Prevention Act 1848; Public Health Act 1848; Public Health Act 1848; Lodging Homes Act 1850; Common Lodging Act 1857; Vaccination Act 1853; General Board of Health Act 1854; Disease Prevention Act 1855. Nuisances Removal Act 1855; Local Government Act 1858; Public Health Act 1858; Public Health Act 1859; Nuisances Removal Act 1860; Vaccination Act 1861; Nuisances Removal Act 1866; Sanitary Act 1866; Sewage Utilisation Act 1867; Sanitary Act 1868; Sanitary Act 1870.
31. Ibid., p.16.
32. Ibid., p.16.
33. Ibid., p.218–219.
34. Ibid., p.241.
35. Gauldie, *op. cit.* (note 21), p.122.
36. *op. cit.* (note 27), p.32.
37. *op. cit.* (note 27), p.335, evidence of J. Liddle.
38. Local Government Board Act 1871, 34&35 Vict. c.70.
39. Lambert, *op cit.* (note 25), pp 515–516.
40. Public Health Act 1872, 35&36 Vict. c. 79.
41. *Hansard*, 3rd ser, vol. 277 (29th May 1873), 2nd reading of the Bill.
42. *Hansard*, 3rd ser, vol. 209, p. 1886.
43. *Hansard*, 3rd ser, vol. 219, p.925, 2 June 1974.
44. The addition of controls on roofs and rainwater were not retained, as there were controls that came into operation after the RSC had reported. Accordingly, they were not incorporated in the recommendations. They were discarded in the process of consolidation.
45. The Public Health Act 1875, 38&39 Vict. c. 55.
46. *Hansard*, 3rd ser, vol. 222, 11th February 1875.
47. *Hansard*, 3rd ser, vol. 223, 19th April 1875, 2nd Reading of the Bill.
48. *Hansard*, 3rd ser, vol. 224, 25th May 1875, Committee Stage.
49. Public Health Act 1875, 38&39 Vict. c 157.
50. Ibid. Section 158. Where the authority incurred expense in the removal of faulty work the cost could be recovered from the person who caused the contravention. These powers would not be available in respect of contraventions which occurred 12 months or more before action for removal was taken by the authority.

51. Ibid. Section 157.
52. Ibid. Section 160.
53. Ibid. Section 25.
54. Ibid. Section 36. The provision of a water or earth closet, privy or ashpit was compulsory. These were powers retained from the Public Health Act 1848.
55. Fraser, W.M. (1950). *A History of Public Health 1834–1939*, p.177. London: Bailliere, Tindall & Cox.

Chapter 5: Bye-laws and the Anti-bye-law Lobby pp 69–89
1. The Royal Commission on the Housing of the Working Classes, 1885, C 4402.
2. *Rivingtons Series of Notes on Building Construction Part 3 – Materials*, pp 164 and 173, (1923). London: Longman, Green & Co.
3. *Knights Annotated Byelaws*, 8th edn, p.93. (1928). London: Charles Knight.
4. Cowan, H.J. (1972). *Science and Building*, p.33. New York.
5. Ibid., p.36.
6. Ibid., p.33.
7. *op. cit.* (note 1), para. 13952.
8. Ibid., para. 13944. Evidence of E. Chadwick.
9. Ibid., para. 8393. Evidence of J. Lawes, Surveyor, responsible for enforcing by-laws in Newcastle-upon-Tyne.
10. 'Jerry-builder'. A term given to bad builders derived from a nautical term 'jury rigged', which referred to the temporary rigging of a sail on a boat. Quite often jury rigging was not done well, and was never successful as a properly rigged sail.
11. Ibid., para. 8393.
12. Ibid., para.12367. Evidence of J. Chamberlain.
13. Ibid., paras. 8855, 12858, 13958.
14. Ibid., paras. 3003, 12927, 52021.
15. The Public Health Amendment Act 1890, 53&54 Vict. c 59.
16. See *Appendix 10* for list of bye-law headings.
17. *Hansard*, 3rd ser., vol. 346, 1233. In reply to Captain Verney who referred to meetings being held in rural areas often in upper floors of buildings where life was endangered due to gas lighting and narrow staircases.
18. The Royal Sanitary Commission 1871, vol. III, C 281–II. Minutes of Evidence, paras. 8471/2 and 8492, evidence of J. Clutton Esq. – paras. 8050/1–8109. Evidence of J. Knowball Esq., Chief Agent to the Duke of Northumberland – para. 7867/9 – 794. Evidence of Lord Penhryn.
19. Green, J.L. (1899). *English Country Cottages*. London: The Rural World Publishing Co. Ltd.
20. Hole, J. (1866). *The Homes of the Working Classes*, p.87. London: Longman Green & Co.
21. Ibid., p.56.
22. Powell, C.G. (1980). *An Economic History of British Building Industry*, p.49. London: Architectural Press.

NOTES

23. Green, *op. cit.* (note 18), p.202.
24. Daunton, M. (1983). *House and Home in the Victorian City*, p.37. London: Edward Arnold.
25. Lucas, R.M. (1906). *Anti-building Byelaws*. Contains articles and correspondence generated by the published articles in 1905.
26. Ibid., p.9.
27. Ibid., p.12.
28. Refers to letters from Lord Carrington in *The Times* and Mr E.W. Lemon in *The Country Gentleman*.
29. Chance, Sir William (1914). *Building Bye-laws in Rural Districts*, p.2. London: King & Son.
30. Lucas, R.M. *op cit.* (note 25), p.17.
31. Chance, *op. cit.* (note 29), p.5.
32. Circular letter from the Local Government Board dated 5th January 1906. The circular makes reference to a survey carried out amongst rural districts as to the type of model bye-laws they had adopted. The survey is contained in 'Byelaws in Rural Districts', p 272, Session 1905.
33. Chance, *op cit.* (note 29), p.4.
34. Ibid., p.5.
35. *Hansard*, 3rd ser, Vol. 143, 1650 (1st reading 30th March 1905).
36. Chance, *op. cit.* (note 29), p.8.
37. *Hansard*, 3rd ser, Vol. 151, 590 (8th August 1905).
38. *Hansard*, 3rd ser, Vol. 154, 518.
39. Ibid., p.519.
40. *Hansard*, 3rd ser, Vol. 156, 1419 (10th May 1906).
41. Chance, *op. cit.* (note 29), p.8.
42. The Public Health (Amendment) Act 1907, Edition 7, Cd 53, 28th August 1907.
43. The Departmental Committee on Building Byelaws 1981, Cmnd 9213. The report on p.15 refers to evidence given by GL Sutcliffe FRIBA, MRSI, Architect for Co-partnership Tenants Ltd.
44. The Departmental Committee on Building Byelaws 1981, p.9214, Minutes of Evidence, p.153. Evidence of T.Alwyn-Lloyd FRIBA Architect. Paras. 3338, 3339, 3343.
45. *op cit.* (note 42), Section 24.
46. Ibid., Section 27.
47. Ibid., Section 30.
48. Perkins, H. (1969). *The Origins of Modern English Society 1780–1880*, p.321. London.
49. The Housing and Town Planning etc. Act 1909, 9 Edw. c 44, 18th August 1909.
50. *Hansard*, 3rd ser., Vol. 12, 1638.
51. Ibid., 1639.
52. The Education (Administrative Provisions) Bill 1911, First Reading 1st March 1911. Second Bill presented 25th May 1911.
53. *Hansard*, 3rd ser, Vol. 29, 2206 – 11th August 1911 – objection by Mr Booth.

A HISTORY OF BUILDING CONTROL IN ENGLAND AND WALES 1840–1990

54. Ibid., Vol. 41, 1912. Bill was entitled The Housing of the Working Classes No. 2 Bill.
55. Ibid., 1912.
56. Local Government Board Circular dated 29th August 1912.
57. *Hansard*, 4th ser, Vol. 50, 452, 13th March 1913.
58. Ibid. Vol. 53, 469, 13th February 1914 – reference to the Housing of the Working Classes Bill 1914.
59. Ibid. Vol. 59, p.2388, 20th March 1924.
60. Muthesius, S. (1983). *The English Terraced House*, p.37. London: Book Club Associates.

Chapter 6: Committees, Commissions and Circulars pp 90–111

1. The committee members were: The Rt. Hon. J. Herbert Lewis MP, Sir Randolph L. Baker MP, A.E. Collins Esq., The Hon. Eustace Pienaes MP, E.J. Cowan Esq., E.V. Kelly Esq., W. Jerred Esq. CB, F.R. Harding-Newman, Esq., J. Pointer Esq., W.T. Postlewaite Esq., Raymond Unwin Esq., Henry Vivian Esq. On the 29th October 1917, Stephen Walsh MP, Col. Sir A. Griffith-Boscowan MP, Major David Davies MP, and W.E. Hart, Town Clerk of Birmingham, were appointed to replace the Rt. Hon. J. Herbert Lewis, Major Sir Randolph L. Baker, Major the Hon. Sir Eustace Pienaes Bt. MP, and E.V. Milly, previously Town Clerk of Birmingham. Report on the Departmental Committee on Building Byelaws 1918, Cd 9213, p.2.
2. Ibid.
3. Ibid., p.232, paras. 4989–4990.
4. Ibid., p.11, para. 24.
5. Departmental Committee on Building Byelaws 1981, Cmnd 9214 Minutes of Evidence, p.263, para. 5703.
6. Ibid., p.308, para. 6775.
7. Ibid., p.307, paras. 6760–6762.
8. *The Builder* (October 26th 1918), *CXV*: 3951, p.1.
9. *op. cit.* (note 1), p.11, para. 21.
10. *op cit.* (note 5), p.263, para. 5711 and p.295, para. 6475.
11. Ibid., p. 300.
12. Ibid., p. 278.
13. *op. cit.* (note 1), p.17, para. 36.
14. Ibid.
15. Gaskell, S. Martin (1983). *Building Control – National legislation and the introduction of local byelaws in Victorian England*, p.49. London: Bedford Press.
16. *op. cit.* (note 5), p.59.
17. *op. cit.* (note 1), p.18, para 42. It was considered that the availability of the LGB to determine differences would be a speedier process resulting in minimal delays in the progress of building work.
18. Ibid., p.42, para. 110.
19. Ibid., p.43, para. 114.
20. Ibid., p.44, para. 115.

21. The government had secured powers under the Education (Administrative Provisions) Act 1911 to exempt educational buildings approved by the Board of Education. Exemption had already been recognized in model bye-laws whereby the bye-laws did not apply to Crown buildings, lunatic asylums, prisons, buildings associated with canals, rivers, docks and harbours and mining workings; buildings approved by the Board of Agriculture, Land Commissions or Agricultural or Fisheries Department, or buildings approved by or in pursuance of any statutory provision on behalf of one of the principal Secretaries of State; buildings used for the treatment of infectious diseases.
22. *The Builder* (January 16th 1919), *CXVI*, No. 2962, p.48.
23. Housing (Building Construction) Committee Report 1918, Cd 9191, 24th October 1918, p.3.
24. Walters, Rt. Hon. John Tudor. 1868–1933. MP for Brightside division of Sheffield 1906 and for Penaryn and Falmouth 1929–1931. Postmaster General in 1919–1921 and 1931. Formerly Chairman of the London Housing Board. Chairman of the Housing (Building Construction) Committee 1918. President of the Housing and Town Planning Trust. Author of the book *The Building of Twelve Thousand Houses*, published in 1927.
25. *op. cit.* (note 23), p.28.
26. Burnett, J. (1978). *A Social History of Housing 1815–1970*, p.221. Cambridge: Cambridge University Press.
27. *Hansard*, 4th ser, Vol. 112, 806, 26th February 1919.
28. The Housing and Town Planning Act 1919, 9&10 Geo. V c.60.
29. *Hansard*, 4th ser, Vol. 116, 896, 26th May 1919.
30. The Housing Act 1923, 13&14 Geo. V c.24.
31. The Housing Act 1925, 15&16 Geo. V c.18, Sections 99 and 101.
32. *Hansard*, 4th ser, Vol. 114, 1742. Sir D. Maclean speaking in the second reading of the Housing Bill 1919.
33. Ibid., Vol. 194, 1364, 22nd April 1926.
34. Ibid., Vol. 251, 1835, 30th April 1931.
35. Report on the Royal Commission on Fire Brigades and Fire Prevention 1923, Cmd 1945.
36. Ibid., p.34, para. 42.
37. Report on the Departmental Committee on Building Byelaws 1918 Cd 9214, Minutes of Evidence, Mr Dolton – Principal of the Legal Department of the LGB, p.1, para. 5.
38. *op cit.*, p.34, para. 42.
39. The Borough of Brighton Building Byelaws 1886, 9th November 1986, Bye-law 21.
40. The Factories and Workshops Act of 1901 required every factory erected after 1892, and workshops erected after 1896, in which more than four persons were employed, to be furnished with a certificate from the local authority that a satisfactory means of escape in case of fire had been provided. Model bye-laws for factories with less than 40 employees were issued by the LGB in 1906 (see *Appendix 13*). However, up to 1919 only 52 urban authorities had adopted such bye-laws, a mere four per cent of the total number of authorities eligible to make and enforce such bye-laws (by December 1922 the number was 71). Even where enforced, the bye-laws did not make satisfactory

provisions for safety. In 1920, 379 fires occurred, resulting in complete suspension of work at some factories and 22 fatalities being reported to the Factory Department. Yet, despite the appalling record of local authorities in enforcing the provisions of the 1901 Act, the Commission recommended that the existing law be strengthened to require local authorities to issue certificates to factories and workshops where more than 20 persons were employed or more than 10 at first floor level. These requirements were to be applied to both new and existing buildings. The Secretary of State had power to make regulations on means of escape which would provide some degree of uniformity between local authorities in their enforcement of such standards. In the event of any alterations, should the building no longer be satisfactory, the local authorities were required to cancel the certificate.

41. Powell, C.G. (1980). *An Economic History of the British Building Industry 1815–1979*, pp. 80, 93. London.
42. Housing financed by a subsidy under the Housing (Additional Powers) Act 1919 and the Housing Act 1923.
43. Ministry of Health Circular No. 332, 1st September 1922.
44. *op. cit.* (note 39), p. 5, para. 30.
45. Ministry of Health Circular, C.46, dated January 1928.
46. Ministry of Health Circular, C.41, 1926.
47. Ministry of Health Circular, C. 343, dated 28th September 1922.
48. Ministry of Health Circular, C.70, dated June 1927.
49. Ministry of Health Circular, C.34A, 1928.
50. *Hansard*, 4th ser, Vol. 280, 2009, 20th July 1933.
51. Memorandum attached to the Ministry of Health Model Byelaws Rural Series 1932.
52. Ministry of Health Circular dated 1st September 1935.
53. Ministry of Health Circular C.46, January 1927.
54. Ministry of Health Circular, 1st September 1935.
55. Ministry of Health Circular C.44, January 1927.

Chapter 7: The Professional Approach pp 112–127

1. Lea, F.M. (1971). *Science and Building – A history of the Building Research Station*, p.13. London: HMSO.
2. The London County Council (General Powers) Act 1909, 9 Edw. VII c. 130.
3. *Hansard* 5th ser., vol. 240, 357, 19th June 1930.
4. Navier's Theory of Bending in 1826 and Euler's Theory of Buckling in 1759 were refined by Rankine in 1857 and Tregold in 1824.
5. Cowan, H.J. (1971). *Science and Building*, p.91. New York.
6. *op. cit.* (note 3), p.567.
7. *op. cit.* (note 1), p.19.
8. Ibid., p. 85.
9. Knowles, C.C. and Pitt, R.H. (1972). *The History of Building Regulations in London 1189–1972*, p.95. London: Architectural Press.

10. Letter to A.J. Ley from the Secretary of the Institution of Municipal Engineers (now merged with the Institution of Civil Engineers).
11. Ibid.
12. Letter from the Secretary of RIBA to A.J. Ley, 9th February 1982.
13. Thompson, F.L. (1968). *Chartered Surveyors – The growth of a profession*, p.181. London: Routledge and Kegan Paul.
14. Local Government Act 1933, 23&24 Geo. V. c. 51.
15. Burnett, J. (1978). *A Social History of Housing*, p.220. Cambridge: Cambridge University Press.
16. Dewsnup, E.K. (1970). *The Housing Problem in England*, p.68. Manchester: Manchester University Press.
17. Second Report of the Royal Sanitary Commission 1871 c. 182 Vol. 35, vol. 1, The report. p. 16.
18. Local Government and Public Health Consolidatory Committee Second Interim Report 1936 Cmd 5059 Minutes of Appointment, p.8.
19. Local Government Act 1933, 23&24 Geo. V. c. 51.
20. *op. cit.* (note 17), p.14.
21. Ibid., p.37.
22. Ibid., p.45.
23. Ibid., p.45.
24. Ibid., p.47.
25. Ibid., p.46.
26. *Hansard*, 5th ser., Vol. 311, 2308, 3rd April 1936.
27. Minutes of Evidence taken before the Joint Committee of the House of Lords and Commons on the Public Health Bill (H.L.) 10th June 1936, p.78, para. 628.
28. *Hansard*, 5th ser., Vol. 101, No. 67, 532, Tuesday 7th July 1936.
29. *Hansard*, 5th ser., House of Lords, vol. 101, No. 67, 532, Tuesday 7th July 1936.
30. Ibid., Vol. 314, 2391, 16th July 1936.
31. Ibid., Vol. 315, 1902.

Chapter 8: Towards a Building Act pp 128–141

1. Lewis, P. (1986). *A People's War*, p.84. London: Methuen.
2. Longmate, N. (1971). *How We Lived Then*, p.134. London: Arrow Books.
3. *Hansard*, ser 5, Vol. 391, 1288, 23 July 1943. Statement by Mr Quibell, MP for Briggs.
4. Ibid., Vol. 398, 321, 15 March 1944.
5. Ibid., Vol. 400, 951, 6 April 1943.
6. Ibid., Vol. 391, 1278, 27 July 1943.
7. Ministry of Works. Ministry of Local Government and Planning (1951). *Housing Manual 1949: Technical Appendices*. London: HMSO.
8. *Hansard*, 5th ser., Vol. 400, 1358, 7 June 1944. Refers to factory housing not complying with building bye-laws or seven Building Acts governing large cities.
9. Ibid., Vol. 410, 974, 26 April 1945.

10. Ibid., Vol. 487, 186, 7 May 1951.
11. Ministry of Housing and Local Government (1953). *Model Building Byelaws 1953*. London: HMSO.
12. *Hansard* 5th ser., Vol. 526, 957, 13 April 1954.
13. Department of Scientific and Industrial Research (1937). Report of the Building Research Board 1936. London: HMSO.
14. Public Health Bill 2nd reading, Vol. 643, 889, 30 June 1961.
15. Public Health Act 1961, 9&10 Eliz.2, c.64.
16. Royal Commission on Fire Brigades and Fire Prevention 1923. Cmd 1945, p.49. London: HMSO.
17. *Hansard* 5th ser., Vol. 595, 875.
18. *Hansard* 5th ser., Vol. 603, 915.
19. The Fire Precautions Act 1971, c.40.
20. Section 9 Factories Act 1959, 7&8 Eliz.2
21. Factories Act 1961, 9&10 Eliz.2, c.34.
22. *Hansard* 5th ser., Vol. 625, 88.
23. *Hansard* 5th ser., Vol. 791, 28.
24. SI 1973 No.1276. The Building (First Amendment) Regulations 1973, which came into effect 31st August 1973.
25. *Hansard* 5th ser., Vol. 657, 106, 10 April 1962.
26. Ibid., Vol. 706, 59, 9 February 1965.
27. Incorporated Association of Architects and Surveyors (1965). *Building Regulations 1968 Practice Notes*. London: Incorporated Association of Architects and Surveyors.
28. *Hansard* 5th ser. Vol. 720, 311, 17 November 1965.
29. Ibid., Vol. 841, 201, 6 July 1972.
30. Ibid., Vol. 841, 1795, 26 July 1972.
31. Ibid., (note 28) Vol. 846, 367, 21 November 1972.
32. Proposals for a Building Bill. Consultative Document. Department of the Environment July 1972.
33. *Municipal Engineering*, 3 November 1972, p.2228.
34. Health and Safety Etc. Act. Ch. 37. HMSO 1974.
35. *Hansard*, 5th ser., Vol. 793, 9, December 1969.
36. Department of Education and Science (1973). *Report on the Collapse of the Roof of the Assembly Hall of the Camden School for Girls*. London: HMSO.
37. *The Daily Telegraph* No. 38544, 9 May 1979, p.1
38. *Building Trades Journal*, 15 September 1978, p.63
39. *Building Design* No. 585, 12 March 1982.
40. Ibid., Vol. 583 p.1, 26 February 1982.
41. The Building (Third Amendment) Regulations 1983. SI 1983 No. 195.
42. Dutton v. Bognor Regis Urban District Council [1971] 2 All. E.R.1003.
43. *Institute of Building Control Officers Journal*, Spring issue 1979, p.9.
44. *Building*, Vol. CCXXXII, No. 21, 27 May 1973 p.47.

NOTES

45. Association of District Councils Circular 1977/80.
46. Command Paper 8179 *The Future of Building Control England and Wales 1981.* London: HMSO.
47. *Building Trades Journal,* 8 February 1980 p.50.
48. *Building Trades Journal,* 18 July 1980, p.7.
49. *Building Design,* 11 July 1980, p.44.
50. *Builder,* 10 August 1979, p.9.
51. The Building (Prescribed Fees) Regulations 1980. SI 1980 No. 286.
52. *Hansard,* 6th ser., Vol. 31, 116. 1st Reading Housing and Building Control Bill.
53. *Hansard,* 6th ser., Vol. 31, 751, 23 November 1982. 2nd Reading Housing and Building Control Bill. 4 November 1982.
54. *Builder,* 10 December 1982, p.27. Article by Peter Jones, Director of Architecture, GLC.
55. *Building Trades Journal,* 22 February 1980. p.7.
56. Ibid., Vol. 184, p.3, 19th August 1982.
57. Ibid., Vol. 184, p.3, 2 December 1982.
58. Ibid., Vol. 185, p.3, 10 February 1983.
59. *Hansard* 6th ser., Vol. 45, 206, 5 July 1983.
60. Ibid., Vol. 65, 663, 24 October 1984.
61. Ibid., Vol. 65, 31 October 1984, p.1389 – Royal Assent.

Chapter 9: A New Beginning pp 142–150

1. Lifting the Burden, Cmnd 9571, July 1984. London: HMSO.
2. The Building Regulations 1985 (SI 1965 No. 1065). London: HMSO 1985.
3. The Building (4th Amendment) Regulations 1985 (SI 1985 No. 488). London: HMSO.
4. *Hansard,* 6th ser., Vol. 89, 13.
5. The Building (Approved Inspectors etc.) Regulations 1985 (SI 1985 No. 1066). London: HMSO.
6. The Building Act 1984 Section 57.
7. Department of Environment Circular 1996, 8th December 1996.
8. *Hansard* 6th ser., Vol. 86, 26, 11th November 1985.
9. *Building Today,* p. 12, 6 July, 1989.
10. Ibid., p.17, 12 July, 1990.
11. *Building,* Vol. CCLV, No. 30, p.28, 27 July 1990.
12. *L.A. Week,* p.8, 30 November 1990.
13. *Municipal Journal,* p.20, 12 May 1989.
14. Ibid., p.6, 5 May 1989.
15. *Hansard,* 6th ser., Vol. 124, 617, 17th December 1987.
16. *Building,* p.12, 7 April 1989.
17. *op. cit.* (note 7) p.5, 13 July 1989.
18. *op. cit.* (note 11) p.16, 27 January, 1989.
19. *op. cit.* (note 7) p.5, 16 January 1989.
20. *Municipal Journal,* 10 June 1988, p.1169.

21. Garnham-Wright, M.J. (1983). *Building Control by Legislation: The UK Experiences. (The Theory and Practice of Building Control)*, p.32. Chichester: John Wiley and Sons.
22. Burnett, J. (1978). *A Social History of Housing 1815–1970*, p.307. Cambridge: Cambridge University Press.
23. *Ibid.*, p.165.
24. Muthesuis, S. (1982). *The English Terraced House*, p.37. London: Yale University Press.
25. Powell, C.C. (1980). *An Economic History of the British Building Industry 1815–1979*, p.63. London.
26. Newsholme, Sir Arthur (1925). *The Ministry of Health*, p.157. London: GP Pitman & Son Ltd.
27. Gaskell, S. Martin (1983). *Building Control – National legislation and introduction of local bye-laws in Victorian England*, p.50. London: Bedford Press.
28. Daunton, M.J. (1983). *House and Home in the Victorian City*, p.36. London.
29. *Ibid.*, p.292.

Bibliography

Primary Sources
Acts of Parliament

Calais Paving Act	2 & 3 Edw. c. 38
An Act for the Better and More Easy Rebuilding of the Town of Northampton, 1675	27 Chas. c. 2 6 & 7 Will. c. 3
Act for the Rebuilding of the Town of Warwick 1694	1 Will. c. 3
An Act for the Better and More Easy Rebuilding of the Town of Blandford, 1731	5 Geo. c. 2
An Act for the Better and More Easy Rebuilding of the Town of Tiverton, 1731	5 Geo. c. 2
An Act for the Better and More Easy Rebuilding of the Town of Wareham, 1763	3 Geo. c. 3
Bristol Building Act 1788	28 Geo.3 c. 66
An Act for the Better and More Easy Rebuilding of the Town of Chudleigh, 1808	48 Geo. 3 c.66
Liverpool Building Act, 1825	6 Geo. 4 c.75
Municipal Corporation Act 1835	6 & 6 Will. 4 c.76
Bristol Building Act 1840	3 Vict. c. 77
Liverpool Building Act 1842	5 Vict. c. 44
Bristol Building Act 1847	10 & 11 Vict. c. 129
Town Improvement Clauses Act 1847	10 & 11 Vict. c. 34
Public Health Act 1848	11 &12 Vict. c. 63
Public Health Act 1858	21 & 22 Vict. c. 97
Local Government Act 1858	21 & 22 Vict. c. 98
Public Health Act 1859	22 & 23 Vict. c. 3
Public Health Act 1866	29 & 30 Vict. c. 40
Stockton Improvement Act 1869	32 & 33 Vict. c. 73
St Helens Improvement Act 1869	32 & 33 Vict. c. 20
Local Government Board Act 1871	34 & 35 Vict. c. 70
Public Health Act 1872	35 & 36 Vict. c. 79
Sanitary Laws (Amendment) Act 1874	37 & 38 Vict. c. 89
Public Health Act 1875	38 & 39 Vict. c. 55
Public Health (Amendment) Act 1890	53 & 54 Vict. c. 59
Local Government Act 1894	56 & 57 Vict. c. 73
Public Health (Amendment) Act 1907	7 Edw. 7 c. 30
Housing and Town Planning Act 1909	9 Edw. 7 c. 44

Education (Administrative Provisions) Act 1911	1 & 2 Geo. 5 c. 32
Housing and Town Planning Act 1919	9 & 10 Geo. 5 c. 60
Housing Act 1923	12 & 13 Geo. 5 c. 24
Housing Act 1925	15 & 16 Geo. 5 c. 14
Public Health Act 1925	15 & 16 Geo. 6 c. 71
Public Health Act 1936	26 Geo. 6 & 1 Edw. 8 c. 49
Clean Air Act 1956	4&5 Eliz. 2 c. 52
Thermal Insulation (Industrial Buildings) Act 1957	5&6 Eliz. 2 c. 40
Public Health Act 1961	9 & 10 Eliz. 2 c. 64
The Fire Precautions Act 1971	1971 c. 40
The Health and Safety at Work Etc. Act 1974	1974 c. 37
Housing and Building Control Act 1984	1984 c. 39
The Building Act 1984	1984 c. 55

Building Bye-laws

Model Building Bye-laws 1st series 25 July 1877
Model Building Bye-laws 1890 Act Bye-laws 1894
Model Building Bye-laws 1899
Model Building Bye-laws Series IV Urban 1912
Model Building Bye-laws Intermediate Series IVc 1928
Model Building Bye-laws Rural Model IVa 1928
Model Building Bye-laws Urban Series IV 1930
Model Building Bye-laws Urban Series IV 1932
Model Building Bye-laws Urban Series IV 1933
Model Building Bye-laws Urban Series IV 1935
Model Building Bye-laws Means of Escape from Fire in Certain Factories and Workshops 1935
Model Building Bye-laws Buildings Series IV 1937
City of Bath Building Bye-laws 28 May 1866
City of Bath Building Bye-laws 12 May 1868
Borough of Barnstaple Building Bye-laws 21 June 1875
Borough of Brighton Building Bye-laws 19 November 1886
City of Exeter Building Bye-laws 13 January 1899
City of Exeter Building Bye-laws 31 May 1899
City of Exeter Building Bye-laws 23 January 1912
City of Exeter Building Bye-laws 8 January 1928
City of Exeter Building Bye-laws 23 May 1939
Barnstaple Rural District Council Building Bye-laws 1 February 1939
Model Building Bye-laws 1952 & 1953

Building Regulations

The Building Regulations 1965

The Building Regulations 1972
The Building Regulations 1976
The Building Regulations 1985
The Building Regulations 1991
The Building (Approved Inspectors Etc.) Regulations 1985

Reports

PP Poor Law Commissioners 4th Annual Report Appendix A 1838
PP Poor Law Commissioners 5th Annual Report Appendix C 1839
PP Poor Law Commissioners Report on the Sanitary Conditions of the Labouring Population of Great Britain 1842 (Chadwick's Report)
PP Bye-laws in Rural Districts 1905 PP No. 272
Report to the General Board of Health on a Preliminary Inquiry into the Sewage Drainage and Supply of Water and the Sanitary Conditions of the Inhabitants, of the Borough of Barnstaple in the County of Devon, by TW Rammell – Superintendent Inspector, London 1850
Report on the Collapse of the Roof of the Assembly Hall of Camden School for Girls. Dept of Education and Science, HMSO, 1973
Proposals for a Building Bill. Consultative Document. Department of the Environment, 1972

Command Papers

The Future of Building Control in England and Wales. Cmnd 8179. HMSO, 1981

Circulars

Local Government Board Circular Letter Attached to First Series Model Bye-laws 25 July 1877
Local Government Board No. 31 1901/02
Local Government Board 7th Annual Report 1877/78 Appendix A Report No. 35 1905/06
Local Government Board Circular Letter 5 January 1906
Local Government Board Circular Letter 29 August 1912
Ministry of Health Circular No. 332 1 September 1922
Ministry of Health Circular No. 343 28 September 1922
Ministry of Health Circular No. 56 January 1926
Ministry of Health Circular No. 44 January 1927
Ministry of Health Circular No. 41 January 1927
Ministry of Health Circular No. 70 June 1927
Ministry of Health Circular No. 43a January 1928
Ministry of Health Circular No. 80 January 1928
Ministry of Health Circular No. 80 1 September 1935
Ministry of Housing and Local Government Circular No. 48/66 September 1966
Ministry of Housing and Local Government Circular No. 10/67 February 1967
Ministry of Housing and Local Government Circular No. 70/67 November 1967

Ministry of Housing and Local Government Circular No. 34/69 May 1969
Department of the Environment No. 1/71 February 1971
Department of the Environment No. 36/72 April 1972
Department of the Environment No. 70/73 December 1973
Department of the Environment No. 44/77 May 1977
Department of the Environment No. 1/96 March 1996
Department of the Environment No. 19/96 December 1996

Parliamentary Records
Hansard Parliamentary Debates 3rd series, 1840–8 February 1892
Hansard Parliamentary Debates 4th series 9 February 1892–14 February 1909
Hansard Parliamentary Debates 5th series 15 February 1909 – onwards
Hansard Parliamentary Debates 6th series, 5th July 1983 onwards

Parliamentary Bills
Building Regulation Bill 1841 No. 302
Building Regulation Bill 1841 No. 339
Building Regulation Bill 1842 No. 33
Building Regulation Bill 1842 No. 52
Building Regulation Bill No. 2 1842 Bill No. 270
Building Regulation Bill No. 2 1842 Bill No. 371
Public Health Act (Amendment) Bill 1905
Public Health Act (Building Bye-laws) Bill 1906 6 Edw.7 Bill No. 347
Housing of Working Classes Bill 1911
Education (Administrative Provisions) Bill 1911
Housing of Working Classes No. 2 Bill 1912
Housing of Working Classes Bill 1913
Housing of Working Classes Bill 1914
Building (Escape from Fire) Bill 1930
Health & Safety at Work etc. Bill 74
Housing and Building Control Bill (as amended by Standing Committee F) Bill 94
Building Bill (HL) (as amended by the Joint Committee on Consolidating Bills) Bill 269

Commissions
PP Second Report of the Commissioners of Inquiry into the State of Health in Large Towns and Populous Districts 1845
PP Second Report of the Royal Sanitary Commission 1871 C. 281 Vol. XXXV
Vol. II Analysis of Evidence – Precis of Oral Evidence C. 281
Vol. III Minutes of Evidence Vol. III C. 281–11
PP First Report of Her Majesty's Commissioners Inquiring into the Housing of the Working Classes 1885 C. 4402
PP Report of the Royal Commission on Fire Brigades and Fire Prevention 1923 Cmd. 1945

Committees

PP Report of the Select Committee on Health of Towns 1840, 17th June.
PP Departmental Committee on Building Bye-laws 1918 Cd. 9213
PP Housing (Building Construction) Committee Report 1918 Cd. 9191 (Tudor-Walters Report)
Report on the Departmental Committee on Housing 1933 Cmd. 4397
PP Local Government and Public Health Consolidation Committee Second Interim Report 1936 Cmd. 5059

HMSO publications

Manual of Safety Requirements in Theatres and Other Places of Entertainment (1934). London: HMSO.
The Housing Manual 1949 (1951). London: HMSO.
Digest 247, March 1981. Building Research Station.

Secondary Sources

Brunskill, R.W.(1982). *Houses*. London.
Buer, M.C. (1926). *Health, Wealth and Population in the Early Days of the Industrial Revolution*. London.
Burnett, J. (1978). *A Social History of Housing 1815–1970*. Cambridge: Cambridge University Press.
Calder, J. (1977). *The Victorian Home*. London: Book Club Associates.
Cave, L.F. (1981). *The Smaller English House*. London: Robert Hale.
Chance, W. (1914). *Building Bye-laws in Rural Districts*. London: King and Son.
Checkland, S.G. (1964). *The Rise of Industrial Society in England 1815–1895*. London.
Cowan, H.J. (1972). *Science and Building*. New York.
Daunton, M. (1983). *House and Home in the Victorian City*. London: Edward Arnold.
de Bono, E. (1971). *Lateral Thinking for Management*. London: Penguin Books.
Dennison, D.V. (1967). *The Government of Housing*. London.
Dewsnup, E.K. (1970). *The Housing Problem in England*. Manchester: Manchester University Press.
Dictionary of National Biography. Oxford: OUP.
Dyos, H.J. (1908). The Speculative Builders and Developers in Victorian London, *Victorian Studies, XI*, supplement.
Entwhistle, F.D.(1974). *Building Regulation, Practice and Procedure*. London.
Finer, S.E. (1952). *The Life and Times of Sir Edwin Chadwick*. London.
Frank, T. P. (Ed.) (1928). *Knights Annotated Model Bye-laws*, 8th edition. London.
Fraser, D. (1979). *Power and Authority in the Victorian City*. Oxford.
Fraser, W.M. (1950). *A History of Public Health 1834–1939*. London: Bailliere, Tindall and Cox.
Garnham-Wright, J.H. (1983). *Building Control by Legislation – The UK Experiences*. Chichester: John Wiley and Sons.

Gaskell, S.M. (1983). *Building Control – National Legislation and the Introduction of Local Bye-laws in Victorian England.* London: Bedford Press.

Gauldie, E. (1974). *Cruel Habitations.* London.

Green, J.L. (1899). *English Country Cottages.* London: The Rural World Publishing Co. Ltd.

Harper, R.H. (1978). 'Evolution of the English Building Regulations'. (Unpublished Ph.D. Thesis, University of Sheffield, 1978, number 4316.)

Harper, R.H. (1985). *Victorian Building Regulations. Summary Tables of the Principal English Building Acts and Model Bye-laws 1840–1914.* London: Maxwell Publishing Ltd.

Hellyer, S.S. (1877). *Water, Air and Light.* London.

Hellyer, S.S. (1884). *The Plumber and Sanitary Houses.* London.

Hole, J. (1866). *The Homes of the Working Classes.* London: Longman, Green and Co.

Incorporated Association of Architects and Surveyors (1965). *Building Regulation 1965: Practice Notes.* London: IAAS.

Knight's Building Regulations. Charles Knight Publishing.

Knowles, C.C. and Pitt, P.H. (1972). *The History of Building Regulation in London 1189–1972.* London: Architectural Press.

Lambert, R. (1963). *Sir John Simon and English Social Administration.* London.

Lea, F.M. (1971). *Science and Building. A history of the Building Research Station.* London: HMSO.

Lewis, P. (1986). *A People's War.* London: Methuen.

Lewis, R.A. (1952). *Sir Edwin Chadwick and the Public Health Movement.* London.

Longmate, N. (1971). *How We Lived Then.* London: Arrow.

Lucas, R.M. (1906). *Anti-Building Bye-laws.* London.

Macdonagh, O. (1977). *Early Victorian Government, 1830–1870.* London: Holmes and Meier Publishing.

Macdonagh, O. (1961). *A Pattern of Government Growth, 1800–1860.* Godstone: Gregg Revivals.

Methesuis, S. (1982). *The English Terraced House.* London: Yale University Press.

Nagarajan, R. (1976). *Standards in Building.* London.

Newsholme, Sir Arthur (1925). *The Ministry of Health.* London: GP Pitman and Son Ltd.

Newsholme, Sir Arthur (1927). *The Last 30 Years in Public Health.* London.

Powell, C.G. (1971). *Mid-Victorian Britain 1851–1875.* London.

Powell, C.G. (1980). *An Economic History of British Building Industry 1915–1979.* London: Architectural Press.

Rickards, T. (1974). *Problem Solving Through Creative Analysis.* London.

Simon, J. (1893). *English Sanitary Institutions.* London.

Thompson, F.L. (1968). *Chartered Surveyors: The growth of a profession.* London: Routledge & Kegan Paul.

Thompson and Yeo (1849/1850). *The Unknown Mayhem.* Selections from the *Morning Chronicle.*

Toulmin-Smith, J. (1851). *Local Self-government and Centralisation.* London.

Wright, L. (1960). *Clean and Decent.* London.

Journals

The Builder
Building Design
Building Today
Building Trades Journal
Institute of Building Control Journal
Journal of the Royal Agricultural Society
Local Authority Week
Municipal Journal
The Times

Index

Compiled by Mary Kirkness

Note: page references in *italics* indicate illustrations/plates

Ackroyd, Colonel, 56
Ackroydon, 56
Adderley, Sir Charles, 59, 201n.28
America, 113, 114, 136
Anns *vs.* London Borough of Merton, 137
Approved Documents, 143
Approved Inspectors, 139, 140, 190–1, 143–4
Arkwright, Richard, 56
Ashley, Lord (Earl of Shaftesbury), 35, 37, 198n.1

back-to-back housing, 7, 28, 51, 77
    and Building Regulation Bills, 13, 16
    in Leeds, 7, 28, 46, *Pls.3a/3b/4a/4b*
Baker, Sir Randolph, 90
Barnstaple: bye-laws, 70
Bath, *21, 48,* 49, *49*
Bedford, Duke of: estate housing, 77–8, *Pl.7*
Belper: philanthropic housing, 56
Birkenhead Sports Hall, 135
Birmingham, 74, 105
Blandford: fire, 2–3
Board of Education, 86, 126
Boards of Health, *see* Health, Boards of
Boscowan, Col. Sir A. Griffith, 90
Bourneville, 56
Bramah valve closet, 47–8
BRE, 112, 133
bricks/brickwork, 38–9, 129
    in footings, 71–2, 100
Brighton: timber buildings, 106
Bristol
    Building Acts
        1788, 3, *4, 5,* 151–3
        1840, 3, 4, 5, 27, 154–6
        1847, 28
    prefabricated buildings, 130, *Pl.9b*
British Constitutional Association, 83
British Medical Association, 59
British Standards, 115–16, 127, 133
British Standards Institution (BSI), 101, 110, 115, 129
Bromyard (Herefordshire), 36
Builder magazine, 93, 97, 139
builders
    and bye-laws/local Acts, 3, 5, 61, 110, 130
    Departmental Committee: evidence, 91–2, 93, 96
    unscrupulous, 63, 100
    see also jerry-building; speculative building
Building Act(s)
    local, *see* Improvement Acts
    national
        1984, 139–41, 142–4, 147, 150, 193
        proposed, xiv, 55, 65, 134
            Chadwick on, 20, 23–7, 37–40
            by Health of Towns Committee, 10–11, 12

Building By-laws Reform Association, 80, 82, 83, 85, 86, 97
    and rural areas, 79–80, 81
building bye-laws, *see* bye-laws
building inspectors, *see* surveyors
Building Legislation, Committee on, 131
Building Regulation Bills
    1841, 13–14, 159–62
    1842, 14–19, 163–4
Building Regulations, 131, 133–4
    1965, 133, 188
    1972, 132, 188–9
    1976, 142, 189
    1985, 142–3, 145, 190
        Approved Inspector, 144, 190–1
Building Regulations Advisory Committee (BRAC), 132–5
Building Research Board (*later* Building Research Establishment), 112, 113, 116, 131
Building Research Department (BRD; *later* Building Research Station), 114–15
Building Research Establishment (BRE), 112, 133
Building Research Station, 116, 119, 124, 129
Building Societies Act 1939, 130
Building Standards (Scotland) Regulations, 142
Burgh Police Act (Scotland) 1902, 100
Burns, Mr (LGB President), 85–6, 87, 88
By-law Reform Association, *see* Building By-laws Reform Association
bye-laws, building, 41, 147–8, 192–3
    administration
        adoption, 96, 97, 103–4, 122
        complaints about, 61–2, 85–6, 125
        enforcement, 74–5, 95–6, 111, 126
        post-World War II, 129–30
        relaxation (policy), 103, 107, 109–11
    exemption, 102, 107, 205n.21
        and Departmental Committee, 97, 101
        for Education Board, 86, 126, 205n.21
        in Public Health Acts (Building Bye-Laws) Bill, 81, 82
    functionality: *vs.* specificity, 149
        and Departmental Committee, 94, 95, 100
        and innovation, xv, 74, 78, 94
        and BRB/BRS, 116, 119, 131
    and health/safety, 62, 91, 106, 136
    vs. local Acts, 43, 51–3, 57–8, 85, 92–3, 126
    and Local Government Act 1858, 23, 44, 45, 49, 50–3, 168–9
    local variations, 45, 46, *47,* 49, 50, 70
    model, 44, 45
        1877/78 (urban), 69–71, 172–3
        1899 (urban), 84, 174–5
        1901 (rural), 80–1, 82–3, 84, 87, 176
        1905 (intermediate), 84
        1912 (urban), 106, 177–9

INDEX

1932 (rural), 110
1935 (on industrial fires), 180
1937 (Ministry of Health), 183–5
1952/53, 130, 186–7
and Public Health (Amendment) Act 1890, 76
in rural areas, *see* rural areas
and science/technology, 47–8, 73, 74, 78, 87–8, 114
   steel, 73, 76, 87, 113, 114
   work of BRD/BRS, 115, 116, 119
and speculative building, 46–7, 124–5
updating
   and LGB, 87, 94, 100
   post-World War I, 94–5, 99–100, 103, 105, 108, 110
   and Public Health Acts, 84, 126, 127, 128
   during 1930s, 123–4
see also Building By-Laws Reform Association; *and under* Departmental Committee on Building Byelaws; Local Government Board

Cadbury: housing, 56
Calais: roofing materials, 3
Calais Paving Act 1548, 3
Cardiff: cavity walls, 94
Carrington, Earl, 83
cavity walls, 94, 99–100, 136
cellars, habitable, 31, 33
cements, 71
   Portland, 38, 71–2, 100
central control: *vs.* local, 148–9
   and LGB, 64, 83, 88–9, 93, 97
   in 19th century, 41, 53, 55–6, 57–8, 61, 67
      Chadwick on, 26–7, 36–7
      Simon on, 55–6, 61, 67, 74
   in 20th century, 103, 123, 126, 129, 131, 149–50
Chadwick, Edwin
   on concrete, 71, 73
   and General Building Bill, 37–40
   and Health of Towns Commission, 31–2
   opposition to, 36–7
   and Public Health Act 1848, 35, 40, 41
   Report on Sanitary Conditions, 20–2, 23–7
   and Working Classes Housing Commission, 71, 74
Chance, Sir William, 80, 91
Cheltenham District Council, 146
cholera, 2, 6, 7, 8, 35
Chudleigh: fire, 2–3
Committee on Building Legislation, 131
compensation claims, 137, 138
competition: in surveying, 143–7
concrete, 38, 71–4, 78
   reinforced, 73, 76, 115, 136
Conservative policies (1979–81), 138–9
Consolidation Committee, 120–1, 122–5
Construction Industry Council, 144
Conversion 10 (warranty scheme), 145
Cooper, Anthony Ashley (7th Earl of Shaftesbury), 35, 37, 198n.1
Copley: philanthropic housing, 56
costs: of building
   and bye-laws, 46, 94
   and health/safety, 22, 148
   see also surveyors: fees
courts (in housing), 7, 13, 16, 31
Coventry: World War II damage, 128
Cubitt, Thomas, 9, 24–5, 32, 119, 196n.28

damp proof course, 43, 47
dampness, 43, 53, *54*
Daunton, M., 78
death rates (1829–40), 8, *21*
demand: for housing
   c. 1900, 57–8
   postwar, 98, 102–3, 107, 129–30
Department of Scientific and Industrial Research (DSIR), 101, 112
Departmental Committee on Building Byelaws, 90–8, 120, 204n.1
   on bye-laws, 89, 98, 100, 122, 125
      enforcement, 95–6, 111, 126
      exemption, 97, 101
      updating, 94–5, 105
   and Fire Brigades Commission, 104–5
   and Housing Committee, 101–3
   on surveyors, 95–6, 118
Departmental Committee on Consolidation, 120–1, 122–5
Dewsnup, E.K., 120
diseases, 2, 7, 60, *see also* cholera
Disraeli, Benjamin, 66
district surveyors, 116–17, 126, 140, 143
documents, approved, 143
Dolton (LGB officer), 93, 108
Dorman Long, 113
double glazing, Chadwick on, 39
drainage
   Chadwick on, 37
   in Public Health Acts, 33–4, 58, 68
DSIR, 101, 112
Dutton *vs.* Bognor Regis D.C., 137

Education, Board of, 86, 126, 205n.21
Education (Administrative Provisions) Act 1911, 86, 87, 205n.21
Engineering Standards Committee, 101
Entwhistle, N.D., 194n.1
estate housing (rural), 77–8, *Pl.7*
exemption: from bye-laws, *see under* bye-laws
Exeter, 105, 106, *Pls.1/2/5/6/8*

Factories Acts
   1901, 131, 205n.40
   1937, 131, 132
   1961, 132
factories/workshops
   health/safety, 106, 180, 205n.40
   and Public Health Act 1848, 33
failures, notable, 135–7
fees, *see under* surveyors
fire, escape/protection from, 15, 65, 105
   in factories/workshops, 72, 131–2, 180, 205n.40
   pre-19th century, 1, 2–3
   in public buildings, 106, 136
Fire Brigades and Fire Prevention, Royal Commission on, 104–5, 106
Fire Precautions Act 1971, 132, 193
Fire Protection, Committee on, 65, 76
fire resistance: and concrete, 72
Fires Bill 1872, 76
flats, 124
floors, Chadwick on, 38
footings, brick, 71–2, 100
formaldehyde foam, area, 136

219

Foundation 15 (warranty scheme), 145
Fovarque, H.W., 94
FRE (Fire Research Establishment), 133
Fuller, Graham, 147
functionality
  of 1985 Building Regulations, 139, 142
  of bye-laws, *see under* bye-laws

garden cities, 56–7, 87
gardens, front, *see* space
gas, Chadwick on, 39
Gaskell, S. Martin, xvi, 17, 50, 95
Gauldie, E., 17, 62
General Building Bill (Chadwick), 37–40
glass, use of, 39
Greater London Council District Surveyors Service, 143
Green, J.L., 77
Guinness, Walter, 85, 86–7
Gutch, Mr (London surveyor), 24

Haig *vs.* London Borough of Hillingdon, 137
Halifax: housing costs, 77
Hammurabi: Code, 194n.1
Harper, Roger A., xvi
Hayes-Fisher, W., 91, 98
Health, Boards of (central/local), 11, 27, 35–6
  abolition, 40, 41, 59
Health, Ministry of, *see* Ministry of Health
Health and Safety at Work Etc. Act 1974, 134–5, 139, 149–50, 193
Health of Towns Bills 1845–48, 32–4
Health of Towns Commission, 30–2
Health of Towns Select Committee, 8–12, 13, 18, 27, 31
health/safety
  and bye-laws, 62, 91, 106, 136
  vs. costs, 22, 148
  industrial, 33, 106, 180, 205n.40
  see also fire
hearths: in bye-laws, 105
Heddle, John, 144
Hennebique, François, 73
Herbert-Lawes, J., 90
Heseltine, Michael, 138–9
Hole, James, 51–2, 53, 55–6
Housing Acts (1923, 1925), 103–6
Housing and Building Control Bill 1982, 139–41, *see also* Building Act 1984
Housing and Town Planning Acts
  1909, 83, 95, 100–1
  1919, 108
Housing (Building Construction) Committee, 98–101, 108–9, 112, 119
  and Departmental Committee, 101–3
Housing Manual, 129
Housing of Working Classes
  Bill, 86–9, 90
  Royal Commission, 71, 74, 75
Howard, Ebenezer, 57
Hull: World War II damage, 128
'Hygienic Closet', 48
Hylton, Lord, 81, 82–3

Improvement Acts, local, 27–30, 51–6
  vs. bye-laws, 43, 51–3, 57–8, 92–3

Chadwick on, 20, 23–7
and Local Government Act 1858, 42
named
  Leeds, 28
  Leicester, 51, 92
  Manchester, 28
  Newcastle, 28
  St Helens, 50–1, 170–1
  Stockton, 50
  see also Bristol; Liverpool; London
and Public Health (Amendment) Acts, 76, 85
see also under surveyors
Incorporated Association of Architects and Surveyors (IAAS), 118, 133, 139
industrial buildings, 72, 148, *Pl.10, see also* factories/workshops
inspectors
  approved, 139, 140, 143–4
  sanitary, 117, 121
  see also surveyors
Institute of Building Control, 139
Institution of Municipal Engineers, 117, 118, 134
Institution of Surveyors, 118
insulation, thermal, 38–9
isolated buildings, 82, 105, 123

jerry-building, 74, 93, 103, 128–9, 202n.10
jettying: of upper floors, 3, *Pl.2*

Kingston (Surrey), 24
Knight's Annotated Model Byelaws, 118

laissez-faire, 41, 64, 199n.18
Lambert, John, 75
Lancashire: bye-law variations, 131
lead piping, Chadwick on, 40
Leeds, *21*, 25–6, 28, 52, 77
  back-to-back housing, 7, 28, 46, *Pls.3a/3b/4a/4b*
Leicester, 51, 92
Letchworth Garden City, 57
LGB, *see* Local Government Board
Liddle, John, 63, 76
'Lifting the Burden', 142
lime cements, 71
Liverpool, 16, *21*
  Building Acts, 5–6
    1825, 6, 157–8
    1842, 27–8, 165–7, 197n.21
    1882, 70
  and bye-laws, 51, 58
  Building Bill 1802, 6, 17
local Acts, *see* Improvement Acts
local authorities
  discretionary powers, 44, 67, 115, 118, 119–20, 149
  and Public Health Bill/Act 1936, 122, 123, 149
  housing, post-World War I, 97, 99, 102–3, 107
  see also bye-laws; central control: *vs.* local; Improvement Acts; surveyors; *and named authorities*
local/central control, *see* central control
Local Government Act Department, 40–1, 43–4, 45, 51, 69
Local Government Acts
  1858, 40–4, 81, 192
    and bye-laws, 23, 44, 45, 49, 50–3, 168–9
  1933, 119, 121–2

220

INDEX

Local Government and Public Health Consolidation Committee, 120–1, 122–5
Local Government Board (LGB), 48, 64, 75, 85, 95
  and bye-laws, 69, 84, 85, 96
    rural use, 80–1, 83
    updating, 87, 94, 100
  and central control, 64, 83, 88–9, 93, 97
Local Government Board Act 1871, 64
London, 77, 128
  Building Acts, 17, 63, 140
    1667, 1–2, 3
    1844, 29–30
    1894, 81
    1909, 114
    1772/74, 2
    1855 (Metropolitan), 25, 33, 63, 117
    vs. bye-laws, 85, 126
    Chadwick's criticisms, 24, 25
  and national systems aligned, 140, 143
  surveyors, 74, 126, 140, 143
    fees, 6, 15, 24, 25, 110, 116–17
London City Council, 113, 115
London County Council, 85–6
Long, Walter, 79
Loudon, John C., 22–3, 197n.5
Lowestoft Corporation Act, 106
Lucas, R. MacDonald, 78–9, 82

Macclesfield, 35–6
McDougal's patent, 40
Manchester, *21*, 28, 136
Medina cement, 71
Metropolitan Building Act 1855, 25, 33, 63, 117
Metropolitan Management and Building Act 1878, 106
Ministry of Health (MOH)
  bye-laws (1937), 183–5
  circulars, 108–11, 116–17, 120
  regulations (1922), 109
Molesworth, Sir William, 36
Morpeth, Lord, 32, 35
mortality rates (1829–40), 8, *21*
Mouchel, Louis Gustave, 73
Municipal Corporations Act 1835, 33
Municipal Mutual Insurance Company, 145
Murphy *vs.* Brentwood D.C., 138

NALGO, 138, 144
National Federation of Building Trades Employers (NFBTE), 91–2
National House Builders Registration Council (NHBRC), 130
National House Building Council (NHBC), 139, 140, 144–6
National Promotion of Local Authority Building Control, 145
negligence claims, 137, 138
New Lanark, 56
Newcastle Improvement Act 1837, 28
Newlands, James, 5, 6, 17, 195n.15
noise control, 124–5
Normanby, Marquis of (C.H. Phipps), 12–13, 29, 30, 196n.32
  and Building Regulation Bills, 13, 14, 15, 17, 18
Northampton: fire, 2–3

nuisances: in law, 10, 58
Nuisances Removal Act, 35

officers, *see* staff
Offices, Shops and Railway Premises Act 1963, 132
Owen, Robert, 56

Palmerston, 3rd Viscount, 37
pan closets, 38, 47, 48
party wall: above roof, 45, 94, 100, 105, *Pls.5/8*
Patten, John, 144
Perkin, H., 41
philanthropic housing, 56, 57, 78
Pick (RIBA witness), 92
Pite, Prof. (of RIBA), 94, 96, 100
Platt, F.W., 92–3, 94
Plymouth, 128, *Pl.11*
Poor Law Act 1834, 33
Port Sunlight, 56
Portland cement, 38, 71–2, 100
prefabricated buildings, 129–30, *Pls.9a/9b*
Pridgin-Teale, Thomas, 52–3, *53*, *54*, 200n.13
professional bodies: and surveyors, 117–18, 119, 134–5
'property rights', 10, 17, 18, 23, 42
public buildings, 50, 63, 76, 106–7
Public Health Acts
  1848, 32–4, 35–6, 38, 40, 41, 42
  1858, 40–1
  1866, 58–9
  1872, 64–5, 68
  1874, 64, 192
  1875, 66–8, 75–6, 122, 192
    and concrete structures, 72, 73
  1907, 111
  1925, 104
  1936, 128, 133, 149, 181–2, 192
    and Bill, 125, 127
  1961, 130–1, 132–3, 149–50, 192–3
Public Health Acts (Building Bye-laws) Bill 1905, 81–2
Public Health (Amendment) Acts
  1890, 52, 53, 75–6, 192
    and 1899 bye-laws, 76, 174–5
  1907, 84–5, 123–4
Public Health Bills
  1873, 65
  1936, 122, 123, 125, 126, 127

Ramsgate Corporation Act, 106
refuse tips, building on, 52, 53, *53*
Regulating Buildings in Large Towns, Bill for, 13–14, 159–62
Rhys Jones Consultants, 145
RIBA, *see* Royal Institute of British Architects
Ridgmont: estate housing, 77–8, *Pl.7*
Roman cement, 71
Ronan Point, 135
roofs, 66, 76, *see also* party wall
Royal Commission on Fire Brigades and Fire Prevention, 104–5, 106
Royal Commission on Housing of Working Classes, 71, 74, 75
Royal Institute of British Architects (RIBA), 69, 117, 118, 139
  and Departmental Committee, 91, 92, 94

221

Royal Institution of Chartered Surveyors, 118
Royal Liver Building, 73
Royal Sanitary Commission (RSC), 59–64, 68, 75, 120
rural areas
  bye-laws, 77–83, 84, 104
    authorities' powers, 62–3, 66, 67
    model
      1901, 80–1, 82–3, 84, 87, 176
      1932, 110
    and urbanization, 122–3
  housing
    Chadwick on, 20–1
    estate (rural), 77–8, *Pl.7*
    Loudon on, 22–3
    Pridgin-Teale on, 53, *54*
Rural District Councils Association, 83, 91
Russell, Lord, 14
Rutland: death rate (1840), *21*

St Helens Improvement Act 1869, 50–1, 170–1
Salford: building control, 92–3
Salt, Sir Titus, 56
Saltaire, 56
Samuel, Herbert, 88, 90
'sanitary house', 147–8
sanitary inspectors, 117, 121
Sanitary Laws Amendment Act/Bill 1874, 65–6, 67
sanitary reform, 147–8
  under Public Health Acts, 33–4, 58–9, 66–8
  and RSC, 59–64
  see also Chadwick; diseases; drainage; sewage; ventilation; water closets
Schwartz's patent, 40
Selby (Yorkshire), 36
sewage/sewers
  Health of Towns Committee on, 11
  and Public Health Acts, 33, 58, 68
Sewage Utilisation Act 1865, 58
Shaftesbury, 7th Earl of (Lord Ashley), 35, 37, 198n.1
Sheffield, 20, 29, 45
Shelley, K.M.C., 90
Simon, Sir John, 41, 75, 199n.20
  on central control, 55–6, 61, 67, 74
Slaney, R.J., 30, 32, 195n.26
  committee (Health of Towns), 8–12, 17, 31
Slater-Booth, George, 65–6
Small Dwellings Acquisition Act 1899, 88
Smith, George, 9–10
Social Science Association, 59
South Stoneham R.D.C., 78
Southwood-Smith, Thomas, 8, 35, 37, 195n.22
space: about houses, 13, 22, 63
  and bye-laws, 42–3, 46, *47*, 69–70, *Pls.5/6*
  see also back-to-back housing
speculative building, 7, 9, 18, 52, 57
  and local Acts/bye-laws, 28, 46–7, 52, 70, 124–5
staff, local authority, 109–10, 121–2
  during 1980s, 137–8, 143–4, 146
  see also surveyors
staircases: in 1890 Act, 76
Stanstead, Lord, 65, 67
steel/steel-framed buildings, 72–3, 87, 113–14

and British Standards, 115
and bye-laws, 73, 76, 87, 113, 114
Stockton Improvement Act 1869, 50
Stokes, Denis, 145–6
Summerland Leisure Centre, 136
Sunderland: bye-laws, 46
surveyors
  and Building Regulation Bill 1842, 14, 15, 16, 17, 18–19
  and bye-laws, 43–4, 74–5, 95–6, 116
  fees/salaries, 6, 14, 25–6
    from 1980, 139, 146–7
    in Bristol, 4, 28
    and Building Regulation Bills, 14, 15, 16
    in London, 6, 15, 24, 25, 110, 116–17
  and local Acts, 6, 14, 25–6, 28–9, 31
    for Bristol, 3, 4–5, *5*, 27
    for London, 1–2, 14, 15, 25, 29
      as district surveyors, 116–17, 126, 140, 143
  local authority *vs.* NHBC, 144–7
  professionalism: criticised, 25, 29, 31, 78, 79
  qualifications, 117–18, 119, 134–5
    as Approved Inspector, 139, 140, 143–4

technology, new: and bye-laws, xv, 47–8, 74, 94, 95, 99–100
  and BRS/BRB, 116, 119, 131
  see also concrete; steel
thatch, 2–3, 45
Thatcher government policies, 138–9
timber
  buildings, 45, 105–6
  use: regulation, 76, 100, 109–10, 129
Tiverton: fire, 2–3
Toulmin-Smith, Joshua, 36–7, 41, 55, 198n.7
Town Improvement Clauses Act 1847, 29–30, 37, 42, 68
Trevelyan, C.P., 86
Truro: death rate (1840), *21*
tuberculosis, 2, 7
typhoid, 2, 7

updating, *see under* bye-laws
Urban District Councils Association, 83, 91

ventilation
  and bye-laws, 42–3, 46, *48*, 49
  and courts/back-to-back housing, 7, 13, 23, 46
Vetch, James, 23, 197.n6

Walters, Sir John Tudor, 99, 205n.24
Wareham: fire, 2–3
Warwick: fire, 2–3
water closets (WCs), 38, 47–8
Weavers Mill (Swansea), 73
Welwyn Garden City, 57
Wilkinson, William, 73
Williams (South Wales builder), 91–2
windows, 39, 49
Woolworths (Manchester), 136
World Wars: and housing needs
  I, 98, 102–3
  II, 128–30